M000266106

LIVING MONUMENTS

R.B. ROSENBURG

LIVING
MONUMENTS

Confederate Soldiers' Homes in the New South

The University of North Carolina Press • Chapel Hill and London

© 1993 The University of North Carolina Press

All rights reserved

Manufactured in the United States of America

The paper in this book meets the guidelines for permanence
and durability of the Committee on Production Guidelines for
Book Longevity of the Council on Library Resources.

Portions of Chapter 4 appeared earlier, in somewhat different
form, in R. B. Rosenburg, "The House that Grady Built: The
Fight for the Confederate Soldiers' Home of Georgia,"
Georgia Historical Quarterly 74 (Fall 1990): 399–432, and are
reprinted here with permission.

Frontispiece (p. iii): Past and present merge in a scene outside
the main building of the Lee Camp Home, Richmond,
Virginia, c. 1910. (author's collection)

Library of Congress Cataloging-in-Publication Data

Rosenburg, R. B. (Randall Britt), 1956–
    Living monuments : Confederate soldiers' homes in the
New South / by R.B. Rosenburg.
        p.   cm.
    Includes bibliographical references and index.
    ISBN 0-8078-2109-8 (hard : alk. paper)
    1. United States—History—Civil War, 1861–1865—
Veterans.   2. Soldiers' homes—Confederate States of
America.   3. Soldiers' homes—Southern States—History—
19th century.   I. Title.
E545.R65   1993
973.7'42—dc20   93-12465
                                                              CIP

97   96   95   94   93   5   4   3   2   1

For Max

CONTENTS

ILLUSTRATIONS

PREFACE

The city of Atlanta had witnessed nothing quite like it before. It was one of those sensational events that people would remember and talk about for years to come: the world premiere of David O. Selznick's *Gone with the Wind* at the Loew's Grand on Peachtree Street. Among the excited throng that night in December 1939 was a quartet of Confederate veterans, all of whom were in their nineties. The aged warriors were invited guests of Clark Gable (Rhett Butler), who had arranged for them to be seated near the front of the packed house. The veterans had a wonderful time. Dressed in their gray United Confederate Veterans uniforms, they posed for the newsreels, spoke over a national radio network, and were greeted with applause as they ambled down the aisle. A few minutes later, Margaret Mitchell, the novelist whose vivid and moving account was about to be enacted on the giant screen, paused to shake hands with them before continuing to her seat. Mitchell's act was more than a symbolic gesture. It was a fitting tribute to the survivors of the original battle of Atlanta, the *real* stars that evening.

Throughout the film, the old men watched intently, often leaning forward in their seats and cupping their hands behind their ears. They clapped, cheered, growled, and jeered, and at times felt like crying, as others in the audience unashamedly did. Afterward, J. A. Skelton, age ninety-two, was asked by a reporter what he thought of the movie. Never before having seen a "moving picture," though he recalled once having viewed some lantern slides back in 1876, Skelton remarked that it was "the gol-darndest thing" he ever witnessed. Equally impressed was James R. Jones, nearly ninety-five, the eldest of the veterans and also the most talkative. Jones, "admittedly the 'ladies' man' of the group," had vowed just days before the premiere to kiss Vivien Leigh, Carole Lombard, Claudette Colbert, or "any of the ladies" if he had the opportunity, and, true to his word, General Jones kissed Scarlett O'Hara that evening—twice! When asked what he made of what he had just seen, the colorful Jones's reply was both memorable and succinct. "The picture's fine," he said. "The war looked just like that!"[1]

At the time of the premiere, Jones and his three companions were living in the Georgia Soldiers' Home, which was only a ten-minute ride from the theater. In fact, they were among the last of literally thousands of Confederate veterans who had resided in institutions such as the Georgia home, which were designed specifically for their needs. The story of those homes is well worth telling and forms the background for this book. But what follows is not simply an institutional history per se. Granted, one purpose of the study is to treat comprehensively the homes, examining why and how they were established and how they evolved over time. Nevertheless, I have attempted to focus less on the institutional side of things and more on the veterans and their caretakers themselves, preferring to allow them to do the talking and the acting, and sometimes the pontificating and the bickering. Moreover, I have tried to assess the societal functions of the homes, arguing that they were meant to reflect much of what those "on the outside" who created and administered them valued and appreciated. In others words, an examination of the history of Confederate soldiers' homes offers insights into the assumptions and beliefs held by people in the post–Civil War years in regard to such significant matters as social welfare, honor, aging, race relations, class resentments, and the role of women—to name just a few.

Antedating the establishment of institutions to take care of disabled and homeless ex-Confederates was the myth that southern soldiers had been heroes fighting for the Lost Cause. It was this myth that inspired concerned citizens to organize benevolence for poor ol' Johnny Reb. And organize they did. As the present study reveals, a well-organized soldiers' home movement emerged late in the nineteenth century and had three distinct stages. The first stage, during the 1880s and 1890s, brought the founding of early homes; the second, after 1900, saw the idea of establishing soldiers' homes spread throughout the South; and the third, after 1920, led states to assume from private boards responsibility for operation of the homes. But as this study also reveals, some harsh realities were in store for those who sought to embody a myth in an institution. Ironically, the same principles of honor, valor, and masculinity found in Johnny Reb that inspired many to do their "sacred duty" of establishing, supervising, and maintaining the homes, compelled others from the outset to disapprove of the charities. Apologists faced serious obstacles in selling their projects to the public and obtaining state funding; in Georgia, for example, detractors succeeded for over a decade in preventing the soldiers' home from opening. Just as troublesome were the day-to-day challenges posed by recalcitrant inmates who resisted having to conform to regiminal deportment standards and apparently resented being told by their social "betters" to act their age and live up to standards befitting true, virtuous "heroes." In some cases administrators were forced to reconsider their own ideas of social responsibility and stewardship, leading them to be more patient with their wards and less diligent in their paternal oversight. Nevertheless, until their breakup around 1920, Confederate soldiers' homes continued to function in much the same fashion as originally intended.

By no means should the following study be regarded as definitive. Its primary focus is on the homes' combined social and cultural functions, from the time of their founding to roughly 1920. After 1920, the institutions evolved rapidly, and the texture of home life changed; management of the homes came completely under state control, and female relatives of veterans were admitted—which is another topic entirely. Moreover, foremost attention has been devoted to homes in the eleven states that comprised the former Confederacy, with secondary references made to the other five homes where instructive. This work is also necessarily limited by the sources available. It has been relatively easy to describe how the home founders idealized the common private soldier, how they viewed his poverty, aging, and disability, and how they conspired to protect and reform inmates, based upon their own assertions, which have been preserved and collected. Achieving an equal understanding of the soldiers' attitudes and motives is more difficult, however. I have attempted whenever possible to reconstruct how soldiers' home residents perceived themselves, their managers, their community, and their places in history and society; and a preliminary socioeconomic profile, based upon the quantitative analysis of a selected sample of inmates, has been provided. Nevertheless, owing to the usually wooden and stylized nature of many official records relative to the homes and the general dearth of documents produced by inmates themselves, their perspective as presented here may be somewhat distorted.

The Confederate soldiers' homes of the New South occupied a significant place in southern history. Several generations of southerners knew about them and selflessly gave their time, energies, and gifts to them. The grounds provided the setting for everything from veterans' reunions and gospel singings to political rallies, vaudeville acts, band concerts, and Easter egg hunts. Presidents, governors, military leaders, movie stars, and other dignitaries occasionally visited the homes; and over the years, glee clubs and Sunday school classes, curiosity seekers and temperance lecturers, preachers and elixir salesmen beat a persistent path to their doors. The homes served as objects of concern, devotion, commercialism, sectional pride, and reconciliation, and sometimes as sources of heated controversy—just as had the aged, poor, and disabled veterans who lived and died (and sometimes resented being) there. As Clark Howell, longtime editor of the Atlanta *Constitution* and avid defender of the Georgia home, aptly put it: "Tombstones and statues crumble and decay, and, even while they stand, their inscriptions fade from sight. . . . But *living monuments* are worth more than all." To southerners of all ages, especially to Johnny Reb, the homes were indeed worth a great deal.[2]

ACKNOWLEDGMENTS

Many persons have contributed to the completion of this book. First are the following scholars, who read large portions of the manuscript and/or offered helpful suggestions and otherwise gave sound advice: Fred A. Bailey, Paul H. Bergeron, James C. Cobb, Gaines M. Foster, Gary W. Gallagher, LeRoy P. Graf, Daniel E. Sutherland, Peter Wallenstein, Wm. Bruce Wheeler, and Charles Reagan Wilson. Each of them has made this a better work than it might have been. Then there are the many directors and staff members of repositories and collections listed in the bibliography, whose courteous and timely service merit recognition here. They expedited my research and generally made life easier for me. The assistance of several persons exceeded the call of duty, and I am compelled to thank, individually, Mark Kennedy of Vanderbilt University and, collectively, the staff of the Special Collections Library at the University of Tennessee, Knoxville. Special recognition also goes to Bill Rambo of the Confederate Memorial Park in Alabama and Keith A. Hardison of Beauvoir, the Jefferson Davis Memorial Shrine, who, in addition to providing research materials, gave me guided tours of the only extant Confederate soldiers' homes. I also wish to thank Ruth P. Graf, who proofread my manuscript before I submitted it to the University of North Carolina Press, where it was transformed into this finished product. At the press, I am especially appreciative of Lewis Bateman, who recognized the work's potential, and Ron Maner, whose careful copyediting proved invaluable. Finally, I am indebted to Lynn and to Jonathan, Joel, and J. Leigh, without whose long-standing support and encouragement none of this would have been possible or worth the effort.

LIVING MONUMENTS

We ... sincerely hope that these poor cripples, the relics of war and a lost cause, may meet with that charity which never faileth.
—New Orleans *Daily Picayune*, June 9, 1866

A land without monuments is a land without heroes. And, gentlemen, this is the monument that has been raised to the Confederate soldiers of Alabama.
—Jefferson M. Falkner, as he stood upon the highest point overlooking the Alabama soldiers' home, April 2, 1904

CHAPTER ONE

Johnny Reb: Hero and Symbol

Geneneral Tennessee Flintlock Sash was an ancient Confederate veteran whom local society venerated and praised. On special occasions Sash, dressed in uniform, was loaned to a museum by his granddaughter, who took care of him, and carefully put on display, surrounded by other relics of the war. As schoolchildren passed by, they were afforded a rare opportunity to see (but not touch) a real, live Confederate veteran—and a general to boot! Yet neither was Sash a former general nor was he wearing his own uniform. In fact, he could hardly remember anything about the war, let alone the details of any engagement that he had supposedly witnessed. Moreover, he inwardly detested being forced to relive his part. Except for the pretty girls who occasionally paid attention to him, Sash could not have cared less for the ceremonial activities.

Not unlike Sash—a character in a story by Flannery O'Connor[1]—thousands of Confederate veterans were dressed in uniforms, publicly exhibited, protected from harm, and required to play a role. They were residents of soldiers' homes, "living monuments" to the South's most sacred virtues of honor and chivalry. At these homes, not only schoolchildren, but southerners of all ages, gathered to celebrate and help relive the achievements of the past. The Confederate soldiers' home served as simultaneously a place of refuge, a museum, a military camp, an artificial city, and a shrine.

As many as sixteen different Confederate soldiers' homes were founded, and their collective histories span more than a century. The first homes were established during the 1880s and 1890s, a period of rampant ex-Confederate activity. In these two decades, at the same time that southerners organized and dedicated themselves to unveil monuments, write regimental histories, decorate cemeteries, preserve battlefields, and participate in reunion rituals—all in an effort to preserve the memory of Johnny Reb—a viable and discernible soldiers' home "movement" developed.

Soldiers' homes were built long before the 1880s. The Hôtel des Invalides, believed to be the first institution of its kind, was constructed in Paris by Louis XIV in 1670, and in 1682 the Chelsea military asylum was established by Charles II of England. In the United States, Congress first authorized an asylum in 1811 for veterans of the American navy; forty years later Senator Jefferson Davis introduced legislation that resulted in the founding of the U.S. Soldiers' Home, with branches in Louisiana, Mississippi, Kentucky, and Washington, D.C. During the Civil War, the U.S. Sanitary Commission created temporary soldiers' homes or lodges, and in the South private residences were converted into makeshift convalescent homes to meet the needs of wounded men. But these "soldiers' homes" were relatively small-scale endeavors compared to the institutions established immediately after the war and during the next several decades in more than two dozen northern and western states to augment the newly created National Homes for Disabled Volunteer Soldiers.[2]

Soldiers' homes were not, then, uniquely southern institutions. In fact, there are striking similarities in the stories behind the creation and administration of Confederate homes and of their national counterparts. The Grand Army of the Republic (GAR) and the Woman's Relief Corps served as primary advocates of soldiers' homes for Union veterans in much the same way that the United Confederate Veterans (UCV) and the United Daughters of the Confederacy (UDC) championed homes for Johnny Reb. All but a few of the Union veterans' homes established in as many as twenty-eight different states from Vermont to California were, like southern homes, founded during the 1880s and 1890s. The dedication of a veterans' home for the "boys in blue," as for the boys who had worn gray, was an important event, featuring bands and uniforms, campfires and speeches, drum corps and reunion tents. The "typical" state home for disabled and poor Union veterans was part military camp, part workhouse, part asylum, and part final refuge, just as it was for ex-Confederates. And national administrators and managers, no less than southern ones, adopted a paternalistic attitude toward their charges; at times worried that they were being overly repressive in maintaining discipline; fought ceaseless battles against inmates' intemperance, filth, and unchasteness; earnestly sought to combat the debilitating effects of wounds and disease heightened by old age; and were generally reluctant to allow women to be admitted to the homes or to serve on governing boards. Moreover, based upon the available evidence, Union veterans who resided in the national homes apparently had much in common with their Confederate comrades. These old soldiers from both sides of the war were poor and semiskilled, and they were mostly single men who either had never married or had recently been widowed. In addition, they were told by their superiors to abide by rules and regulations, encouraged to attend worship services, warned about the evils of imbibing alcoholic beverages, and, above all, enjoined to conduct themselves as gentlemen or risk receiving a dishonorable discharge.[3]

At the same time, Confederate soldiers' homes and those for Union veterans were different in at least two fundamental respects. First, despite yearnings by a group of well-meaning individuals, the southern homes never received monies from Uncle Sam. By contrast, in addition to regular legislative appropriations and occasional contributions from veterans' groups, each state home that accommodated Union veterans received an annual per capita subsidy from the National Homes for Disabled Volunteer Soldiers, a federal government agency. For example, beginning in 1888 the Wisconsin Veterans' Home near Waupaca received $100 per year for every veteran admitted.[4] By 1922 total federal funding for veterans' homes had reached $777,757. A stronger financial base invariably eased the economic burden at homes caring for Union veterans—Southern homes always seemed to be strapped for funds— affecting in the long run both the level of service and the quality of care provided there. Furthermore, in accepting federal money, home officials were required ultimately to report to Washington and conform their operations to certain governmental standards. Confederate administrators were accountable to their individual state legislatures instead of a centralized bureaucracy responsible for coordinating veterans' care in all southern states and therefore generally exercised greater autonomy.

Second, the Confederate homes, unlike national ones, excluded veterans of other wars. This difference had important consequences, too. Both Confederate and U.S. soldiers' homes possessed symbolic as well as purely functional roles. Yet, because survivors of the Indian Wars and the Mexican-American War—and, in time, veterans from the Spanish-American War and World War I—were admitted to the national homes, they could not help losing much of their symbolic significance. No longer were they homes for veterans of the Union army exclusively. But the Confederate homes remained forever Confederate, even if their military character was altered when most of the veterans had died and widows and other female relatives were admitted as a matter of policy. While the functional significance of homes for both Confederate and Union veterans increased over time—as their populations aged and required greater custodial care—Confederate soldiers' homes continued to serve a vital symbolic function for southerners of all ages even as national homes were losing their symbolic power and appeal.

Up until now, the Confederate soldiers' home movement, which began in the 1880s, has received scant attention. William W. White's standard work, *The Confederate Veteran*, devotes only four brief pages to the topic. Judith Cetina's ambitious dissertation, "A History of Veterans' Homes in the United States, 1811–1930," apportions less than a dozen of nearly 500 pages to the

"THE OLD BRIGADES
MARCH SLOWER NOW—
THE BOYS WHO
WORE THE GRAY—
BUT THERE'S LIFE AN'
BATTLE-SPIRIT IN A HOST
O' THEM TODAY!

THEY HEAR THEIR COMRADES
CALLIN' FROM THE WHITE
TENTS FAR AWAY;

AND ANSWER WITH THE
RINGIN' ROLL OF

'DIXIE!'"

Images of Johnny Reb, like this one, helped inspire the establishment of homes for wounded, poor, but brave, ex-Confederates. (author's collection)

Confederate homes of Louisiana and Maryland and the South Carolina institution for needy women. Only three concise summaries—concerning the Virginia, North Carolina, and Oklahoma homes—have appeared in print. Therefore, any attempt to treat several homes at once and to place them in their proper historical context will enhance our current knowledge and understanding of these homes.[5]

Although not concerning themselves with the soldiers' homes per se, at least two scholars have interpreted them within a larger framework. Charles Wilson views the Lost Cause as a conservative "cultural revitalization" movement, arguing that Lost Cause enthusiasts (particularly ex-Confederate organizations) feared that certain southern values were threatened and sought to safeguard those values by preserving or reliving the past. Preservation or revitalization, according to Wilson, took various forms: monument dedication, archival work, holiday and reunion rituals. Therefore, if Wilson is correct in identifying the appeal of the Lost Cause, Confederate soldiers' homes were created as means of resisting progress and preserving tradition. In other words, the Confederate soldiers' home was a manifestation of the struggle to reconcile "progress and tradition."[6] More recently, Gaines Foster has interpreted the "celebration" of traditional southern values by predominantly middle-class Confederate veterans' groups in the late 1880s and early 1890s as a direct reaction to various social and political upheavals and tensions that gripped the South following the war. The rituals of this celebration, he points out, above all praised the common soldier—by building monuments or writing histories, by awarding pensions or establishing veterans' homes—as a means of re-forming society and promoting social unity.[7]

An in-depth investigation of Confederate soldiers' homes necessitates testing these prevailing interpretations. As this study reveals, the southern soldiers' home movement cannot be isolated from other attempts by the public to memorialize Johnny Reb, and reactionary Lost Cause zealots (or even southerners in general) were not the only ones who took part in the movement. Although they founded soldiers' homes of their own, Union veterans actively participated in the establishment of similar southern institutions. Also, at the forefront of the movement were southerners like Henry Grady, John B. Gordon, Lawrence "Sul" Ross, Francis P. Fleming, and Julian Shakespeare Carr, men who championed national as well as sectional values. Thus, Confederate soldiers' homes cannot be viewed solely as another ritual for preserving a special southern identity but must be seen also as a vehicle for achieving sectional reconciliation.

As Gaines Foster has suggested, the Confederate soldiers' home movement was, indeed, a class-specific reform movement. Predominantly middle-class members of society eagerly responded to the needs of indigent but "worthy" veterans by founding institutions and administering them; and it was this same group of people who consistently viewed their charges as objects of benevolent paternalism requiring comfort and care, as well as moral guidance and discipline. Camp Nicholls, the second soldiers' home of Louisiana,[8] for example, was made possible through the combined efforts of two strong veterans' societies headquartered in New Orleans. Born during a period of intense political strife, the first of these organizations, the Association of the Army of Northern Virginia (AANV), was chartered in 1874, about the same time that more than a dozen different militia companies united to oppose the Radical Republican administration of Governor William P. Kellogg. The

White League attracted to its ranks men with military backgrounds, many of whom were former Confederate soldiers. In September 1874 they handily defeated state troops commanded by, among others, General James Longstreet, in what came to be known as the battle of Liberty Place, and forcibly removed Kellogg from office. The second organization, the Association of the Army of Tennessee (AAT), also had ties with the White League. Some men already belonging to the prestigious Washington Artillery joined the AAT when it was formed in 1877. Three years earlier the unit had fought alongside other militia groups during the battle of Liberty Place.[9]

In spite of the political activism of some members, both the AANV and the AAT, like most fraternal orders of the period, functioned primarily as benefit societies, preferring to identify themselves as "benevolent" and incorporating the word as part of their official names. Benevolence took two forms, one for members and another for nonmembers. Each association aimed to provide its dues-paying members and their dependents with assistance during personal and unavoidable crises: sudden unemployment, poverty, and "extreme cases of want and sickness." When a member "in good standing" died, for example, he could count on his comrades to give him a proper and decent burial in the group tomb the veterans had paid for and erected.[10] Like other fraternal organizations, the AANV and AAT in reality operated as exclusive social clubs rather than as fraternities open to all ex-Confederates. More than two-thirds (67.9 percent) of AAT members had proprietary or professional occupations. Influential men—attorneys, physicians, clergymen, merchants, and elected officials—also dominated AANV membership rolls. Each group established and originally enforced stringent membership guidelines: the association was opened to anyone of "good moral character" who had served honorably, subject to a two-thirds vote of the membership. The bylaws drafted by each organization permitted honorary memberships for local dignitaries, particularly leaders of other veterans' organizations. Yet the same rules barred survivors of different Confederate armies from joining. As for needy veterans not belonging to a particular society—or those men entitled to membership by virtue of their military record but unable to afford to pay monthly dues—they had to look elsewhere for comradeship and assistance.[11]

Nonmembers, but comrades nonetheless, received second priority in the benevolent activities of the AAT and AANV. In response to the yellow fever epidemic that devastated New Orleans in 1878, each association created and maintained for many years veterans' benefits and relief committees that supervised the distribution of funds and other donated items of clothing, food, and medicine to "worthy" recipients. In the depression era of the mid-1890s several prominent members of the AANV founded a job agency in order to assist able-bodied comrades (and their spouses and children) in finding work.

Headed by James Y. Gilmore, a journalist, and Hamilton Dudley Coleman, a local plantation machinery manufacturer and dealer, the Confederate Veterans' Employment Bureau of New Orleans published and circulated a small pamphlet containing the names, addresses, and occupations of scores of "exemplary and law-abiding" applicants.[12] The two veterans' groups sometimes coordinated relief activities as well. In one instance of such a dual effort, in 1880 they convinced state legislators to enact a bill providing either artificial limbs or cash payments for crippled ex-Confederates. Both societies continued to lobby successfully for similar legislation throughout the decade. Beginning in 1884, for example, owing largely to the efforts of the AAT and AANV, the state granted a quarter section of land to disabled and indigent Confederate veterans and widows. Another combined project a year earlier had resulted in the establishment of a soldiers' home in New Orleans.[13]

Among the first veterans' organizations to establish a home for the "invalid and infirm" were other ex-Confederates who comprised the Robert E. Lee Camp No. 1 in Richmond, Virginia. Formed in 1883, the group was primarily dedicated to "minister[ing] ... to the wants of" disabled comrades languishing in poorhouses throughout the South. Its roughly forty charter members, consisting largely of skilled craftsmen and clerical workers, elected Captain Charles U. Williams, an attorney, as their first commander and chose other former Confederate officers—in civilian life a publisher, a druggist, and a dentist—as their executive committee. Subsequently, Richmond's mayor, William C. Carrington, succeeded Williams as commander; he was followed by Generals John R. Cooke and, in 1885, Fitzhugh Lee (who would become Virginia's next governor).[14] Within a few years the camp's membership rolls boasted the names of many more prominent and respected individuals, men like former Confederate general Peyton Wise, a tobacco inspector; Major Lewis Ginter, the city's largest tobacco manufacturer; and James B. Pace, a bank president. By the 1890s Richmond's middle class clearly dominated the veterans' group, which numbered about 700 members; more than two-thirds pursued professional occupations. As membership numbers and overall socioeconomic status rose, the camp expanded its scope, or, in the words of member Henry R. Pollard, "ennobled its objects," when it formed a historical committee to collect and publicize the "gallant deeds and pure motives and high character of Southern soldiers."[15]

Like the Lee Camp, the AAT, and the AANV, Nashville's Benjamin F. Cheatham Bivouac No. 1 drew its constituency largely from the upper socioeconomic ranks. Named in honor of a recently deceased popular Confederate general, at its zenith this group would function as the parent society for more than 3,000 veterans residing throughout the South. Its strict bylaws limited membership to men who had fought "honorably," had maintained an

Confederate veterans, like these on the grounds of the Lee Camp Home in the late
1930s, were dressed in uniforms, publicly exhibited, and required to play a role.
(courtesy of Virginia State Library)

"unimpeachable" war record, and had remained citizens "of good standing"
since war's end. Fully two-thirds of its members held professional positions
considered compatible with the emerging New South; only about one-fourth
were farmers. A surprisingly large number were not native sons, but surnames
such as Cockrill, Overton, and Porterfield testified to the presence of the old
Nashville elite. Attorneys, physicians, and businessmen dominated this group
of Nashville's leading men.[16] Some members were inveterate joiners, and their
behavior proved to be contagious. For example, the bivouac's first president,
George B. Guild, also served as vice-president of the state veterans' association
and (with his wife) was a contributing member of the Confederate Monumental Association. The latter organization was at one time presided over by
another bivouac member, Marcus A. Spurr of Commerce National Bank,
whose wife (along with the wives and widows of other veterans) was numbered among its members. Attorney John P. Hickman held the elected office of
secretary in five organizations concerned with the well-being of Confederate
veterans or the commemoration of the Confederate past; his wife joined the
nationwide monumental association and worked tirelessly with the UDC,

The Confederate soldiers' home was part military camp and part artificial city, as this view of the North Carolina Soldiers' Home in Raleigh, c. 1910, suggests. (courtesy of William R. Perkins Library, Duke University, Durham, North Carolina)

while their offspring actively participated in the city's two Sons of Confederate Veterans chapters.

The Cheatham Bivouac resembled the New Orleans organizations more than the Lee Camp in that it advocated from the outset a historical and archival mission. According to its official charter, members committed themselves to honoring their late comrades who had died in service or since the war by writing about their heroic deeds and collecting and preserving "all material of value" for later historians. At least two of the bivouac's members utilized this collected material: charter member William J. McMurray, a one-armed physician, former Klan organizer, and future president of the state health board, wrote a respectable account of his old infantry unit, the Twentieth Tennessee, and President Guild wrote a history of the Fourth Tennessee Cavalry, a regiment formerly commanded by his brother-in-law, Colonel Baxter Smith. At one monthly meeting the Cheatham Bivouac unanimously adopted a resolution—presented by its history committee chairman, Nashville *Banner* editor Gideon H. Baskette—condemning a state textbook, John J. Anderson's *History of the United States*, as "mischievous in tone and sentiment, untruthful in statement and tending to perpetuate the resentment of the civil war." At another meeting of the organization, several prominent members proposed establishing a Tennessee soldiers' home.[17]

Thus, many of the leading men of such New South cities as New Orleans, Richmond, and Nashville were the people who started Confederate soldiers' homes, formed their governing boards, and became officers of the institutions. They were motivated not only by a sense of comradeship and humanitaria-nism but also by what they themselves defined as their "sacred duty." For to take care of their less fortunate brethren who had fought in a glorious cause was not just a matter of regional pride for southerners; it was a matter of honor.

In a speech at the opening of the Lee Camp Home in Richmond in 1885, Archer Anderson praised the "supreme manliness" of the "devoted" Confeder-ate soldier, who by virtue of self-discipline had attained "moral perfection." Not all soldiers, he admitted, had reached this ideal, but "they strove to attain it." As a result many veterans who had fought under Robert E. Lee and Joseph E. Johnston had become "useful, loyal and zealous citizens" since the war.[18] A few days after a bill to establish Tennessee's soldiers' home was introduced in the state legislature in 1889, the Nashville *Banner* printed an address delivered to the Cheatham Bivouac by the paper's editor, Gideon Baskette. His speech, as much rhetorical as it was autobiographical, focused on the Confederate private soldier, "who bore so large a share of hardship" during the war. Baskette recounted how he had seen with his own eyes comrades who were poorly armed, barefoot, and hatless, with clothing that made them "often the more ragged than any beggar." Despite Johnny Reb's sometimes "picturesque, gro-tesque, unique," appearance, Baskette recalled, he was the "model citizen soldier, the military hero of the nineteenth century!" Confederate veterans are "the men who made the grandest fight that the world has ever seen," ex-claimed former governor E. W. Rector of Arkansas at a meeting to discuss erect-ing a home in his state. "The whole world was their enemies—they fought the universe!" Surely men of such caliber merited special care and attention.[19]

"These old soldiers cannot be with [us] much longer," wrote General Joseph Wheeler in 1902, some four years before his own death. "They are rapidly nearing the sunset of their lives, and the present generation must be saved the remorse which in after years they will feel, if, looking back, they see that during the short time these brave heroes were with them, they were allowed to spend their last days in want and suffering."[20] It was this image of the Confederate soldier, if not of any specific group of individuals, that soldiers' home advocates wanted to protect, preserve, and (as some would charge) exploit. The myth of Johnny Reb was persistently conjured up, nurtured, and promoted as a means of advancing a host of causes, including the building of Confederate soldiers' homes.[21] To the predominantly middle-class men and women who sought to perpetuate his memory, Johnny Reb served as a living relic—the very sort represented by Tennessee Flintlock Sash—from a mythic past to be preserved and enshrined.

CHAPTER TWO

Southern Poor Boys

After visiting an old acquaintance in Chimborazo Hospital No. 4 in Richmond, Virginia, on August 23, 1864, Colonel William Ward hastily scribbled in his diary, "Poor fellow, he will never be well." Ward aptly summarized the military career of Henry J. Dawson, a private in the Seventh Tennessee Infantry, who spent fully half of the war incapacitated by a host of ailments—dysentery, bronchitis, chronic rheumatism, something diagnosed as "catarrah & debility"—unable even to walk or at times to feed himself. His weight plummeting to only ninety pounds, Dawson was mercifully granted a medical discharge in January 1865 at Petersburg, where he lingered until after Lee's surrender.[1] In the late spring of 1865, Dawson, like thousands of other former Rebel soldiers, finally returned home. Intending to get back to the routines of life interrupted by war, many would have little time left, for less than half survived until 1890.[2] Miraculously, Dawson, though only barely, had beaten the odds and persevered. In January 1894, his sixty-second year, no longer able to support himself by painting houses, his constitution completely "broken down," illiterate, never married, and living with "poor relations," Dawson had no other choice but to apply for a Confederate pension. He was not able to subsist on the pension, however, so the following year he entered the Tennessee Confederate Soldiers' Home, where he breathed his last in 1906.[3]

Dawson's postwar career typifies that of many indigent, homeless, and dissatisfied ex-Confederates who eventually applied to relief agencies for help. They were men who during the prime of their lives had bravely shouldered a musket and marched off to drive the Yankee invaders from their lands. Perhaps the most startling characteristic of these men was their relative youth. Among the first beneficiaries of the homes for ex-Confederates were men who had been born in the late 1830s or mid-1840s, who had taken up arms in defense of the southern cause in their late teens or mid-twenties, and who found themselves out of work and impoverished in their forties or early fifties (see the Appendix, Table 6 and Figure 1).[4]

To be poor at middle age was deeply disturbing to many Confederate veterans not only because it left them in material need but also because it was thought to raise serious questions about their manliness and morals. According to the prevailing assumptions of the period, a man should accumulate wealth with age; thus, to become dependent upon others was to admit failure. "The thought of having to go to the Paupers Home is a horor & a dread to many of us old vets," an ex-Confederate stated, "to beg we are ashamed; to except the charity of friends in case we have them, is humiliating." To accept charity was practically unthinkable, for, as a Confederate Memorial Day speaker in Alabama put it in 1902, honor is "dearer to [the ex-Confederate] than the laurel wreath that crowns the victor's brow." Governor Francis P. Fleming of Florida, a veteran of such bloody campaigns as Seven Pines, Gaines's Mill, Sharpsburg, and Gettysburg, who surrendered with Joseph E. Johnston's forces in May 1865, viewed pensions as an "evil" that "tends to lower" a Confederate veteran "from that high standard of honorable distinction." For these reasons, charity carried with it a nasty stigma that repelled many proud veterans.[5]

But the sad reality was that an estimated one of every five Confederate soldiers was wounded during the war. Soldiers' homes were places for wounded men and broken lives. In the Texas and Louisiana institutions, for example, fully one out of five residents was counted among the "war wounded." In the North Carolina, Georgia, and Tennessee homes, the ratios were considerably higher, about one out of three (see the Appendix, Table 7).[6]

Those who chose to acknowledge their poverty were quick to attribute their embarrassing financial circumstances to a service-related disability of some kind. "A man with one arm cannot be expected to make as much as one with two," explained John B. Glynn of Franklin, Louisiana, whose total earnings as a carpenter in 1885 amounted to only $245. Hundreds of other men who appealed for medical and monetary assistance from various New Orleans fraternal groups in the 1870s and 1880s claimed that the wounds they had received in the course of the fighting had not yet healed. In each case, the loss of a limb, blindness, or the inability to stand upright without flinching had seriously curtailed a veteran's postwar economic activity.[7]

The same was true wherever ex-Confederates resided. Despite a disabling wound received at Chickamauga, J. E. Roebuck "worked and managed to support [him]self honorably and very comfortably" until 1906, when he became ill and without means and "as a last resort" applied for admission to the Mississippi home. Excruciating pain plagued Nathan J. Lewis of Alabama, whose right leg had been shattered at Petersburg some twenty years earlier. By 1893 William J. McNairy of Aberdeen, Mississippi, still had not fully recuperated from the wound he had received at Gettysburg, nor had he been able to hold down a decent job. As a private in the Sixth Virginia Cavalry, Samuel Corbett had been wounded five different times and taken prisoner twice. His health impaired and his property lost because of the war, he became a "wanderer," drifting aimlessly from Virginia to Maryland to Texas and finally back east to North Carolina. S. J. Spindle, formerly of Harpers Ferry, spent nearly twenty years in Mexico before showing up in Austin, Texas, penniless, unemployed, and agonized by an old war wound. Among the first to enter the Alabama home was one Thomas Brown of Mobile, a seventy-one-year-old Irishman and veteran of the Seventeenth Alabama Infantry. Like many veterans, Brown had been unable to recover from the ravages of war. Poor, unmarried, and without living relatives, he decided that the state veterans' institution was the place for him.[8]

The war had adversely affected the lives of veterans in less visible ways as well. Before the fighting began, James B. Hale had been a "gentleman," a member of one of the most prominent families of East Tennessee. When he returned home, he discovered that he had lost everything: his slaves had been freed, his fields trampled, and his buildings plundered. And within a few years all of his immediate family members died. R. A. Toon returned after the surrender "without a cent to live on." Upon finding his home burned and his livestock slaughtered, Toon, like thousands of other dispossessed ex-Confederates, migrated to the city to rebuild his fortunes, but he never succeeded. His wife forced him out of the house and sued for divorce. Hugh L. Fry, on his journey home after the war, was arrested in Knoxville on a charge of treason; he swore an oath of allegiance, posted bail, and then hid out in the mountains of Georgia for three years to escape further prosecution. Fry never recovered financially. Neither did John M. Karr, whose father's undertaking business in Franklin, Tennessee, had been completely destroyed when the retreating Federals set the town ablaze in 1864.[9]

Other veterans could point to certain postwar events as the source of their poor health and abysmal deprivation. After a yellow fever epidemic struck New Orleans in 1878, scores of needy veterans and their families appealed for monetary assistance in order to to fill prescriptions, purchase groceries, pay rent, or discharge debts to undertakers and other creditors. Napoleon Saucier and George Boden lost their wives and children to the epidemic. The youngest of Charles E. Caylat's daughters died. Too infirm to report to work, Caylat lost his job. For the next six years he remained out of work, subsisting on the scanty contributions of his more fortunate comrades.[10] Other veterans, like James T. Holt, were victims of financial panics. Losing thousands of dollars when the National Bank of Petersburg failed in 1878, Holt spent four months in jail owing to bankruptcy and never recouped his losses. William O. Reese of

Standing in front of the Arkansas Confederate Home near Little Rock, c. 1908, are some of the deserving but down-on-their-luck veterans the home was established to care for. (author's collection)

Trenton, Georgia, saw all of his postwar savings, earned as a prison guard and convict lease warden, vanish in the panic of 1893. A few years later, he lost all of his property in bankruptcy court as well.[11] In March 1902 Thomas W. Booth of Montgomery had a most unfortunate accident. While working as a carpenter upon a high trestle of a streetcar line, he lost his balance and fell to the ground, a distance of twenty feet. Both of his feet were crushed, and he

suffered multiple breaks in both legs—the same limbs through which a minié ball had passed at Seven Pines nearly forty years earlier—rendering him paralyzed below the waist. Living in a day when there was no such thing as workers' compensation, Booth had no means to support himself and his family.[12]

During economically depressed times some aging veterans experienced even more hardships, and countless numbers of displaced men gravitated to the city. John M. DeSaussure went to New Orleans in 1893, after his former employer had replaced him with a boy working at half wages. William E. Todd trekked from New Orleans to Birmingham and finally to Washington, D.C., in search of "honest" work but succeeded in obtaining only low-paying temporary positions. H. C. Belcher, after being forced to retire from his job as a teacher in Monroe County, Tennessee, relocated in Nashville, where the only work he could find was as a street peddler.[13] Other ex-soldiers complained of what they regarded as blatantly discriminatory acts. Sixty-four-year old W. T. Vaughn of Louisville, Kentucky, was discharged from his bridge building job on account of his gray hairs. R. B. Clements's boss informed him he could no longer keep his job as a janitor in a Richmond armory because he had only one arm. "Truly it seems to me that the time has come when 'No Maimed Confederate Need Apply,'" observed Charles Moore, Jr., of Alexandria, Louisiana. For some time after the war, Moore had done remarkably well for himself and his family of five, despite having had his leg amputated at Gettysburg. But in 1878 Moore lost his clerking job. For the next few years he applied for positions all over Rapides Parish, only to be told over and over again that the situation had been awarded to some "Planter's Son or Relative." Eventually Moore appeared in New Orleans with only four dollars in his pocket, his health completely broken, and his family evicted from their home.[14]

Postwar life for other veterans residing in rural areas had been just as unrewarding. In contrast to the more recent misfortune experienced by some planters, theirs was merely one link in an unbroken chain of disappointment and deprivation. Although more than half of all Confederate soldiers had given their occupation as "farmer" upon enlistment, many had actually owned no real estate. In fact, a number had held no real or personal property at all. The rank and file of the southern army had consisted largely of "wool-hat boys," "crackers," "hayseeds," "strawfoots," and "clay-eaters": whatever derisive sobriquets were applied to them or they used to refer to themselves, they were landless, impoverished common folk whose families had for years eked out a hardscrabble existence.[15] The war had done little to improve their economic condition. Downward mobility was more characteristic of their experience than upward movement, and in the years following the war many continued to own no land, subsisting instead as sharecroppers, tenant farmers, or menial laborers. Plagued by declining health and plummeting crop prices, marginal farmers moved off their lands, which often had been too poor to cultivate successfully anyway. It was from this rather large pool of displaced common people that the soldiers' homes would draw a majority of their residents. More than one-half (58.6 percent) of all ex-Confederates who resided in these institutions had been either yeoman farmers, agricultural workers, or other unskilled laborers; only a relatively small fraction (16.4 percent) formerly held professional or clerical positions (see the Appendix, Table 8).

Exactly who were these southern common people who wound up in soldiers' homes, and how did the war create the preconditions for their application for poor relief? An analysis of a selected group of veterans who ultimately
resided in the Tennessee Soldiers' Home (see the Appendix, especially the
tables cited in the following paragraphs) provides some answers. It reveals, for
example, that at the outset of the war more than one-fifth (23.8 percent) of the
143 veterans and their families had owned, on average, estates worth only
$376. That figure fell far below the mean ($3,978) reportedly held by all
southern adult white males in 1860.[16] In addition, a somewhat larger proportion (27.9 percent) had owned no property at all. The starkly uneven distribution of wealth is attested by the fact that 30.6 percent of those sampled
controlled 94 percent of the 1860 total family wealth; veterans in the poorer
half of the sample owned slightly more than 1 percent (see the Appendix,
Table 9).[17]

Treating the Confederate military rank of the inmates sampled as a proxy
for their antebellum socioeconomic status, one can confirm historian Fred
Bailey's findings that a high proportion (85.6 percent) of men from poor
Tennessee families served as privates, while men from elite families dominated army leadership positions. Bailey broadly defines "poor" as those having
insignificant or no property and "elite" as those possessing prewar assets
greater than $5,000.[18] Of those whose rank could be positively determined,
men whose prewar wealth fell in the lower two categories of the sample (zero
and $1,000 or less) served predominantly as privates in the Confederate army.
On the other hand, men from families whose antebellum estates were considerably more valuable tended to hold higher military ranks. In fact, Bailey's
figures for the service rank of 188 men of "elite" standing and the figures
resulting from the analysis of the soldiers' home sample—which is a much
smaller sample than Bailey's—are nearly identical (see the Appendix, Table
10).[19]

The general economic disparity that marked the prewar condition of
soldiers in the Tennessee home sample persisted five years after the war. Four
of the five groups that had owned property in 1860 were somewhat poorer in
1870, undoubtedly reflecting their loss of slaves and other personal assets, as
well as depreciated real estate values. Nevertheless, the richest veterans and
their families in 1870 controlled a predominant share (82.9 percent) of the
wealth, while those in the other three wealth categories held on to the
remaining fraction. Of those sampled, 40 percent owned nothing in 1870,
eclipsing the percentage (27.9) of the previous decade (see the Appendix,
Table 11).

Although the foregoing results of the analysis of the Tennessee home
sample cannot be considered statistically reliable because of the restricted

Inmates and staff of the South Carolina Confederate Infirmary are displayed along
with other relics of the war in this group portrait from the 1920s.
(courtesy of South Carolina Department of Archives and History, Columbia)

sample size, together they suggest that many of those who would one day
occupy the wards of Confederate soldiers' homes had been poor at the outset of
the war and that these same men's fortunes had not improved ten years later.
As one ex-soldier remarked, these veterans were "penniless before the fight
and are so yet; but they fought for us."[20]

What happened to these veterans in the ensuing decades? Unfortunately,

family wealth cannot be traced beyond 1870 since subsequent manuscript censuses exclude individual economic data. Available tax lists, deed books, and other alternate sources would probably confirm what is already known; by all accounts, the years from 1870 to 1890 were characterized by increasing impoverishment and dependency. The financial conditions of most southern white farm families deteriorated steadily. These families increasingly failed to raise adequate foodstuffs for market, became heavily indebted, and lost their land. Indeed, it seems inconceivable that the material well-being of men who had always lived on the margin, with a bare minimum of land, education, and worldly goods, would significantly improve during a period of general economic tribulation.[21] The Tennessee veterans' economic and physical conditions immediately prior to enrolling in the home support this conclusion. Of the 143 men whose cases were examined, nearly 20 percent had been confined in poorhouses, while another 20 percent had been out of work for at least five years. Ninety percent of these men had been on the dole, and fully two-thirds reported having had no family to support them. Estimated income among those who had been employed ranged from $1.00 a day to $5.00 plus board a month. Low body weight and poor health at the time of enrollment were further indices of the debilitating consequences of these veterans' poverty.[22]

A few veterans in the sample, however, did appear to overcome adversity and attain some measure of success after 1870. When John Young, who had spent most of the war in a Union prison camp, returned home to Nashville, the ex-Confederate had to rely chiefly upon his own resources for economic advancement, as his father had died years earlier. For a while Young worked as a farm laborer picking cotton, and he eventually put away enough money to pay for medical training. In 1878 he moved to Texas, where he practiced medicine for the next thirty-eight years. William Wade, a day laborer in antebellum Memphis who was wounded at Shiloh, secured a position as bookkeeper for a Minnesota-based railroad by 1880 and continued to work for the same company until he retired at age seventy in 1910. Andrew J. Denton of Maury County and Clement Nance of Bedford County were propertyless agricultural workers when they joined the Confederate army, but by 1880 the two Tennesseans had purchased their own modest farms. All of these veterans, with the exception of Wade, ultimately found refuge in the Tennessee home for indigent ex-Confederates. Young was admitted in 1916, having obtained a transfer from the Texas home. His body was wracked by rheumatism, and at age seventy-two he was a widower with no children. Nance and Denton, both in their seventies and bachelors, were admitted in 1905 and 1909, respectively. Reportedly, family problems more than anything else led to Wade's application to the home in May 1911. According to one sympathetic observer, the veteran had "very foolishly" married a woman some forty years his junior, who was "indolent & self indulgent" and constantly upbraided him. Although his application was approved, Wade, acting "very plucky," refused to enter the home in Nashville, protesting that he would rather stay put and "take care of himself." He did, however, accept the winter clothing tendered him by the Minneapolis chapter of the UDC, which arranged a proper burial and ceremony for Wade upon his death in February 1912.[23]

For the majority of Tennessee veterans sampled, the years from 1860 to 1870 played a pivotal role in fostering the preconditions for home admission. Three-fourths (75.8 percent) of those who resided in or applied for admission to the Tennessee soldiers' institution during its first decade of operation had owned property valued at $1,000 or less at the outset of the war. Fifty-two-year-old Andrew J. Bonner, the first inmate admitted, in February 1890, had been a landless day laborer in Bedford County some three decades earlier. In 1870 Bonner, then a farmer and schoolteacher residing near Shelbyville, possessed $300 in personal property but still owned no real estate. Apparently, veterans who had formerly held substantially more wealth managed to avoid the institution longer. The richest and oldest veteran in the sample, ninety-year-old William H. Maney, whose father's prewar Williamson County estate was valued in excess of $85,000, was admitted in 1909, some twenty years after Bonner. Men who gained admittance to the home after 1901 had been, on the average, about three times more affluent than the men who preceded them in entering the home (see the Appendix, Table 12).[24]

The war years were crucial in other respects too. Early admittance may also have depended on whether and how badly a soldier had been wounded. The wiry constitutions of some veterans allowed them to remain active and self-supporting for many years despite their physical infirmities. For example, Samuel Roe, a gunsmith from Tipton County, had been wounded four separate times during the war, but he did not apply for admittance to the Tennessee home until 1910 when he was eighty-two years old.[25] Nevertheless, of the forty-eight Tennessee veterans in the sample who claimed they suffered from a war wound, 58.3 percent were admitted to the home before 1901. Slightly more than three-fourths (77.5 percent) of all known Confederate soldiers' home residents who claimed a service-related disability had been admitted during the first decade of their respective homes' operation. In all probability many of these same men never married; nearly one-third (31.8 percent) of all inmates remained single, and about half of them applied for admission before the turn of the century (see the Appendix, Table 13). There is also some evidence to support the contention that a significant number of those who did marry after the war, regardless of whether they were admitted before or after 1901, may have been sterile and consequently produced no lineal descendants to care for them as they grew older or more feeble. Whether they had never been married or were recently widowed, some veterans also may have suffered from severe social and psychological problems that significantly reduced their ability to adapt to a stress-inducing institutional environment, thereby increasing their vulnerability and heightening mortality rates.[26]

Some veterans, as sons of planters, had access to enough wealth, education, and family support to aid them in their postwar recovery and defer institutionalization until relatively later in their lives. For example, William Nevins of Rutherford County relied upon his father's wealth and family connections to take care of him for many years after losing his leg at Murfreesboro in 1863.

Tennessee lawmakers set aside part of Andrew Jackson's Hermitage estate for construction of a home for the state's indigent and homeless Confederate veterans, some of whom pose before the home in this photograph taken late in the 1890s. (courtesy of the Hermitage—Home of Andrew Jackson)

When the war closed, Thomas Stokley Vinson worked as an overseer on his father's rice and sugar plantations near Centerville, Louisiana, for several years before he returned to his birthplace of Gallatin, Tennessee, where townspeople who still remembered his grandfather and father elected him to various public offices. Henry Clay Nolen's father had been sheriff of Haywood County. After the war ended, young Nolen returned home, got married, had seven children, and served as mayor of Brownsville for a number of years. Greenberry Dobbins, a former member of the Ninth Tennessee Cavalry, borrowed money from his father and "went west." Eventually, even these veterans from more affluent backgrounds applied for admission to the Tennessee home. In 1911 Nevins, at age seventy-one, with only his unmarried sister residing with him, was finally forced to enter the Tennessee institution. Vinson, at age sixty-five, and Nolen, at age seventy-six, entered the home in 1908 and 1918, respectively. After Dobbins returned to Tennessee, he fell on hard times. In 1913 his wife died, and he had suffered a stroke not long before her death. With his estate totally exhausted and his nearest kin residing in Utah, Dobbins, at age seventy-seven, finally applied for admission in 1918. At least some veterans who had begun life with relative advantages could point to personal failings as the source of their postwar economic downfall. After his release from the prisoner of war camp at Johnson's Island, Ohio, Joseph B. Scobey returned to manage his family's Wilson County plantation. Never married, he squandered much of his inheritance on racehorses. Edwin Whitmore, who had been one of General Nathan Bedford Forrest's men, a scion of a formerly prominent Fayette County family, lost the bulk of what had been bequeathed to him by taking "too much liquor occasionally."[27]

Whatever the reasons for their condition, veterans not only in Tennessee but across the South aroused attention in the early 1880s. By that time the disabled and indigent ex-Confederate had become a visible problem. In urban areas he appeared on the scene jobless, half-starved, weary, ragged, excessively dirty, and sorrowful. He sat with shoulders sagging in a vacant doorway, desperately waiting for someone to pass by and offer him a job, a meal, or some spare change and perhaps another drink. Or he huddled next to a meager fire in a vacant lot by the railyard, reflecting on painful memories. Or he lay dying of consumption amid the foul conditions of the city almshouse. An unidentified poet described him and his plight:

> A battle-scarred old veteran
>   One who had worn the gray,
> And fought beneath the Southern flag
>   With glory as his pay;
> Now bent with age and worn by time,
>   Stands waiting at the door,
> And asks the State for shelter—
>   He's homeless, old and poor.[28]

Wherever the South's poor boys were found, their suffering pricked the conscience of their fellow citizens and moved them to action.

CHAPTER THREE

The Sacred Duty

On April 9, 1884, the nineteenth anniversary of the surrender at Appomattox, an enthusiastic audience, comprised mostly of veterans, assembled to hear a series of speakers discuss the establishment of a home for needy ex-Confederates. Perhaps the most unusual aspect of the meeting was that it took place neither in Richmond, the proposed site of the institution, nor for that matter in any other city of the South, but in New York City.[1] The large, flag-draped hall of the Cooper Union Institute resounded with cheers and hearty applause that evening, as several luminaries held forth from the speaker's podium. Among them, ironically, was the so-called Hero of Appomattox himself, a recently retired Georgia senator, General John B. Gordon, who chaired a committee of Confederate and Union veterans promoting the Richmond home.[2] Gordon spoke at great length about a southern home "movement" that had commenced with the determination of men of opposing armies to become comrades. The general was referring to the Blue-Gray reunions of the previous two summers, during which Union veterans visiting New Orleans and Richmond had told of national homes generously subsidized by a "grateful government" and had volunteered to contribute to similar projects in the South. "This movement," Gordon predicted confidently, "will do more to cement a reunited country than all political harangues and platforms."[3]

Echoing Gordon's conciliatory keynote was legless Corporal James Tanner, Brooklyn's tax collector, the future GAR commander in chief and U.S. commissioner of pensions, as well as "moving spirit" behind the establishment of the New York Soldiers' Home at Bath. Tanner declared that it was the "sacred duty" of the GAR to "do something for the poor soldiers of the South." Human decency and the "common doctrines of Christianity" demanding it, "let us reach out the hand of sympathy," Tanner concluded, "now that we are one country, one flag and one destiny from Maine to the Gulf!"[4] More than half a dozen other prepared speeches—by Ohio carpetbagger Judge Albion W. Tourgée, for example, and by former Union general Wager Swayne and brevet brigadier James R. O'Beirne, the latter a congressional medal of honor recipient—filled the hall that night. All of the speeches expressed the theme of reunion, as did the red, white, and blue bunting with the gilded inscription BLUE AND GRAY that stretched behind the speakers' platform. Reunion was likewise the theme of a medallion specially designed for the meeting that featured Johnny Reb and Billy Yank shaking hands, a medallion proudly worn by many in the audience.[5]

The Cooper Union Institute meeting was but one of several remarkable fund-raising extravaganzas planned and coordinated by Gordon's committee on behalf of the Richmond home. The following month Tanner and the GAR sponsored a "Testimonial and Entertainment" at the Academy of Music in Brooklyn. The meeting featured an opening address by former abolitionist Henry Ward Beecher and a stirring "lecture" by an Andersonville prisoner of war. Throughout the evening musicians played such crowd pleasers as "The Star-Spangled Banner," "Dixie," and "Marching through Georgia"; the audience especially cheered "A Knot of Blue and Gray," superbly rendered by a Richmond tenor. When it all ended, nearly $2,000 had been raised, much more than the amount donated during a special performance of *Richard III* at the Metropolitan Opera House the previous week.[6] Before long, Gordon's efforts on behalf of the southern soldiers' home at Richmond had captured the nation's attention. President Grover Cleveland endorsed the project. Former president and general U. S. Grant gave his "hearty approval" in the form of a $500 check. William W. Corcoran, an influential Washington banker, donated ten times that amount, and the Appleton publishing family presented a comparable gift. Dozens of Union veterans' organizations scattered from Sing Sing, New York, to Butte, Montana, contributed. A theatrical troupe in St. Louis and another company touring the South set aside one-half of their proceeds from special performances for the home. Coloradan C. A. Spencer, a former officer in the Eleventh Vermont Infantry, who said he considered Robert E. Lee "the Greatest General of modern times," donated his entire $1,200 annual pension, claiming that he voiced "the feelings of nine-tenths of all" his old comrades when he asserted he had "no better and truer friends" than the "old Soldiers of the Confederacy." For months, similar promises of both moral support and financial contributions poured into the R. E. Lee Camp No. 1 headquarters, temporarily located at Monticello Hall, on Broad Street in downtown Richmond.[7]

With a successful fund-raising drive behind it, the Lee Camp moved rapidly to establish the home. Fitzhugh Lee, as expected, accepted the camp's nomination to head the board of trustees (soon renamed board of visitors), which by November 1884 had purchased for $14,000 a thirty-six-acre farm and homestead formerly belonging to Channing Robinson located on the outskirts of northwest Richmond. Eventually cottages bearing the names of prominent benefactors—Corcoran, Pace, Appleton and Ginter—were constructed adjacent to the Robinson House. On February 22, 1885, Washington's birthday, the Lee Camp Soldiers' Home (its official name) opened with a procession that commenced at Monticello Hall at eleven o'clock. Active camp members in gray uniforms marched to the site, where they heard Archer Anderson—son of Confederate general and Tredegar ironworks owner Joseph Reid Anderson and treasurer of the Tredegar works as well as a fellow member of the Lee Camp—present the dedicatory address.[8] Anderson paid homage to those who had fulfilled their "sacred and solemn duty" by contributing to the "pious and beneficent work": fellow veterans; southern women, with their "magic fingers" and "witching will"; and especially Grant, "The Great Captain," who, after having "waged fierce and relentless war, stretched out a friendly hand and bade us hope and prosper." He then turned his attention to the home's future beneficiaries, or "recipients" as he preferred to call them, private soldiers of "honorable record" who had since become disabled, poor, and "unfit to earn their own livelihood." They now lacked food, clothing, and shelter. Anderson rhetorically asked: "Shall we let these men starve, while we write books to emblazon their heroic deeds, and erect statues to their leaders?" It would be a shame for more fortunate fellow soldiers not to come to the rescue. Anderson concluded by emphasizing that the Lee Camp Soldiers' Home was not only a building but also a "monument to a re-united country," the same theme that Gordon and the other Cooper Union Institute speakers had stressed some ten months earlier.[9]

To speak of a "movement," as General Gordon had done, implies a coherent process with a beginning and an end. Yet at the time when Gordon spoke no one accurately could have predicted that the movement that had its origins in the second decade following the end of the Civil War would finally end more than eighty years later when the last Confederate soldiers' home formally closed its doors. Nor could it have been properly stated that the movement was limited to one state, anymore than it could have been truthfully asserted that Gordon and the Virginians were the initiators of the movement, since ex-Confederates in as many as sixteen different states ultimately got involved and acted largely independently of each other. In fact, the inauguration of the so-called Confederate soldiers' home movement that Gordon so proudly heralded in 1884 did not begin in Virginia, or in any of the former Confederate states for that matter, but instead commenced some three years earlier in the border state of Kentucky. Admittedly, nothing much became of the Confederate Soldiers' Home and Widows' and Orphans' Asylum at Georgetown, Kentucky, though its founder, Captain James E. Cantrill, one of John Hunt Morgan's men

From the perspective of those on the "outside," Confederate soldiers' homes were idyllic and serene places, as the Lee Camp Home appears to be in this photograph from the 1890s. (courtesy of Virginia State Library)

and a former lieutenant governor, predicted during the summer of 1881 that the home would "stand as an enduring monument" for the relief of the "crippled and indigent Confederate." After only a few years in operation, with more than $5,000 remaining to be paid on the buildings and grounds and $8,000 still owed by subscribers, the home suspended operations indefinitely in November 1883.[10]

Perhaps the main prerequisite for the establishment of a soldiers' home was the existence of a statewide Confederate veterans' organization to supply the initial resources, manpower, and political clout needed for such an endeavor. Surely one contributing factor for the failure of the short-lived Kentucky institution had been the lack of an effective organization like the Lee Camp of Richmond. Two decades passed before a Confederate soldiers' home was refounded in Kentucky in 1901, when members of the state UCV adopted a report proposing the institution's establishment. In March of the following year, the legislature passed an act incorporating the Kentucky Confederate Home and appropriating $10,000 for the endeavor, to be added to the more than $17,000 previously raised through private subscriptions. In addition, A. W. Gordon, a veteran, donated Villa Ridge Inn and its forty-acre plat at Pewee Valley, about sixteen miles outside Louisville, for use as a home. But "it is no charitable institution," proclaimed the speaker at the home's dedication ceremonies on October 23, 1902, as a crowd estimated at 10,000 looked on and cheered, amid the strains of "Dixie," "My Old Kentucky Home," and other southern airs. Not "since the Civil War," reported the *Courier Journal*, "has there been a gathering of old Confederate soldiers, of their families and friends in Kentucky filled with more enthusiasm for the South and all things Southern."[11]

In Louisiana there were two strong veterans' organizations, the AAT and the AANV, each capable of organizing benevolence for a soldiers' home. In fact, it was during a meeting of the AAT in New Orleans on June 13, 1882, that Walter H. Rogers, a state appellate judge—whose obituarist credited him with having played a prominent role in the White League Revolt of 1874— proposed that the veterans petition the legislature again, as they had before, for the establishment of a home. The AAT and AANV had just spent, collectively, $35,000 on a tomb for their own members, but they were unable to allocate enough funds to meet the more pressing demand of caring for their living comrades. A state-supported relief program offered, in the veterans' view, a twofold panacea. Their impoverished comrades would be cared for, while at the same time the veterans' organizations would be spared the brunt of the financial burden. When the AAT president, Joseph A. Charlaron, put the proposal to a vote, the forty-five AAT members in attendance—several of whom held state Senate and House seats—voiced their approval. Charlaron then appointed Judge Rogers to chair a joint committee of AAT and AANV members charged with drafting the appropriate legislation.[12]

The amendment to Act No. 103 (the measure that had created the original, abortive soldiers' home of Louisiana in 1866) mandated a modest appropriation of $5,000 over a two-year period. Some "sticklers," as Charlaron later referred to them, considered the enabling act, House Bill No. 309, unconstitutional. Most notable in this camp was Senator William W. Leake, of West Feliciana Parish. Regarded by his peers as a "devoted and gallant Confederate soldier," Leake argued against the amendment because he believed it violated Article 51 of the Louisiana Constitution of 1875, which, according to his interpretation, prohibited the state from funding private charities. The rightful responsibility for the welfare of Louisiana's "infirm, disabled paupers," he pointed out, belonged to the parishes. Had the bill been worded differently, so as to force the parishes rather than the state to appropriate the money, Leake declared, he might have been persuaded to support it.[13]

Were Leake's arguments only a ruse? Did his real objection actually lie in his unspoken conviction that *true* men are responsible for their own lives and should never look to others for assistance? Given the overwhelmingly negative attitude of many veterans and the public at large toward institutional relief, opposition to the home is understandable.[14] In fact, Charlaron remarked in a historical account written in 1901 that the trustees of Louisiana's first soldiers'

The Texas Confederate Home for Men, shown here, stood atop an eminence overlooking the Colorado River in Austin that is now occupied by married student
housing for the University of Texas.
(courtesy of Austin History Center, Austin Public Library, Austin, Texas)

home had "found it no trifling task" to overcome among veterans their own
"disinclination" toward the home; the new board, he added, encountered the
identical "prejudice." As one veteran revealed, he felt a certain "humiliation"
in applying for admission to a home, because one invariably "loses caste" when
entering such an institution. For similar reasons many ex-Confederates renounced pensions. Apparently nothing aroused an ex-Confederate's indignation more than a perceived assault on his manhood, regardless of the source.
When Gilmore and Coleman published their list of unemployed New Orleans
veterans in 1895, they carefully emphasized that the men listed the "worthy
class of citizens" who desired an "opportunity to work," not charity. A state-
supported home—or indoor relief of any kind—violated the principle of manly
self-sufficiency. When AAT and AANV members read a mistaken report that
Leake, in debating the bill's legality, had publicly called *them* "paupers," each
association passed resolutions condemning his "unjustified language."[15]

The bill's proponents employed potent oratory in order to counter such
attacks. They spoke of the state's long-standing obligation to provide "compensation" and a "dignified retirement" to the "brave, worthy men"—one

senator actually dubbed them "living monuments"—who took up arms in the state's defense. *Times-Democrat* editor John Augustin, a former Crescent City White Leaguer, currently AAT executive committee chairman, wrote that the home would provide a place where the "maimed, crippled and destitute survivors of so many glorious battlefields" could find "rest and peace for their old age." Future governor Murphy J. Foster echoed the editor's remarks, stating that Louisianians owed the "helpless and dependent champions of our rights and liberties" not only a debt of gratitude but also a "full share of veneration and love." An AANV officer conceived of the home as a "resting place" for "deserving" ex-Confederates.[16] Each of the spokesmen emphasized that the proposed home would be the payment due for services rendered, not an outright gift. This important distinction served as the crux of their arguments and a rationale for their enterprise. The sensitive issue apparently dogged the Louisiana home founders long after the legislature had passed the bill and Governor Samuel D. McEnery, a veteran, had eagerly approved the measure on June 30, 1882. Nearly thirty years later, in a report to the AANV, Julian S. Levy, a member of the board of directors, concluded that it dishonored no man to reside in the home, for "that institution [was] no charity, but a monument erected by the state of Louisiana for the benefit of her brave defenders."[17]

The contest in Louisiana would not be the last occasion for people to object to a state-supported Confederate soldiers' home. In Texas, for example, the establishment of a home was not greeted with universal acceptance. The Texas institution had a direct link with the Richmond endeavor: in November 1884, after procuring a copy of the Lee Camp's constitution and bylaws, Major Joseph H. Stewart, a Maryland-born banker and attorney, summoned a number of fellow veterans to his office in the old state capitol building to form the John Bell Hood Camp. Original members included two former Texas governors (Senator Richard Coke and State Treasurer Francis R. Lubbock) and a future governor (Congressman-elect Joseph D. Sayers) as well as several state officials, Travis County businessmen, and a handful of ex-Confederate generals, one of whom (R. Lindsay Walker) the group elected as its first commander.[18] During the next year and a half the Hood Camp concentrated its efforts on fund-raising. By July 1886 the veterans had purchased a seven-room house and more than fifteen acres atop a high knoll overlooking the Colorado River in Austin. The home admitted its first inmates in November 1886. Four months later the Hood Camp held dedicatory ceremonies for the Texas Confederate Home for Men.[19]

The attempt to obtain public funding for the Texas home officially commenced in March 1887, about a week after the institution had been formally dedicated, when Senator John H. Harrison of Waco introduced a bill that set aside proceeds from state land sales as an "endowment" for the institution. By this time Confederate veterans practically controlled the state government, occupying 60 of 131 House and Senate seats, as well as the governor's office and all of the posts in the cabinet. Although referred to the Committee on Public Lands, which in turn recommended its passage, Harrison's enabling legislation saw no further action. Apparently many legislators doubted the bill's legality, as had lawmakers some six years earlier when they narrowly defeated a $2.5 million appropriation for artificial limbs for ex-Confederates. Austin attorney Fred Carleton, a founding member of the Hood Camp, joined by other sympathizers, had voted against the measure, because he believed it violated the Texas Constitution, one article of which strictly prohibited the state from allocating public monies to any "individual, association of individuals, municipal or other corporations whatsoever," except in cases involving "public calamity."[20] The article did not, however, restrict forms of assistance other than the expenditure of funds. Thus, in 1881 the Texas legislature had been able to grant land certificates of 1,280 acres for every permanently disabled and indigent Confederate veteran and widow residing in the state, although the act had to be repealed in 1883, after the public domain was declared "exhausted."[21]

Stymied, the Hood Camp eventually figured out how to circumvent the constitutional barrier. Under a plan developed by Attorney General James S. Hogg and approved by Governor Lawrence "Sul" Ross, the group obtained in March 1889 a ten-year lease of the old capitol building, at $5.00 per annum. This arrangement enabled the veterans' organization to rent office space to various private individuals and, therefore, derive a permanent revenue for the home.[22] But much more funding was needed. In the 1890 general election, the Hood Camp and other Texas ex-Confederate organizations made full state appropriations a campaign issue. The veterans pledged to vote against any candidate who failed to support the endeavor. They easily obtained the endorsement of Governor Ross, who believed the state must fulfill its "sacred duty." They also succeeded in having their demands fashioned as a plank in the platform adopted by Democrats convening at San Antonio. During a speech at Rusk, Texas, in April 1890, Democratic gubernatorial nominee Hogg declared that the state should "endow, support and maintain a Confederate Home." Perhaps Hogg, a veteran himself, intended to ease conservatives' qualms when he added that "no inmate would feel as a pauper" in the home but would instead feel as if he were "an independent proprietor surrounded by all the comforts of the home he lost when he responded to his country's call." After Hogg was elected, he continued to press for a state-supported home; in his inaugural address of January 21, 1891, he called the creation of a home a "noble task" that lay "deep in the hearts of Texans." When "a state orders her

Inmates had plenty of opportunities to sit, talk, and reminisce, as these veterans at
Louisiana's Camp Nicholls appear to be doing, c. 1902.
(courtesy of Howard-Tilton Library, Tulane University, New Orleans)

men to fight," he reasoned, "it accepts the obligation to care for . . . maimed,
tottering helpless men . . . too proud to accept pity."[23]

Two days after Hogg's address, Austin representative Alexander W. Terrell,
a Virginia-born ex-Confederate colonel, introduced legislation authorizing the
establishment of the home as a state institution. House Bill No. 242 stipulated
that, in return for $75,000 in public funds, the Hood Camp would transfer the
home property to the state. Under the plan a board of five ex-Confederates
would retain control of the home's management. By the third week in
February, the legislature passed the bill by a combined vote of 101-16. The
bill's few opponents rightfully doubted its constitutionality, while the majority
of legislators considered it "a debt" the state owed. "It is signed. Bully!," a
House clerk scribbled on the bill before forwarding it to Governor Hogg, who
signed it into law the following day, March 6, 1891.[24] But the home's legal
status remained in jeopardy until the constitution was officially amended
several years later to permit the legislature to levy a special tax for the benefit
of the state's disabled and indigent Confederate soldiers and sailors and their
wives and widows. Ratified in the election of November 6, 1894, the amendment was proclaimed adopted six weeks later. In April 1895 the Confederate
home bill was approved all over again, this time with legislators voting in favor
of the measure 109-2.[25]

By this time the Louisiana home was beginning its second decade of operations. In April 1883, a year before General Gordon's Cooper Union speech, the
AAT and AANV had jointly elected ten managers to serve without recompense
as home administrators, financial consultants, and an admissions review board.
For chairman the board chose, unanimously, the current AANV president,

Francis T. Nicholls, a one-armed, one-legged, one-eyed ex-Confederate brigadier, a former (and future) governor. The board members also appointed AAT
president Charlaron and second vice-president Alfred J. Lewis as home treasurer and secretary, respectively. Duly organized, the board then proceeded to
accomplish the half dozen tasks prescribed for it by law.[26] By June 1883 the
managers had found a suitable location in the New Orleans vicinity for the
home. They bought a large lot nicknamed, ironically, "La Folie," on Bayou St.
John, off Esplanade Avenue, from ex-Confederate naval lieutenant Joseph R.
DeMahy. That purchase having absorbed the lion's share of the state's annual
appropriation, the managers then appealed to parish police juries, as well as to
the public directly, for contributions. Upon hearing of the project, General
Gordon himself donated $600 in lecture proceeds. Other revenues originated
from a lottery and a two-day sham battle held at the state fairgrounds. Before an
estimated 7,000 paid spectators at the fairgrounds, the combined forces of the
State National Guard and a local GAR post, on cue, repeatedly, but futilely,
"charged" a Confederate fort manned by AAT and AANV members. The battle
organizers naturally assumed the role of defenders, and, befitting the occasion,
some gallant veterans suffered slight casualties, including one AANV member
temporarily dazed by a shell burst. Anticipating such injuries, the AANV
chaplain, the Reverend Darius Hubert, could be seen "everywhere on the
battlefield" resuscitating soldiers by giving them a few sniffs of a "very valuable
and important canteen."[27]

The much publicized fund-raising stunts, like the "medicinal" therapy, had
proven remarkably successful. Home managers netted more than enough
profits (about $7,000) to cover the cost of several buildings, designed by local
architect William A. Freret, which construction crews had completed within
eight months. On February 5, 1884, the institution admitted its first inmate,
James Adams, a one-legged veteran of the First Louisiana Infantry. About five
weeks later, the Louisiana soldiers' home—known as Camp Nicholls—officially opened its doors. The opening ceremonies, attended by more than 600
people, centered around the home's seventy-foot flagpole, in front of the main
building, where the daughters of Generals Lee, Jackson, and D. H. Hill
proudly presented and hoisted the home's adopted blue and white flag,
handmade by Stonewall's widow. Applause, hoorahs, and Rebel yells, accompanied by a thirteen-gun salute fired by the Washington Artillery's howitzer,
"Redemption," filled the air. On this spring day, March 14, in New Orleans, the
Confederacy lived again![28]

More celebrations were forthcoming. The philanthropic efforts so aus-
piciously conducted by the New Orleans veterans and the Lee Camp provided
an immediate model for ex-Confederates residing in several other states. The
earliest known attempt at organizing benevolence in North Carolina, for

example, occurred in Charlotte in May 1884, when several prominent Army of Northern Virginia veterans publicly announced that they would begin soliciting and accepting donations for the "unfortunate victims of the Lost Cause." The recognized leaders behind the movement were undoubtedly well acquainted with John Gordon and certainly mindful of the Richmond and New Orleans homes. Zebulon B. Vance, a former Confederate general and North Carolina governor, then serving as a U.S. senator, and Julian Shakespeare Carr, a popular Durham entrepreneur, were chosen to serve as the first chairman and secretary, respectively, of the North Carolina Confederate Home Association, as the group promoting a home initially called itself. The association attracted many of the state's premier conservative Democrats, including Governor Alfred M. Scales and other elected officials, who willingly volunteered their reputations and influence as directors and trustees. In spite of a formidable start, however, the movement stalled and was practically abandoned until March 1889, when the group reorganized under the name Confederate Veterans Association of North Carolina and dedicated themselves anew to completing their task.[29]

With the aid of the Wake County Ladies Memorial Association, the Confederate Veterans Association raised enough money by September 1890 to lease an eight-room house located on Polk and Bloodworth Streets, near downtown Raleigh; by the following month, five veterans had been admitted. Further organization took place on Valentine's Day, 1891, when eighty-eight members of the Confederate Veterans Association officially constituted the Soldiers' Home Association of North Carolina as an administrative body. According to the terms of the charter, the state deeded Camp Russell—a five-acre plot, also in Raleigh, upon which a Confederate hospital had formerly stood—to the association. A $3,000 annual appropriation, paid in quarterly installments, accompanied the measure that had been approved in the North Carolina General Assembly by a unanimous vote. As Julian Carr later recalled, "dire necessity" had finally "impressed upon [the] hearts of [the] people" the need to provide a residence for unfortunate ex-soldiers.[30] On March 24, 1891, the "people" celebrated the opening of the new facility. Speaking on the refurbished home grounds, Lieutenant Governor Thomas Holt treated listeners to an account of the "patriotic movement" that had culminated in the most "important event in our history." He praised Colonel William F. Beasley, a former president of the North Carolina Confederate Home Association, and saluted future inmates of the home as "honored guests." Later that afternoon, in the office of Raleigh mayor Fabius Busbee, the Soldiers' Home Association selected a board of directors, with one of General Lee's former lieutenants, William P. Roberts, as chairman, and Samuel A'Court Ashe, a well-known historian, as secretary. The board also rewarded Carr and William C. Stronach, a prominent Raleigh merchant, by appointing them to serve with Busbee on the executive committee. In April, after considerable preparation, the superintendent welcomed nine inmates to their new quarters.[31]

Within the next few years, ex-Confederate organizations in several more states had established homes of their own—but not without additional controversy. In Tennessee, for example, during a November 1888 meeting of the Cheatham Bivouac in Nashville, veterans discussed for the first time a home for the state's disabled and infirm ex-Confederates. Nashville physician Robert G. Rothrock, one of the bivouac's original incorporators, who served at the time as the bivouac's surgeon and as the third vice-president of the Association of Confederate Soldiers, introduced the proposal.[32] The proposal was agreed to, and president John "Jack" Moore appointed a five-man committee (consisting of Nashville *Banner* editor Gideon Baskette, physician William J. McMurray, merchant Furgeson S. Harris, former judge Frank T. Reid, and Rothrock as chairman) to formulate plans. Then, the veterans' group notified the eight other bivouacs that comprised the statewide Confederate veterans' organization of their plan and requested their cooperation.[33] In February 1889 Shelby County Democrat James M. Crews, a former private under General Forrest, introduced the project to the Tennessee General Assembly as Senate Bill No. 210, "an act to provide a home for disabled ex-Confederate soldiers." The envisioned home was to be on the grounds of the Hermitage, the former estate of Andrew Jackson and his heirs, which had long since been deeded to the state. The property was to be entrusted to the Association of Confederate Soldiers, Tennessee Division, for a period not to exceed twenty-five years, in return for which the veterans promised to provide and maintain homes for needy ex-Confederates of "good character," with their "widows and their orphan children." All able-bodied residents would be expected to work. Income generated through the proper cultivation of the large, more than 400-acre farm, or through the development of suitable cottage industries, would be reinvested in the nonprofit enterprise. Finally, in order for the "charity" to be set on a firm basis, the bill stipulated an outright grant of $10,000.[34]

Approval of the Crews bill appeared highly likely in 1889. In the preceding six years, in response to veterans' demands, the state of Tennessee had implemented two modest pension programs for disabled ex-Confederates. In addition, proponents could now point to the homes already operating in Louisiana, Virginia, and Texas, as well as to those in the planning stages in Missouri, Arkansas, and Florida. Numbers were decidedly on the veterans' side. Ex-Confederates pervaded state government, while conservative Democrats—those most likely to be susceptible to Old South loyalties—overwhelmingly controlled both the Senate (24-9) and the House (66-26) in the state legislature.[35] If selected newspaper editorials accurately reflected popular sentiment on the issue, then most Tennesseans favored the undertaking. The Memphis *Daily Appeal*, for example, regarded it as "a measure which commend[ed] itself to every right thinking citizen of the state." Even Governor Robert L. Taylor, from traditionally Republican East Tennessee, referred to the public's support of the proposal as a "sacred obligation" and could be counted among the veterans' staunchest allies. "Our legislature," he declared, owed a special debt of gratitude to the state's "decrepit heroes of the Lost Cause."[36]

The veterans' lobby represented a formidable force indeed, but surprisingly the measure to create an old soldiers' home did not glide effortlessly through the legislature. Dissenters objected to the bill for a variety of reasons. Several senators argued against furnishing the needed appropriation, claiming that the state could ill afford to subsidize the venture. Other legislators took exception to an act benefiting only former Confederates; they urged that deserving Mexican-American War veterans as well as honorable Federal volunteers from Tennessee with service-related disabilities be admitted on an equal basis. One East Tennessee legislator went so far as to recommend additional, but separate, facilities for black veterans. Horrified at the latter suggestion, Confederate home supporters succeeded in having his motion tabled immediately. In the House challengers formally managed to amend the Crews measure in favor of all white soldiers, but ultimately their parliamentary maneuvers failed and ex-Confederates alone remained the objects of the bill's provisions.[37] Ironically, the most serious roadblock originated from an unlikely assortment of men and women in Nashville, many of whom were Confederate veterans, wives, or widows or ex-Confederate sympathizers. As one of the original organizers of this group recalled, "We were all . . . Confederates."[38] They worried that using the Hermitage grounds would "detract [from] or overshadow" Old Hickory's memory. One member feared that, if the Crews bill passed, "the remains of Jackson and his wife would be removed to Mt. Olivet, their relics and heirlooms scattered to four corners of the earth, and the home would forever pass out of existence." By mid-January 1889 the group, which had come to be known as the Ladies Hermitage Association, petitioned the legislature to sell them a sizable portion of the Jackson estate. The revenue the state derived from the sale, they pointed out, would be sufficient to establish a soldiers' home someplace else.

Anxious Cheatham Bivouac representatives immediately requested a conference with the Hermitage group. During a mass meeting on February 11, veteran John Hickman proposed that the Crews bill be amended so as to entrust the mansion and the adjacent twenty-five acres to the association's caretakers, but Mrs. Andrew Jackson III reportedly refused to agree to "anything of the kind." The two organizations remained deadlocked, until the

Ladies Hermitage Association reluctantly accepted the Hickman compromise.[39] As expected, the ex-Confederate lobbyists ultimately triumphed in the legislature by a comfortable margin of thirty-three votes. Consistent supporters of the Crews bill as amended were either Democrats or confirmed independents who hailed primarily from the state's middle and western regions; roughly one-quarter of these men satisfied both criteria.[40] Middle Tennessee senator Clement J. Moody, though not a veteran, spoke for the majority. In his "brief, earnest [and] eloquent appeal" before a chamber filled with many visitors (including a number of Hermitage ladies), the Democrat said that it was high time for the state to demonstrate its appreciation for the brave men who had returned from the war "in tatters and rags to look upon the ashes of their ruined homes." House member Joel Battle Fort of Robertson County, also "too young to know which side was right," voted aye, he said, because the federal government had already helped Union soldiers, while the state had practically "done nothing" for ex-Confederates. East Tennessee Republicans, Union veterans, and representatives from counties that had voted against secession comprised the bulk of the forty-one legislators voting against the bill. Thomas O. Morris, the bill's House sponsor, attempted to win over their votes by stating that "Republicans should show manhood and do justice to men who gave their lives and property in behalf of a cause they believed to be right." Republican Stephen C. Pyott of Hamilton County apparently listened to Morris's arguments, for he supported the "just and proper" measure, maintaining that since the former Confederate leaders "had been cared for" by electing them to political office, it was only fair that the "men who bore the muskets" should be given a home "to rest their worn out bodies." Another East Tennessee Republican senator, calling ex-Confederates the "brave[st] men as ever lived," endorsed the bill. Once it cleared the House and Senate, the act became official with Governor Taylor's signature on April 4, 1889.[41]

Almost a year later the Tennessee Soldiers' Home admitted its first veteran. By February 1891 the total inmate population rose to twenty, while at least three times that number awaited entrance into the home. Believing that future inmates could not be adequately cared for in the available facilities, the board of directors requested an endowment of $25,000 toward the construction of a single large building and an additional $10,000 for maintenance during the next two years. Each request experienced little difficulty gaining state legislative approval.[42]

The main building officially opened with dignified fanfare on May 1, 1892. The dedication activities began early, with a number of Nashville's leading citizens (including Dr. and Mrs. J. Berrien Lindsley, of the Ladies Hermitage Association) as participants. Representatives of veterans' groups and ladies' auxiliaries from across the state congregated in the capital in order to attend

Fully one out of four veterans who resided in the Confederate homes had been wounded during the war, as had some of those pictured here, in the 1920s, in front of the Mississippi home at Biloxi.
(courtesy of Mississippi Department of Archives and History)

the long-awaited celebration. They rendezvoused at the new headquarters of the Cheatham Bivouac, at 31 Baxter Court. Shortly after eight o'clock the procession of "pleasure wagons" started moving through the streets, and it arrived at the Hermitage about an hour later. The ceremonies commenced sharply at eleven with an invocation given by the Cheatham Bivouac's chaplain, who was followed by Captain Mark R. Cockrill, president of the home's board of trustees since 1889. Professor William R. Garrett, the day's orator, deemed it perfectly fitting that Tennessee's Confederate veterans should be cared for and buried on the estate formerly owned by Jackson, who had loved the soldiers of the Volunteer State.[43] After a brilliant speech by local attorney Allen G. Hall of the Young Men's Democratic Club, George B. Guild, Nashville's mayor, offered a host of resolutions: one praising the "blessed" men and women who conceived of the idea of erecting such a "monument"; another in honor of the home's architect, W. C. Smith; and a third declaring the home as "an asylum of perfect rest, joy and comfort to the old, indigent and disabled Confederate soldier who gave his all for the cause of his people." Before the day ended, three charter members of the Cheatham Bivouac (Mark R. Cockrill, McMurray, and Richard H. Dudley, a prominent Nashville merchant) were publicly commended for their "indefatigable" efforts, time, and money given to the home.[44]

Acting almost simultaneously with the Tennesseans were veterans in Arkansas. The first public discussion of a home in that state occurred in 1888 during an informal meeting of a number of prominent ex-Confederates in Little Rock. Participants in the meeting included Governor James P. Eagle, a Bourbon Democrat, who championed railroad legislation as well as educational, penal, and tax reform; R. A. Little, publisher of the Arkansas *Gazette*; John D. Adams, bank president and board member of the state insane asylum; W. P. Campbell, clerk of the state Supreme Court and former commissioner of state lands; and John Gould Fletcher, one of the state's most eminent citizens, a former mayor of Little Rock, who was at the time sheriff for Pulaski County. The group issued a call for other veterans to meet with them to effect a permanent organization of Arkansas veterans, so that they might better care for the state's infirm and disabled Confederate soldiers. Noting that "there are movements all over the country looking toward the provision of means for taking care of the disabled soldiers who fought for the 'Lost Cause,'" the veterans vowed that "Arkansas will not be behind in this."[45]

The called-for meeting took place in the hall of the House of Representatives on May 8, 1889, when forty-five "good citizens" assembled shortly after 8:00 P.M. Assuming the chair, former governor E. W. Rector declared that he was in "hearty and entire sympathy" with the movement. Confederate veterans, he said, were "a proud race of men," who would rather "suffer from

Confederate soldiers' home officials endeavored to meet inmates' every physical
need; this receipt indicates that Florida home inmate J. S. Cooley was provided
with "1 full set of teeth" for $20.00 in 1902.
(courtesy of Jacksonville Public Library, Jacksonville, Florida)

hunger and cold in their little cabins by the obscure roadside" than ask for aid,
but they now had no other choice. Campbell announced that he personally
knew many veterans who were poor and disabled and who, he feared, would, at
their deaths, "sink into obscure graves unnoted, unhonored and unmourned."
He was certain that the legislature would help, however, once "it sees what we
are doing." Fletcher predicted that $25,000 could be raised by the citizens of
Little Rock alone, and another $25,000 by people all over the state. The whole
$50,000 could then be used as a sinking fund on which the home would
operate. The home would be open to all, Fletcher vowed, whether they
belonged to the Republican Party, the Knights of Labor, or "anything else." A
committee was then appointed to begin enlisting subscriptions for the proposed home. Some $3,400 was pledged that day, with Little, Adams, and
Fletcher giving $500 each, and Governor Eagle, $200.[46]

Later that summer, when the Ex-Confederate Association of Arkansas had
been formally organized in Little Rock, a board of managers for the home was
appointed and empowered to continue receiving subscriptions and select a site
for the home. "No matter where you locate it, in Hamburg, Bentonville or
elsewhere, my money and affection will go with it," pledged board president
Fletcher. By the following summer, with nearly $9,000 in hand, the association
purchased the Otis Patton homestead, which included more than fifty acres of
land a few miles southeast of Little Rock on the Sweet Home Pike. The old

frame house was remodeled, several additional "barracks" were erected, and the home was formally opened on December 1, 1890.[47] The following April the state legislature passed an act, approved by Governor Eagle, that not only granted a pension to Confederate veterans but also appropriated $10,000 for the erection and maintenance of an improved home. With the completion of the new and larger building, ownership and control of the home were officially transferred to the state in August 1892.[48]

During that same month, ex-Confederates in Florida made a down payment of $1,500 toward a ten-acre lot and seven-room house situated along the Saint Johns River, about three miles from Jacksonville. Formal opening of the Florida Old Confederate Soldiers and Sailors Home took place on April 6, 1893. Making the dedicatory address was Major Albert J. Russell, the state's superintendent of education, who had served as president of the Florida Soldiers' Home Association since its founding in 1888. Russell was also (according to Governor Francis P. Fleming, one of the members of the association) the originator of the effort to obtain state funding for the home that came to fruition with passage of an act by the legislature in June 1893.[49]

By the spring of 1893 the dedication of a soldiers' home had become a familiar ritual. Already Confederate veterans literally across the nation had celebrated the achievements of Johnny Reb as well as those of people whose moral and material contributions had rendered institutions such as the soldiers' homes possible. By this time institutions had been established in nine states, including some that had not belonged to the Confederacy. In Maryland, for example, on June 27, 1888, the Maryland Line Confederate Soldiers' Home, under the direction of General Bradley T. Johnson and other officers of the state veterans' association, had opened its doors—a move made possible by a $5,000 appropriation from the state, as well as the gift of the old barracks at the U.S. arsenal in Pikesville, where the home was located.[50] The following year a charter for a Confederate home in Missouri had been secured by representatives of the state Confederate veterans' association. In 1890 the association selected a 365-acre farm, located about one mile north of Higginsville, as the site for the home. Within a few years a main building had been constructed, paid for, and appropriately dedicated, owing largely to the determined efforts of the state's Daughters of the Confederacy. "No Confederate soldier in Missouri need . . . go to the poor-house or beg on the streets" any longer, commented one Missouri ex-Confederate. Another boasted that the home was "a monument to Missouri." But the veterans and ladies of Missouri, soon finding it more difficult to run the institution than to build it, reluctantly appealed to the state legislature for emergency relief. Beginning on June 1, 1897, the state assumed control of the institution, funding the home for the next fifty-four years.[51] There was even talk on at least two separate occasions of establishing a Confederate soldiers' home in West Virginia, but that project never materialized.[52]

Thus far, with the exception of the false starts in West Virginia and Kentucky, the "movement" for organizing benevolence on behalf of destitute Confederate veterans had been a remarkable success. Sympathetic southerners and northerners alike had responded with measured alacrity and zeal once they perceived the needs of homeless and disabled ex-Confederates. Former enemies had demonstrated time and again that it was the sacred duty of a civilized people to compensate those who had forfeited their health and fortune in defense of a cause. Perhaps the universal acceptance of this principle made events in John B. Gordon's home state of Georgia all the more incredible. And the fact that Confederate veterans residing in the Deep South states of Alabama, Mississippi, and South Carolina had yet to be heard from was just as puzzling.

CHAPTER FOUR

The Home That Grady Built

A t eight o'clock in the morning, on September 30, 1901, the Georgia Soldiers' Home in Atlanta suddenly and mysteriously caught fire. Within an hour the whole structure had been reduced to a jumbled pile of smoldering ashes and blackened chimneys. Fortunately, the night watchman had alerted the staff and residents in time, and everyone escaped unharmed. But the building itself, which had long been embroiled in controversy, had vanished in smoke and flames. "It seemed that the fates were against it," bemoaned one observer, "and its future dark and uncertain."[1]

Indeed, the home must have seemed jinxed. It had been in actual operation for only a few months before the conflagration, the latest in a series of misfortunes that had beset the institution since its formal inception over a dozen years earlier. For most of the time between the completion of its construction in 1891 and the fire in 1901, its doors had been closed, and the edifice had been all but abandoned. On four separate occasions the state legislature had refused to appropriate money for it; forced into bankruptcy, it was ordered auctioned to the highest bidder. No other soldiers' home experienced as much trouble getting started. Georgia farmers had been frightened by it, politicians viewed it as an unnecessary expense, and even some Confederate veterans railed against it. But for the sheer determination of a handful of dedicated men and women, the home would not have opened at all.

Among the home's most stalwart proponents was Henry W. Grady, the editor of the Atlanta *Constitution*, who, in addition to espousing the benefits of modernization for the South, also promised that the "New" South would always honor the "Old." Grady's involvement began as early as March 1889. At that time, Major Joseph H. Stewart was in New York City directing a fundraising campaign for the Texas home, after having completed a successful winter tour in Boston. Stewart met with influential GAR members and prominent ex-Confederates and tentatively set April 9, the twenty-fourth anniversary of the Appomattox surrender, as the date for the kickoff event in New York. Two days before the scheduled date, however, an article appearing in the New York *Herald* produced such a "howl" that it forced Stewart to postpone the event indefinitely. The newspaper carried an editorial entitled "Shall We Go Begging for Them?" as it had appeared originally in the Atlanta *Constitution* on April 6. More than two years earlier Grady had caused quite a stir when he delivered his landmark address, "The New South," before New York City's fashionable New England Society. Now Grady's editorial regarding the Confederate home in Texas had a similar effect.[2]

Grady opened his editorial by stating that the "sorry tale" of "our old veterans" had been "dragged through the North" long enough, and he called upon Major Stewart to "come home!" He claimed that he had never supported Stewart's campaign, in which ex-Confederates were exploited. Although operating in New York for over a month, Stewart had little to show for it. Had New Yorkers been more sympathetic, and had they given more freely, Grady explained, that would have been acceptable; but the "painful spectacle" of "prolong[ed] begging" was disgraceful, if not "humiliat[ing]." Therefore, "Come Home, Major Stewart," he demanded, and allow southerners to fulfill their "sacred duty" of taking care of their own "poor and helpless heroes." Grady's scathing remarks did nothing to boost Stewart's efforts in the North and, in fact, as one contemporary recalled, they "greatly chilled the ardor of the people in that section." The New York *Journal* angrily retorted that the Atlanta editor was unjust to criticize the slow response by northern citizens, since southerners themselves had taken nearly a quarter of a century to do anything for their veterans. Grady agreed. Indeed, the delay had been "piteous," but "that is past," he vowed; Georgians would now commence building a home of their own.[3]

The idea of a Confederate soldiers' home in Georgia had been discussed for almost two years, but no one seemed to have made much progress. Supposedly, E. J. Roach, an Atlanta physician, had suggested a home to members of the Confederate Survivors Association (the Eighteenth Georgia Infantry) meeting in Acworth in August 1887, but the veterans took no definite action. State senator Tom Massengale later boasted that he had argued, while stumping at Warrenton sometime the following summer, that Georgia "owed" veterans "a monument . . . building in which they might find shelter."[4] In contrast to the Acworth meeting, another meeting that took place in August 1887, in the parlor of Atlanta's Young Men's Library, featured plenty of speeches and action. Members of the Atlanta Ladies Memorial Association and over a dozen members of the Fulton County Confederate Veterans Association discussed founding a home in order to ameliorate the condition of needy ex-Confederates. Some of Atlanta's "first citizens" attended, including Captain John Milledge, the state librarian; ex-Governor Alfred Colquitt, one of Georgia's U.S. senators, who less than a year later gave one of the dedicatory addresses for the Confederate home in Maryland; W. Lowndes Calhoun, Fulton County's ordinary; W. A. Hemphill, Constitution Publishing Company treasurer; and Samuel M. Inman, reputedly one of the state's richest men and Grady's confidant. The group proposed "prompt steps" for raising money; but when the public's response was not as favorable as anticipated, the group pondered its next move.[5]

Grady's so-called "immortal" editorial injected a potent dosage of enthusiasm and publicity into the project. Philanthropic motivations notwithstanding, the editor's involvement with the home appears to have emerged from a basic desire to foster his own image and to influence and mobilize popular support for another scheme altogether. Grady was certainly not averse to exploiting the Lost Cause, for he had played upon ex-Confederate sympathies before.[6] Although not a veteran (his father, a Confederate officer, had died from wounds suffered during the battle of the Crater at Petersburg in 1864), he held an honorary membership in the Fulton County Confederate Veterans Association. Inman and Hemphill were, for that matter, charter members of the association, while Judge Calhoun was its president in 1887. Originally numbering about 200 strong, the group had organized in response to a call from Milledge on April 19, 1886, just prior to a widely acclaimed visit to the city by Jefferson Davis, who had accepted an invitation to dedicate a statue to the late senator Benjamin H. Hill. In characteristic fashion Grady seized the opportunity to resurrect the political career of General (and former senator) John B. Gordon, who, having abandoned his business ventures in New York, agreed to reenter Georgia politics, running for governor. Grady arranged for Gordon to accompany Davis on a special train for his journey from Montgomery to Atlanta. The train also carried as an honor guard a host of other dignitaries, including Grady, Hemphill, and Evan P. Howell, the principal owner and editor in chief of the *Constitution*. The publicity stunt ensured not only Gordon's gubernatorial victory but also the continued dominance for at least another term of Georgia's "New Departure" Democrats—Democrats who, like Grady, continued to laud the Confederacy and the Lost Cause while promoting the New South.[7]

The 1886 state election had also been a triumph for the "Atlanta Ring," a loose political federation with broad interstate connections based principally in New York. The ring represented merchant, banking, railroad, and planter interests. Grady, Howell, and Gordon, joined by Senator Colquitt and his colleague Joseph E. Brown, dominated the group that conspired first and foremost to maintain and tighten its control over state politics and, secondly, to make Atlanta, the "Gate City," the premier city of Georgia or even the capital of the New South. Opposing the Atlanta Ring were hordes of disaffected farmers already mobilizing in March 1887. Grady feared that, if white farmers formed a third party, then Republicans, supported by easily duped black voters, could influence or win elections.[8] In order to avert such a disaster, Grady sought to mollify disgruntled farmers by strenuously advocating an agricultural program that featured crop diversification, scientific methods, and a protective tariff. Farmers, however, balked at the attempt to put "new wine in the bottles of ring politicians." The *Constitution* grudgingly admitted the program's failure, but not before June 1888, when Grady and Gordon (seeking reelection) finally embraced the Georgia Alliance movement. The strategy worked: Gordon remained in the chief executive's office, the party of the New Departure won another victory, and the incipient populist rebellion subsided, temporarily.

Grady's advocacy of a soldiers' home in April 1889 must be placed against this complex background of political intrigue. Immediately following the 1888 election, the *Constitution* embarked on another massive campaign to convince farmers that the Atlanta was their friend. For three months Grady set aside a full page in Sunday editions and occasional dailies to discuss the plight of farmers and reassure them that the future looked bright. Beginning in late March 1889, and throughout the summer, Grady personally delivered his message to farmers at mass meetings in Georgia's piedmont and western black belt regions, Alliance strongholds. Earlier in March he had urged ex-Confederate William J. Northen, a wealthy planter from Hancock County, to adopt the role of peacemaker between Georgia's commercial and agricultural interests. Northen subsequently obtained the endorsement of the Alliance and in 1890 won the governor's chair.[9] So the movement to build a Georgia home may indeed have been yet another effort, at least on Grady's part, to demonstrate to farmers that "wool-hat boys" and "silk-hat boys" shared common interests. The institution would provide shelter for countless impoverished veterans, many of whom resided in rural Georgia. A large number of ex-Confederates and their sons filled the Alliance ranks. In the forthcoming legislature of 1890, known Alliance members would hold as many as 102 of 175 (58.3 percent) House seats; more than half (59.8 percent) of the Alliance legislators were Confederate veterans, and another 30 percent were sons of veterans. Surely Grady must have thought that farmers would not oppose the state's establishment of a home.[10]

He initiated the Georgia Confederate home subscription drive in 1889—on the day he penned his eloquent appeal of April 6—with a donation of $1,000. Various members of the Atlanta Ring followed suit. Governor Gordon endorsed the project, though he cautioned Grady about the shortsightedness of eschewing northern philanthropy. Senator Brown matched Grady's gift, as did James Swann, the absentee president of Atlanta National Bank; Marion C. Kiser, a wealthy shoe manufacturer and close associate of both Grady and Howell; Sam

Inman and his younger brother John, the renowned "Carpet bagger in Wall Street"; and railroad lawyers Patrick and John C. Calhoun, grandsons of the Great Nullifier, both staunch supporters of Grady.[11] Other compeers of the ring (notably, former mayors George T. Hillyer and James W. English and current mayor John Thomas Glenn) gave liberally to the cause. John Temple Graves's Rome *Daily Tribune* announced that it stood solidly behind the "movement," adding, "it is better to build homes for live heroes in need" than to memorialize the dead. As expected, members of the Fulton County Veterans Association welcomed the assistance. Amos Fox, a respected physician, police commissioner, and part-time elixir salesman, the group's treasurer, dubbed Grady's campaign the "grandest movement," while Lowndes Calhoun reemphasized the veterans' desire to build a home, not a "poor house."[12]

The project's ability to transcend publicized disagreements between Grady and his longtime nemeses seemed even more remarkable. Former Republican governor Rufus B. Bullock donated $750 on behalf of the Atlanta Cotton Mills. Diehard ex-Confederate Charles C. Jones, Jr., who in the past had decried Grady's vision of a New South, wrote that the "sacred obligation has too long been neglected." Augusta *Chronicle* editor Patrick Walsh, one of Grady's fiercest intrastate critics, viewed the home not as a charity, but as a "holy duty." Fellow Augustan James C. C. Black, another Grady antagonist, sent a few dollars, some favorable words of encouragement, and the promise of a speech in support of the institution.[13] Donating money to Grady's home soon became the rage. By April 14 nearly $35,000 had been pledged by over 3,000 people, about half of whom resided in Atlanta. On the night of April 16, a "very enthusiastic gathering" of local home subscribers convened at the city's Chamber of Commerce building. Called to the chair, Evan Howell spoke briefly about the heroism of the Confederate soldier. While Howell was speaking, Grady walked into the room, greeted by applause and cheers beckoning him to address the crowd. Adept at making impromptu speeches, Grady spoke for nearly an hour.[14]

Grady reminded his audience that it had assembled that evening in order to establish a "different" kind of institution. He then reiterated the four-point plan he had outlined in his columns a few days earlier. First, an "ideal" soldiers' home, as he envisioned it, would permit families to reside with veterans. "Don't make a home for veterans only," he warned. Southern women shared "suffering" and "poverty" when their husbands returned home "crippled and disabled," so do not separate them now! Second, he recommended that the home should offer employment opportunities. "Give every man in the home a patch of ground," he advised (an obvious appeal to Alliance members) "so that visitors may find them tilling the soil, the most ancient and honorable of all" trades. (A great standing ovation followed.) Third, he advocated adop-

Staff of the Confederate Soldiers' Home
of Georgia

Left to right: Miss Philpot, Dr. Corley W. E. McAllister,
Dr. L. F. Patton and Mrs. Card

COMPLIMENTS

Coca-Cola

COMPANY

Atlanta ∴ Georgia

The Confederate soldiers' homes were objects of sectional pride and of commercialism long after Henry Grady's time, as demonstrated in this 1928 advertisement.
(author's collection)

ting a cottage system rather than a central building plan. Finally, Grady favored locating the home in the Atlanta vicinity. He claimed he had personally received proxies "from all over the state" approving such a location, and he was confident that the legislature would agree to maintain the home; several members had already assured him of support. Grady then sat down, but afterward he frequently interrupted the meeting, delighting the audience with several amusing anecdotes and with announcements of new pledges.[15]

A host of other speakers followed. Legislator Augustus M. Foute of Cartersville, whose citizens had donated over $400, promised to do all that he could in the Assembly. "Only one man voted against the soldiers pension bill in the last session," he bragged, "and he has been sorry ever since!" "Establish the home," Mayor Tom Glenn cried defiantly, "and if the state can't or won't sustain it, Atlanta will!" Attorney William D. Ellis, an ex-Confederate colonel from South Carolina, assured everyone that Georgia had no constitutional barriers that would prevent the home's public support. Cheered as he entered the room, General John R. Lewis, a Vermonter, asserted that he spoke on behalf of every "true Union soldier" when he considered it "a privilege to stand shoulder to shoulder with [them] in a cause like this." Erstwhile carpetbagger Hannibal I. Kimball, the owner of Atlanta's grandest hotel, confessed that, had he been southern-born, he could not have been "more behind the movement." After the speeches ended, Sam Inman proposed that the subscribers proceed with the business at hand and elect a board of twenty-five directors. Thirteen would be from Fulton County, and Mayor Glenn, Governor Gordon, and Senators Brown and Colquitt would serve as honorary vice-presidents. The motion carried. A specially appointed committee then retired from the room, only to return within a few minutes with the names of its nominees. The committee tapped Grady, Howell, and Inman, as well as other men who had been associated with the home from the beginning— Lowndes Calhoun, Hillyer, Fox, English, Massengale—to hold director positions.[16]

Meeting on the following day, the new board elected officers. For president, Howell proposed, no more qualified man could not be found than the one who had conceived the whole idea and "pushed the boat out from the shore himself," Henry Grady. All seventeen of the directors in attendance, except the nominee, stood up and voiced their unanimous consent. Grady protested, preferring instead that the group bestow the honor on a veteran, but the men would have none of it. Speaking for the group, Ellis answered that the home would properly be considered a gift from Georgia's "rising generation," whom the young editor represented marvelously. With this, Grady accepted.[17]

Under Grady's direction the board went to work immediately, fearing that any delays would cost between 20 and 30 percent in pledges. On May 8 it decided to locate the home on Madame Emmy Vonder Hoya Schultze's prime 119-acre farm, about three miles from downtown Atlanta and one mile east of Grant Park. By June 1 the board completed the transaction to purchase the farm, which required an immediate outlay of more than $9,000. The first sign of trouble came in the form of a dispute over the institution's proposed design. Grady, joined by Tip Harrison and other directors, had envisioned and pub-licly advocated a "community" of cottages, each inhabited by a veteran and his family, arranged around a central administration building. But cost projections for such a layout greatly exceeded capital earmarked for construction of the home. According to the most conservative estimates, fifteen cottages, each with four rooms and a kitchen, could be constructed for about $1,000 per unit. On the other hand, for approximately the same $15,000, a large building that provided ample space for around one hundred residents without families could be completed. So, when dream met reality, or (to borrow from social historian David Rothman) when conscience met convenience, the latter triumphed, as the board voted to construct the main building first and, if funds permitted, to add the cottages later.[18]

The compromise proved especially costly when Grady's closest friends— Howell, who served as building chairman, and Sam Inman, the finance committee head—resigned over the disagreement. Nevertheless, the directors proceeded as best they could. Judge Calhoun granted a charter to the Confeder-ate Soldiers' Home of Georgia, as the institution was officially called. County commissioners approved and supervised the construction of a road to the site. Work crews cleared and surveyors marked off the land. The respected architec-tural firm of Bruce and Morgan—the same company responsible for Grady's and Hillyer's residences and the governor's estate, as well as downtown stores and offices for Senator Brown and Sam Inman—designed a handsome seventy-five room, three-story mansion, modern, imposing, and efficient. By December the Atlanta construction company that had been awarded the contract, had finished the home's foundation, begun erecting the wooden framework, and projected a completion date of sometime in July. Then, unfortunately for the home, on the day before Christmas Eve, 1889, Grady died.[19]

The board's "saddest meeting ever" occurred on January 21, 1890, when the directors confronted the unthinkable task of choosing a suitable replacement for Grady. Certainly they would have to press on; Grady would have demanded that, remarked Lowndes Calhoun, who was selected as his successor. Moreover, the home would now be more than a building, for it would be a living memorial to an esteemed comrade. As the years pass by for the old veterans who will inhabit the home, the board suggested in eulogizing their departed colleague, the "very last survivor will go down to his grave worshipping at the shrine of Lee and Jackson, and loving the memory of Grady!"[20]

On April 26, 1890, Confederate Memorial Day, a "vast multitude" participated in the home's cornerstone dedication ceremonies. Hymn singing, band
playing, prayers, and Masonic rites comprised the liturgy for the solemn affair,
and cherished relics from a collective past had been lovingly placed inside the
four-foot-square white marble stone. Seated on the speaker's stage were
Governor Gordon and his staff; the featured orator, Augusta's James C. C.
Black; new board chairman Calhoun; and several distinguished visitors, not
the least of whom were Generals Edmund Kirby Smith, James Longstreet, and
Joseph E. Johnston. Near the stage and the scaffolding that buttressed the
unfinished home sat Grady's mother, Mrs. Ann E. Grady, who commented
after the activities had concluded that her son "would have been truly
happy."[21]

The slow progress made by the work crews, however, would not have
pleased Grady at all. When July came, the building was still not ready: the
veranda had not been erected, and the interior was only two-thirds completed.
Furthermore, work on the home's cisterns had not begun, and gas lighting had
not yet been installed. The contractor said he fully expected to have the facility
open no later than September 1. There was little to do but wait and hope that
he was right. Meanwhile, a committee appointed to·tender the property to the
state proceeded with the drafting of a bill to be presented in the upcoming
term of the Alliance-controlled legislature. On November 21, 1890, Colonel
Allen S. Cutts of Americus, a "prominent Allianceman" himself, introduced
the measure, which provided for the state to maintain the home for twenty-
five years, after which the property would revert to the state "for charitable
purposes only." Already Georgia Democrats had approved an act providing
artificial limbs and a pension bill for disabled and indigent veterans; and in the
legislature's previous fall session modest benefits had been extended to a small
group of Confederate widows. But Cutts's soldiers' home bill would be lost in
the finance committee, when committee members, convinced that the state's
title to the home ought to be "absolute and unconditional," struck out the
charity proviso. Rather than agree to the compromise, the home's directors,
during a called meeting at the capitol on December 6, recommended that the
bill be withdrawn and resubmitted when the legislature convened the following summer.[22]

By mid-July 1891, a year behind schedule, the building was finally completed. Even so, half a dozen different cost overruns had depleted Grady's
subscribed endowment of more than $39,000 and left the directors with
operating capital of only $41.01. Nevertheless, Clark Howell, Evan's son, the
new *Constitution* editor and Speaker of the House, expressed confidence that
the upcoming legislature would pass the bill by a "big vote."[23]

Cutts reintroduced a slightly modified version of the home bill on August

13, 1891. Made special order of the day for August 19, the measure was put off twice until the whole House had an opportunity to consider it for the first time on August 25. Proponents marshaled and deployed what had become the standard arguments in favor of a veterans' home. Cutts called upon all those who harbored "any ill feeling towards" Atlanta to push it aside and do "their duty to the old soldiers." "It is a labor of love as well as of duty," added E. W. Martin of Fulton County. Albany's William E. Wooten invoked the name of Grady and reminded his fellow legislators that "every other state [was] moving in the same direction," citing Virginia, Tennessee, Texas, and Louisiana as examples, so why not Georgia? Macon's John T. Boifeuillet favored the venture as "a sound business proposition," while William H. Fleming of Augusta explained that the bill would provide for a "class" of homeless, unmarried veterans rendered dependent by poverty and disability. Fairburn banker William T. Roberts, whose father had been killed at Gettysburg, vowed that he would never see the day when a Confederate veteran languished "in the county poorhouse."[24]

Such strains of eloquence, admittedly, had little effect upon certain realists, many of whom resented the Atlanta Ring as members of the ruling class and viewed the home as a means of lining its subscribers' pockets. Long active in Georgia politics, Dr. Isaac A. Hand, an Allianceman and a fiscal conservative, viewed the home as a "white elephant," not worth the costs and of "no real benefit." Webster County representative W. M. Sears, a veteran and a member of the Alliance, argued that the state could ill afford being saddled with such "unnecessary expenses." Of the $15,000 appropriated for the project, he predicted, fully one-third would go toward administrative costs, not to veterans directly. "Don't let sentiment" fool you into voting for the bill, warned James T. Chappell, a veteran from Laurens County, who questioned its constitutionality. W. C. Bryan, a Primitive Baptist preacher from Floyd County, declared that the home was a "waste of money"; besides, the soldiers in his district would rather receive additional pension benefits than this "class legislation." Veteran M. L. Everett of Lumpkin boasted that his constituents in Stewart County could build a "far better home" for a fraction of the cost. "Money is not the object," roared one Allianceman from Brooks County, "it is a matter of principle": we "don't want the home"; we "never asked for it!"[25]

Former Macon mayor William A. Huff, the House finance committee chairman, decided he had withstood the rhetorical barrage long enough. "I am not an Allianceman," he proclaimed as he took the floor. The farmers "came here to protect their rights, and I sympathize with them." But, he continued, they must understand, "it is a home" that is being proposed, not a poorhouse or a prison; "there is no trick about it!" Nevertheless, M. A. Baldwin, a veteran and a "zealous" Allianceman, interrupted Huff with the pointed interrogatory:

then why force veterans to leave their families for the home? "Do you know of any soldiers who would go there?" Huff responded by producing a list of seventy-five needy applicants from all over the state. He also sent a copy of Grady's "Shall We Go Begging for Them?" editorial of April 6, 1889, to the clerk's desk to be read, adding: "The men who come to the home" are "wandering about" without families, wives, sisters, or aunts to care for them. "It is not a question of money. . . . It's a question of honor!"[26]

Such lively, often intense, debate raged for nearly two days, until on August 26 the measure finally came up for a vote in the form of a last-minute substitute bill. It resembled the one the home directors had already rejected in the previous session. Submitted by home antagonist James Chappell, the bill tendered the home property to the state, in fee simple, unconditionally. House members also agreed to report the bill adversely; that is, an "aye" vote was considered a vote against the bill. Augusta's Fleming abruptly moved that the vote be by roll call, and his parliamentary maneuver also carried. In the end, ninety-four members of the House sounded out in favor of the bill, sixty-two opposed it, and nineteen abstained from voting. The legislation accepting on behalf of the state the home that Grady built had been killed.[27]

"Defeated! . . . Old Soldiers Repudiated. And The People's Gift To Them The State Rejected. A Day That Will Be Remembered": thus fumed the *Constitution* the next day. Several Grady associates expressed disbelief and regret over what had happened. Having observed the debates with "deep concern," Lowndes Calhoun was "exceedingly sorry" and thought the legislature had made a grave error. Similar sentiments were registered by Hemphill, English, and Ellis. "For some reason the Alliance members fight every measure that would benefit Atlanta," Ellis grumbled. The home "is not an Atlanta project, but . . . a broad, philanthropic enterprise!"[28]

Reaction from across the state and throughout the nation virtually echoed Ellis's remarks. Americus, Savannah, Macon, and Augusta were "disgusted," "indignant," and "astonished." La Grange considered the action "niggardly," "unwise," and "unpatriotic." Sparta "deplore[d]" the bill's defeat, while Albany "condemned" the followers of "Mrs. [Mary E.] Lease," an Alliance leader, and "others of the ilk." "Oh! For a word from the lips of dead Grady," remarked the Athens *Daily Banner*, Grady's hometown newspaper, "to say to Georgia veterans: 'Be patient yet awhile! Chide not your people for this deed, for it is not their own.'" One report from New York City had ex-Confederates walking the streets "with bowed heads"; supposedly, no event since Grady's death had "caused such a sensation." Confederate carpetbaggers in Chicago were "dumbfounded"; the city's *Inter Ocean*, for example, condemned the "discreditable act" and claimed to have neither "sympathy . . . nor respect for a legislature so devoid of humane sentiment or of moral principle." The Cincinnati *Gazette* dismissed the argument that veterans would not go to the home, pointing out that those who "seek relief" usually have neither families nor shelters. New Orleans veterans believed Georgians had every right to be upset, for no one was fond of a party that "forgets its obligation to Confederate soldiers." In North Carolina, where Colonel Leonidas L. Polk's Southern Farmers' Alliance had no qualms about sponsoring the founding of a soldiers' home in Raleigh, people thought the action of the Georgia legislature was, indeed, a bit "strange." And a Little Rock newspaper, decrying the "miserable, cheap John economy and demagogy" at work in the bill's rejection, speculated that if someone had told a Georgia soldier in 1864 that sometime later a Georgia farmer would object to the state's acceptance of a home, he would have "shot down the slanderer in his tracks."[29]

At an "indignation meeting" held in Atlanta on the night following the bill's defeat, a "great crowd" numbering perhaps as many as 5,000 was told whom to blame: it was Leonidas F. Livingston, the president of the Georgia Farmers' Alliance, and "Sockless" Jerry Simpson or perhaps Mrs. Mary E. Lease of Kansas, notorious Alliance organizers, who had conspired to defeat the measure and were the cause of this "treachery."[30] This "is what we might expect of the third party should it get into power," one speaker declared. "Grady has been mocked," exclaimed the demagogic Reverend Sam Small, adding: "Let us send our Cincinnatusses of the alliance back to their plows!" Another orator suggested that the names of the ninety-four who voted against the home be inscribed on a marble tablet. "Make it black marble," another man yelled, "and turn its face to the wall in shame!"[31]

When the legislature convened the next morning, "excitement ran high" after Cutts moved to have the vote against the home reconsidered. Several members protested that they were "personally insulted," having been "branded" traitors at the indignation meeting, which eventually resulted in at least two separate challenges to a duel. Warner Hill of Greenville, one of "the Ninety-Four," as the home's opponents came to be called, condemned the "raging mob" as a bald-faced attempt to "bulldoze" the legislature and vowed that he and his comrades would not capitulate: "No! Let them indignate. We have sworn to support the constitution and we will do it!" Hill then revealed that sixty-one veterans had voted with him against the home and twenty-nine home advocates were members of the Alliance. Both groups had indeed split their votes. Among those voting for the home were Robert H. Jackson, the first state president of the Georgia Alliance; former Granger John L. Branch of Polk County; future Populist Lucius C. Mattox of Clinch County; and, of course, Cutts himself—all four of whom were Confederate veterans. Although neither a veteran nor an Allianceman himself, Hill admitted that he had answered Grady's call and contributed his "little mite to build the home."

Outraged over the rejection of the Georgia soldiers' home bill in August 1891, the
Atlanta *Constitution* published this drawing—based on an actual photograph of one
Virge Moses of Dahlonega, Georgia, while he was a prisoner of war at Camp Chase,
Ohio—as an editorial comment on the necessity of caring for the state's indigent
veterans. (author's collection)

Even so, he had voted against the home and he called on his fellow members to "stand by their convictions . . . and show the world that [they] did what [they] thought was right in the sight of God and men!" (Cries of "We'll do it, we'll do it" resounded throughout the chamber.)[32]

Future governor William Y. Atkinson, the son of a planter from Coweta County, and a friend of Hill, also made a violent speech against the home. "Don't be influenced by the yells of mobs and the cries of demoniacal preachers," Atkinson warned. Although we "have nothing against Atlanta," he insisted, "we will not accept a "little kitchen apartment" located in that city. Home champions E. W. Martin and John Goodwin, a former Atlanta mayor, countered by denying that there was anything said or done at the meeting that could be construed as "disorderly or undemocratic." Atkinson's cross-state rival, William Fleming, added that it had been "an honest meeting" composed of "honest citizens" who had exercised their constitutional right of peaceful assembly. (This statement brought those seated in the gallery to their feet, cheering and applauding, for several minutes.) After the House finally came to order, Atkinson asked whether his ninety-three allies would stand by him in defeating Cutts's motion to reconsider. ("Yes! Yes!," could be heard.) Would they defend their honor and demonstrate that they could not be bullied? ("Yes! Yes!," the clamor grew louder.) "Let's vote down" the motion, he concluded, and the House did just that, overwhelmingly (94-44), before adjourning. Thus, on August 28, 1891, three of the "wildest and most exciting" days in the history of the Georgia legislature came to an end.[33]

When the home's directors met with Governor Northen on September 9, somewhat cooler heads prevailed. President Calhoun analyzed the situation in this manner: even though the building had been completed and was currently out of debt, there was no money left to maintain the institution. And, since the legislators had in their "wisdom" deemed it proper to reject "the gift," what action should the board now take? A proposal to organize a joint-stock company, with capital set at a quarter of a million dollars, evoked some discussion. But to do that, according to Evan Howell and others, would take a year or more of litigation and would ultimately involve thousands of people. Nelson Tift suggested selling the property and dividing the proceeds among its incorporators at a pro rata share. The directors agreed that do so would be "impracticable," if not premature. The board also dismissed a motion to have the city of Atlanta assume operation, opting instead for a plan to close the home temporarily until the next legislature convened. Wait until the people can "express their will," counseled Sam Inman; then if the home is rejected again, the board would accept the fact that the people do not want a veterans' home. Meanwhile, director Clement A. Evans of Augusta issued an address calling on all Georgians to rally behind "this good and great cause." The unoccupied building, guarded by a lone Confederate veteran, he said, deserved a better fate, and would be opened, no matter how long it took.[34]

The directors hoped to succeed not only by cultivating popular sentiment but also by profiting from party loyalty. By the time the new legislature convened, the wisdom of the wait-and-see strategy had become apparent. The hotly contested home issue (as well as others throughout the session) had revealed deep divisions within the Alliance. Farmers had failed to give solid support to their own platform. Only a small minority of Alliancemen bolted the Democratic fold and formed a new party. The legislature that emerged was indeed "new": only 17 of the 175 House members from the previous session retained their seats. A scant eleven of the much-maligned Ninety-Four—headed by Warner Hill and W. M. Sears—were back; meanwhile, home advocates Martin and Boifeuillet had also returned.[35]

After a thirteen-month recess, the board met again and gave unanimous consent to the proposed soldiers' home legislation. The directors voted to amend the previous bill by reducing the state's annual maintenance appropriation from $25,000 to $20,000 and granting the state "absolute" control five years earlier than had been originally requested. To introduce the measure, the board handpicked William Fleming, who presented the bill at roll call on October 27, 1892. There was every reason to be optimistic about the bill's fate, remarked the *Constitution*, since many new members had pledged their support. With a different House, Fleming was more confident and emboldened than ever, predicting that his bill would "go through like a greased streak of lightning." At the same time, Lowndes Calhoun and other members of the Fulton County Veterans Association waged an aggressive campaign, culminating in a pre-debate home inspection tour arranged specifically for a number of "antagonistic" representatives and senators.[36]

The debate on the bill finally began on November 23, 1892. Fleming spoke "calmly" for nearly one hour, emphasizing the "sound investment" the project represented during a period of economic uncertainty. According to his calculations, the property would quadruple in value in twenty years. Bill Smith, a veteran from Gwinnett County, adopting a more emotional tactic, appealed to the "young men" of the House to approve the bill for the sake of Grady, of needy ex-Confederates, and of the "dear, dead old South of long ago." Sears of Webster County, the first to speak for the opposition, claimed that he knew of relatively few old soldiers who were willing to enter the home. Another representative from southwest Georgia said he disapproved of the institution because he feared that veterans would invariably have to "knuckle [under] to the nods and wiles" of their former "superior officers." Harvey Johnson of Fulton County disputed these assertions, arguing that it would cost less to support the veterans in the home than on county poor farms. But the most impressive speech on behalf of the bill came from William H. Styles of Liberty County, one of only two black members of the House. A former body servant of a Confederate soldier, Styles asserted that he was willing to do anything he could to relieve "the distresses" of Confederate veterans. If the federal government provided homes for Union veterans—and "hundreds of colored soldiers benefit from these," Styles declared—then certainly Georgia should have a home of its own. In fact, his fellow blacks would "be willing to be taxed now" to support the institution. For this reason, Styles cheerfully cast his vote for the "monument" to the patriotism of Grady and all other Georgians.[37]

Endorsements by Styles and others helped push the soldiers' home bill through a gauntlet of amendments. First, one legislator wanted to limit appropriations to no more than $15,000, a suggestion that the House adopted. Next, Warner Hill, no friend of the home, moved that the bill be submitted to a direct vote of the people in January 1893. This motion the members grudgingly approved (75-71). A motion that only Confederate veterans were eligible to vote in the special referendum failed, but the legislators agreed to a provision that only veterans could serve as home officers. The House also determined that a veteran could not receive a pension and reside in the home simultaneously. Finally, it defeated a recommendation that fathers of veterans could be admitted. When the measure as amended finally came up for a vote on December 3, 1892, it passed by a substantial margin (121-43).[38]

Yet it was a Pyrrhic victory. In analyzing the opposition's votes, the *Constitution* noted that all belonged to the Populist Party, which had recently adopted a plank against the home. Indeed, seven members representing the "terrible" Tenth District, in counties lying northwest and west of Augusta, and nine members from counties situated south and east of Columbus (both third party strongholds) remained loyal to their party's directive. Also voting against the bill were four remaining stalwarts of the Ninety-Four, three of whom were now active Populists. "It is remarkable," Clark Howell noted wryly, that men who supposedly championed popular referendums should vote against a measure that contained one. But the hidden irony at the time was that not everyone who voted in favor of Fleming's omnibus bill actually sympathized with the home. Warner Hill, for example, and three of his colleagues who had formerly opposed the institution switched their votes in the 1892 session, as a disingenuous ploy ultimately to derail the project.[39]

At least that was how contemporaries interpreted Hill's amendment requiring a popular referendum. A few days after the bill had already gone to the Senate for approval on December 9, Fleming revealed publicly that he and his supporters had erred by acquiescing to Hill's amendment. Fearing that any dispute over this "technicality" would jeopardize the home entirely, they had made no "attack," hoping that their allies in the Senate would be able to strike the referendum. But the bill had already emerged from the Senate finance committee with Hill's amendment intact, and on December 13, just hours before Fleming made his disclosure, the bill passed. If allowed to stand, Fleming warned, the measure would invariably be declared unconstitutional, since the legislature lacked authority to delegate its power. Moreover, the referendum frightened Fleming and others into thinking that, once the legislation had been turned over to the people, "the black vote" controlled by the Republicans and Populists would surely reject it. Reluctant to risk rejection, Senate sympathizers moved on December 14 that the measure be indefinitely postponed, and they prevailed by a vote of 23-16. "The third party was determined to kill the bill under any and all circumstances," concluded the *Constitution.* "The mischief is done. . . . There is little more to say."[40]

Stunned by the bill's failure, the home directors who met in the capitol on January 12, 1893, were in no mood, having been thrice rejected, to "await another turn" and ask the state to help again. Of the several alternatives suggested that day—adopt the old joint-stock company plan, convert the home into a reform school for delinquents, collect voluntary subscriptions, or sell the home outright and refund the money—the board chose, reluctantly, the last-named option. Toward this end, on February 14, John Milledge filed a petition in court for the right to amend the home's charter and dispose of the property. But not until mid-December 1894 was a bill of equity finally granted. Afterward, Lowndes Calhoun announced that he would soon call a meeting of the board to discuss the best method of selling the home and property (which he said had cost "something over" $50,000) either privately or by public auction, adding, "That is really the only thing we can do."[41]

Assembling on January 28, 1895, after a two-year hiatus, the board discussed for several hours a deal wherein the state's Free Arch Masons would pay $25,000 for the home, to be used as a "refuge" for orphans. Several directors— including James English and Clement Evans—belonged to the Masonic order, which promised to allow as many as ten disabled veterans each year to reside in the home. But upon further deliberation the next morning, the board declined the offer, fearing that it lacked authority to give control of the home to "any one or any order" unless the support of ex-Confederates was guaranteed. Perhaps the board was also disappointed by the low bid and hoped that the home would fetch a higher price in the near future.[42]

During this period of general economic instability, a better proposal was not forthcoming. Over the next few years, as the property was advertised for sale or lease at various intervals, the committee charged with disposing of the home received no bids whatsoever. Inasmuch as the home had been plagued by adversity from the outset, apparently no one wanted to borrow trouble. Meanwhile, the scanty contributions received since July 1891 were totally

The controversial home that Grady built for Georgia's veterans, shown here in an 1898 photograph, remained unoccupied for nearly a decade, until it was finally destroyed by fire in 1901. (author's collection)

exhausted, and the home, which stood vacant, closed and guarded, as a "silent monument," fell deeper into debt as insurance premiums went unpaid. Calhoun successfully negotiated a substantial loan at zero interest through fellow director and home treasurer Paul Romare, who served as vice-president of the Atlanta National Bank. But that evasive action succeeded in keeping the home solvent only until October 1897, when a court order finally forced the board to attempt to sell the property at public auction.[43]

On the day before the home was scheduled to be "exposed for sale" in April 1898 at the Fulton County Courthouse, the *Constitution* reported that certain UDC chapters, headed by the wives of Ellis, Hemphill, and Evans, had determined to "save the home Grady built." The newspaper admitted that it had all but written off the failed endeavor. "Would to God" that history had been different, the article read, and the votes against the home had been fewer, "but no, the denial cannot be made. The empty hallways, the cheerless rooms, the air of wildness and desolation and desertion which marks out the building as a haunted castle, forbids any denial!" Grady's call for Major Stewart to come home, the "sacred fund" drive that Grady spearheaded, and even Grady's death could not overcome "some little technicalities of the law, some little jealousy of location." But the ladies of the UDC will come to the rescue, the *Constitution* boasted.[44]

According to a prior agreement reached with Calhoun, Evans, Romare, and others members of the board, the ladies would purchase the home for $5,000, a modest price, but one that would nevertheless be enough to cover the home's indebtedness and prevent it from falling into unfriendly hands. It had been rumored that several independent parties were interested in purchasing the property and making it into a reformatory, a sanitarium, a summer hotel, or even a college. But the ladies believed that it would "disgrace" the state were the home to be used for anything other than what Grady had envisioned.

It is unclear whether the board actually intended to go through with the sale or whether it was simply using the UDC as a means of delaying foreclosure. In either case, the April 5 auction did not go as the UDC planned. Following Lowndes Calhoun's proclamation of the opening of bids for the property, Mrs. Hallie A. Rounsaville, state president of the UDC, made her bid official as expected. As the auctioneer (William "Tip" Harrison) was about to declare that the home had been sold, "an outsider," E. G. Willingham, owner of a lumber company, startled the crowd by bidding $10,000. After hurriedly consulting with the other commissioners, Calhoun stated that the bids were "too low," and promptly declared the sale off, an announcement that the crowd greeted with "hearty applause and cheering." For his part, Willingham, a veteran, was censured by various UCV camps in the days that followed, until the *Constitution* finally disclosed that he had been secretly planted in the crowd by some of the directors to ensure that they not lose the home. In spite of the confusion—or perhaps because of it—the board had somehow avoided sacrificing the home that Grady built.[45]

In the ensuing months the home received a desperately needed boost. From July 20 through 23, 1898, upward of 50,000 visitors "invaded" the Gate City to participate in the festivities of the eighth annual United Confederate Veterans reunion. In honor of the occasion, the *Constitution* published a special commemorative issue devoted entirely to the celebration of the Confederacy's achievements. The paper featured numerous pen sketches of famous southern patriots, personal reminiscences of the war, and histories of Sherman's march through Georgia, the siege of Atlanta, and other important battles. More important, it also carried an account of the "unhappy" and "pathetic" history of the soldiers' home and related how Grady had conceived the "noble plan" but the state legislature had prevented veterans from benefiting from it. The author of the article wrote that he thought the home's history in the courts was "too well known to be repeated." After the veterans adjourned, the committee in charge of local arrangements for the reunion announced that it would donate nearly $4,000 in surplus funds to the home, provided that the Georgia Assembly accept it as a state institution by January 1901. The committee was headed by Clement Evans, and its other members were Calhoun, Harrison, Fox, Hemphill, and Howell, all avid supporters of the home.[46]

Also at work during the 1898 reunion in Atlanta was the fact that America was at war with Spain and some ex-Confederates were serving under the Stars and Stripes, upholding the nation's honor. Veterans at the reunion endorsed the war effort and called on their fellow citizens to take up arms against the foreign foe. The war unleashed a strong sense of patriotism, of duty to one's country, and, in turn, of the country's obligations to all veterans.[47] The extreme form of enthusiasm, pride, and militarism generated by the Spanish-American War invariably nurtured the Confederate soldiers' home movement. Home advocates pointed to the war as a demonstration of Johnny Reb's loyalty and courage. When members of Congress convened in December 1898, they heard for the first time proposals that not only would allow ex-Confederates to be admitted to the national soldiers' homes but also would permit Confederate soldiers' homes to receive federal funding. In addition, following the war Confederate veterans' groups in Alabama, Mississippi, and South Carolina began organizing benevolence on behalf of soldiers' homes in their states. As one superintendent later put it, the soldiers' homes were "sustained by the sentiment of patriotism, and . . . reverence for a hallowed and heroic period of the past, dear to every true Southern man and woman."[48] The home that Grady built would benefit from the same sentiment.

Under legislation introduced in November 1898 by Joe Hall of Bibb County, the home would again be offered to the state in fee simple. The UCV's cash donation, together with the state's unexpended widows' pension fund, would be enough to support the home during the first twelve months of operation. If too few Confederate veterans entered the home, the property would then be sold or donated to another charity. Hall was especially prudent in attaching independent funding to the bill, since Georgia then faced a huge budget deficit and many legislators favored retrenchment. In spite of these precautions, however, Hall's bill eventually bogged down in the finance committee before the whole House had time to consider the measure. Understandably discouraged, the directors were forced to recommit the home to the auction block in May 1899, but in the wake of another of the *Constitution*'s public outcries, "light bidding" convinced the court commissioners to deny the sale. Although the home that Grady built was closed, there still remained a glimmer of hope that it could somehow be revived before the 1901 deadline.[49]

With time running out, Major William T. Gary, in an apparent last-ditch effort to salvage the home endeavor, introduced another bill on October 29, 1900. Finally emerging from the finance committee, the bill was made special order of the day for December 3. Gary, a veteran and a railroad lawyer from

Augusta, made an "impassioned and eloquent" speech on behalf of the "unfortunate" men across the state who had neither shelter nor families and would benefit from the Atlanta home. He exclaimed that "God, on Mount Sinai, had commanded that we honor our fathers . . . and they would be honored if the home was given to the veterans." Critics turned a deaf ear to such an appeal, replaying a scene that had occurred in the House on several previous occasions. The proposal, they charged, was unnecessary, their county poorhouses were "good enough," the requested $15,000 annual appropriation would "take away" from the veterans' pensions, and there was no reason "from an economical standpoint" why the bill should be passed.[50]

The home's proponents had heard it all before, though conspicuously missing from among the various objections raised was the rabid anti-Atlanta bias that had formerly consumed the home's most stalwart foes. Even so, by a narrow two-vote margin the bill failed to receive a constitutional majority. Believing that many of the bill's friends were absent, and since only three more votes were needed, Gary moved for its reconsideration. This time, the bill passed (106-50) and was transmitted immediately to the Senate, where the bill's co-author, Bill Smith of Buford, an advocate of the home since its founding, guided the measure through committee and brought it safely to the floor for debate. Supporting him were Clark Howell, the Senate president, and Senator George M. Tatum, a former Allianceman from Walker County, one of the Ninety-Four, who now confessed that he favored the bill "with all his heart." Tatum's self-confessed conversion was, however, by no means indicative of a general reversal in sentiment by home detractors. In fact, the favorable action in the House had probably resulted from a substantial change in personnel. Only eight members of the 1900 Assembly, for instance, had occupied seats in either the 1890 or 1892 lower house. Although three advocates of the 1892 legislation now supported Gary's bill, Populists J. R. Hogan and M. L. Everett, among the original Ninety-Four, cast their votes against it. Also, three others who had abstained from voting in 1891 split their votes in 1900, including Lectured Crawford, McIntosh County's black representative, who voted against the measure.[51]

Representing the Populist minority in the Senate was James Dennard of Wilcox County, who, like Tatum, had been one of the infamous Ninety-Four. Dennard echoed the reservations voiced by his House colleagues Hogan and Everett and claimed that the veterans' institution would needlessly "burden" the state. Several others said that they refused to be wooed by the appeal to sentiment. Nevertheless, on December 15, 1900, time had come for the Senate to vote on the measure. A large number of veterans seated in the galleries and gathered on the floor anxiously awaited the bill's outcome. Finally, to the delight of the crowd, the bill passed (25-10) and was sent to the governor's office for his signature.[52]

After over eleven years of "expectant waiting," Governor Allen Candler, a veteran, who in his last message to the Assembly had recommended the state's acceptance and maintenance of the Confederate Soldiers' Home, signed the bill into law on December 19. Four days later Candler named eleven of his fellow ex-Confederates, one from each congressional district, to serve as trustees. At its first meeting the board elected Lowndes Calhoun president and began liquidating the home's debt, making necessary renovations on the building "from garret to cellar," drafting the rules and regulations, interviewing candidates for superintendent, and reviewing applications for admission.[53]

On January 19, 1901, Robert E. Lee's birthday, during a special awards ceremony at the state capitol, the UDC honored Major Gary, Senator Smith, and Lowndes Calhoun for their "magnificent fight" by presenting each of them with a medal of achievement. The medal's principal design consisted of a laurel wreath encircling a facsimile of the Stars and Bars; the reverse side bore an inscription in reference to the home, "Monumentum Aere Perennium" (a monument more enduring than bronze). In presenting the medal to Gary, Clark Howell stated that he thought it "providential" that the original bill had been defeated a decade earlier, "for it [had] aroused the state to a recognition of its duty to the Confederate soldiers." No other state had been more generous in granting pensions during the 1890s than Georgia. Indeed, by 1899 pension payments totaled nearly $5 million, representing on average more than 10 percent of the state's total expenditures during the decade.[54]

Finally, on June 3, 1901, Jefferson Davis's birthday, the institution for which Grady had worked so diligently admitted its first veterans, some forty "gray hair remnants" from twenty-six different Georgia counties, including several former third-party strongholds. During the opening ceremonies Governor Candler praised the home, not as "a pauper's retreat"—"God forbid it shall ever be looked on in that light!"—but as a gift to which the state's veterans were entitled. When Lowndes Calhoun spoke, he reminded everyone of the long years of "struggling and waiting" that had passed. He publicly thanked the fine people who stood before him—the UCV and UDC, the Sons of Confederate Veterans (SCV), the Order of Robert E. Lee, and the Children of the Confederacy—for never surrendering, and he promised those admitted that day that "everything possible will be done to make the hours you pass here pleasant and agreeable, not tedious and burdensome." Bill Smith also spoke, making several references to Grady, and was "warmly applauded" as Grady's mother, mother-in-law, and daughter, who were seated on the speaker's platform, nodded in polite approval.[55]

A new home for Georgia's Confederate veterans was erected in place of the one that burned down; the main building, shown here in 1910, stood until 1967, when it was razed. (author's collection)

Formally rededicated and officially declared open, the home, rejoiced the *Constitution*, was "at last a fact!" Little did anyone know that in a few short months fate would once again strike a swift and terrible blow against the home that Grady built. The September 1901 fire ravaged the institution, but Calhoun and the new board of trustees were as committed as ever to see it opened again. Leasing Atlanta's Thompson Hotel as a temporary facility, the board on October 28 had Major Gary introduce a bill in the state legislature granting an additional $20,000 for the rebuilding of the soldiers' home. In late November the House approved (94-36) the measure, and a few days later the Senate concurred (29-6). By October 1902 a new southern colonial style brick building had been finished and stood ready for occupancy, barring any other unforeseen tragedy.[56]

In spite of the multitude of setbacks and obstacles encountered in the past, Grady's vision had become reality. Georgia had finally established a home of its own, paid for primarily by southerners, in recognition of the Confederate common soldier's achievements. The Atlanta Ring, worn threadbare prior to Grady's death, had since completely unraveled. The dreaded fusion of the state's farmers, blacks, and Republicans had never fully taken place. Georgians had largely remained loyal to the Democratic Party, Populism had become a vanishing creed, and the black vote had been effectively neutralized. Yet the home remained—until it was completely demolished in 1967—and eventually an estimated 1,200 veterans resided there. Its survival was significantly more than a memorial to one man. It was a tribute to the powerful and enduring sentiment that had given impetus and meaning to the founding of all Confederate soldiers' homes in the New South.

With the fight for the Georgia home successfully concluded, three other original Confederate states—Alabama, Mississippi, and South Carolina—still lacked a soldiers' home. But that would soon change. In Montgomery, Alabama, for example, on November 13, 1901, more than 2,000 members of the newly formed state division of the UCV unanimously adopted a resolution calling for the establishment of a home. The veterans also pledged their influence in urging the legislature to enact a law that would not only provide sufficient appropriations but also "build houses and furnish stock and farming implements" for a home. Such an institution had been frequently discussed in the aftermath of the Spanish-American War, but the first serious effort to make it a reality had not commenced until Captain Jefferson M. Falkner, a veteran and an attorney for the Louisville & Nashville Railroad, announced that he intended to donate some forty acres of land near Mountain Creek Station in Chilton County to be used as a home site. Already more than $250,000 in pensions were being appropriated by the state each year; Alabama's constitution mandated that ten cents out of every dollar in state revenue go toward Confederate pensions, one-third the amount earmarked for public schools. But the veterans had decided during their first reunion in the state capital the previous year that the "small pittance" given by the legislature was not adequate to meet the needs of the Confederate pensioner. "The home for the old heroes is at last in sight," rejoiced the Montgomery *Advertiser*, whose president and editor in chief, W. W. Screws, was also an ex-Confederate and a former Alabama secretary of state.

By early April 1902 construction of the main building began, and work on several cottages would soon follow, financed wholly through voluntary contributions and various public events, including a highly publicized lecture by former Tennessee governor Robert Taylor, a favorite orator among ex-Confederates since his retirement from public office. Both the Senate and the House passed the bill appropriating state monies for the institution, with a total of only five dissenting votes; and although the state faced a severe revenue shortfall (as had Georgia), Governor Thomas Jelks signed the measure into law on October 6, 1903. Although there certainly were needless appropriations in the state budget, explained the Montgomery *Advertiser*, the Falkner home was "paramount, and we believe that the State can afford to make [the appropriation for] it." Moreover, Alabama's politicians simply could not afford to oppose it. "What leader or politician would dare oppose the

Confederate soldiers?," one representative asked. "God save the man who begins a race for any office in Alabama from United States senator to justice of the peace by antagonizing the Confederate sentiment!"[57]

The same could have been said next door in Mississippi, where on December 10, 1903, the Jefferson Davis Memorial Home for Confederate Soldiers and Sailors opened at Biloxi. A decade earlier people had discussed establishing a home in Meridian, and in the meantime the UDC had successfully lobbied the state legislature for the building of a Confederate Veterans' Annex to the state hospital at Vicksburg. But the opportunity for founding a home was not fully realized until February 1903, when Varina Davis, the former first lady and now the venerated "Queen Mother" of the Confederacy, officially transferred the Davis homestead, Beauvoir, to the newly incorporated state division of the SCV, for the express purpose of converting the property into a "perpetual memorial sacred to the memory" of her late husband. Legislators—nearly 20 percent of whom were Confederate veterans—voted overwhelmingly in favor of accepting temporary control of the institution, and Governor James K. Vardaman eagerly signed the bill creating the home on March 4, 1904. In his inaugural address three months earlier, Vardaman (a member of the SCV) had warned his fellow citizens that "as long as there is one [veteran] left . . . I want it understood that I care not how heavy the burdens of taxation may be, just as long as the money is needed and properly expended for the support of the helpless ex-Confederate soldier." With the governor's imprimatur on the soldiers' home bill, Mississippians had little reason to question his resolve.[58]

Meanwhile, in South Carolina, in the three decades following the war, millions of dollars in artificial limb payments and disability pensions had been appropriated for needy veterans, and a home for Confederate widows and daughters had been started in Charleston. The first known attempt to establish a home for ex-soldiers took place in 1900, when a veteran in Laurens County announced a fund-raising campaign, because the "poorhouse [was] no place" for ex-Confederates. In the following year, the UDC and the board of regents of the State Hospital for the Insane informed Governor Miles B. McSweeney of a potential site for the home. The regents declared that Bellvue Place, property near Columbia formerly belonging to Colonel William Wallace but recently acquired by the hospital, could be "adapted to all the uses of the veterans," since the existing farmhouse could form the nucleus for a "few wooden buildings." But the legislature did not act upon the recommendation until several years later, when Senator J. Hampden Brooks of Greenwood, a distinguished veteran and brother of the late congressman Preston Smith Brooks (of Brooks-Sumner fame), introduced a bill creating the South Carolina Confederate Infirmary.[59]

According to Brooks's bill, the state would provide $12,000, which was to be used to construct a facility on the land donated by the state hospital. Sent to the House on February 9, 1907, but held over and made special order in the second session a year later, the bill was soon approved in a close vote (55-47) and ratified by the Senate shortly afterward. Some lawmakers objected to the home's being established at Columbia, while others no longer saw a need for the home and worried that it would not be a good investment. As for those who voted against the measure, fumed one angry veteran, they "ought to be ashamed, . . . and if they are not, I feel sure some of their constituents are ashamed for them!" When the new Assembly convened the following year, after Brooks had retired from office, thirty-nine-year-old Mendel Lafayette Smith of Kershaw County, a former House speaker, introduced a bill repealing the act establishing the infirmary. When the bill reached the Senate, the UDC made "such a beautiful plea" that it was killed without a dissenting vote, and every penny originally set aside for the project was restored.[60]

On Memorial Day, May 10, 1909, the home opened, and three weeks later, on June 3, Jefferson Davis's birthday, formal dedication ceremonies were held at the home, featuring a speech by Governor Martin F. Ansel, appropriate remarks by Brooks, and an emotional tribute by Senator Francis H. Weston of Richland County, one of the home's most stalwart proponents and an officer in the SCV. The twenty-one old men who were now in the home "seem[ed] perfectly content," commented a Columbia reporter after touring the building. "They are treated with as much consideration as if they were lords. Their rooms are comfortable, their table fare adequate and wholesome, their supply of literature elevating and pleasing." And no one at the time had any reason to doubt that this was all true.[61]

Exactly why ex-Confederates were late in establishing soldiers' homes in Alabama, Mississippi, and South Carolina—the very heart of Dixie—is open to speculation. Whether there was a direct relationship between Grady's highly publicized and drawn out endeavor and the postponed start of the other three homes is unclear. State finances do not seem to provide an answer either. As noted earlier, legislators in all three states were willing to provide pensions, artificial limbs, and other forms of direct assistance to needy Confederate veterans, even when deficit financing was required. A possible explanation is that veterans in these states were not organized well or soon enough to establish a home any earlier. Ex-Confederates in Alabama, for example, waited until the turn of the century, when they were likely spurred by the intense patriotism and consciousness of veterans raised by America's war with Spain, before forming a state division of the UCV. But what Alabama Confederate veterans lacked in organization and effective leadership until 1900, their counterparts in the border states of Maryland and Missouri had lacked in numbers and political influence before they established homes in their states.

And there is no indication that a large number of veterans in South Carolina, Mississippi, or Alabama fervently opposed a soldiers' home in principle, viewing it as degrading charity, in the way some ex-Confederates had done in other states. In sum, there is no satisfactory answer that helps explain why the first states to secede were the last states to join the Confederate soldiers' home movement.

CHAPTER FIVE

A Discipline for Heroes

The movement to create soldiers' homes in the New South began as much with ideas about honor and social responsibility as with the underlying assumption that an indigent but worthy ex-Confederate deserved better than a bundle of straw in a county almshouse. The philanthropists who conceived, founded, supported, and governed the South's first veterans' institutions felt compelled to use their wealth and free time to ameliorate the lot of their less fortunate brethren. Life within a filthy asylum cluttered with alcoholics, tramps, blacks, the insane, and "the roughest sort," they argued, was unnatural, impersonal, and demeaning for old soldiers. And the almshouse was no better alternative, they reasoned, representing as it did a loss of autonomy, and being a place where the indigent veteran would be degraded and manipulated.[1] On the other hand, the benefits of a "home" atmosphere and the solicitude of "family" members would provide ideal conditions for comfort and rest, without the stigma of pauperism. "It is" indeed "a lamentable sight to see a battle-scarred soldier of the Confederacy in a poorhouse," exclaimed the Richmond *Dispatch* in 1892. "It is disgraceful that any worthy veteran . . . should be forced to live like a pauper." As Georgia's Clement Evans had put it two years earlier, "true men" should never be forced into the poorhouse to become the "common objects of uncertain charity" or "face the frown of impatient and heartless strangers."[2]

The central purpose of the Confederate soldiers' home, therefore, was to provide a viable alternative to what many considered a substandard and demoralized institutional care system for aged, infirm, and poor men. Almshouses, pauper farms, insane asylums, hospitals, and, in some cases, jails were to be replaced by a new institution that better suited the veteran's needs and special status. For some home advocates, providing a "new" institution meant simply adopting and applying the best features of established, modern benevolence. For others, however, it meant being willing to try something different, in an effort to improve upon existing conditions. For example, Jefferson Falkner of Alabama derived his idea of a veterans' home from the cottage system, wherein each veteran and his family resided in a "small house" or cottage and enjoyed "home privileges," such as being able to get a "glass of milk or a roll in the kitchen between meals at will, instead of being housed with hundreds of others, [and] eating, sleeping and living by rule and the clock." In time, the Jefferson Manly Falkner Soldiers' Home at Mountain Creek consisted of more than twenty different buildings of various sizes and functions: an eclectic mixture of large dormitories and small houses distributed around a crescent-shaped drive that served as the lifeline of the "beautiful village" in Alabama. William "Tip" Harrison's conception of a "model home" for Georgia's veterans was a large farming cooperative of 3,000 acres, divided into ten-acre plots for each veteran and his family. Siding with Henry Grady, Harrison opposed a central edifice design, as he explained, because "this makes the place appear like a prison or poorhouse, leaves no room for employment [and] creates discontent after the novelty wears off." Yet it was just such a design that well-meaning and concerned veterans in Tennessee, Arkansas, Missouri, Kentucky, Oklahoma, and ultimately South Carolina, adopted for their indigent comrades. In the end, Georgians reluctantly abandoned the cottage plan in favor of a central building too.[3]

Although individual cottages were easier and cheaper to build, were available upon completion for immediate occupancy, and could be constructed and furnished in a relatively short time, a central building was more economical, since more veterans could be housed together at less cost over a longer period— or so it was argued. The Tennessee home, for example, was fully equipped to provide solicitude and compassion to large numbers of old and disabled men who might otherwise have lived out the remainder of their lives alone, uncared for, and forgotten. The brick, two-story building consisted of a pair of symmetrical wings adorned with wide galleries, rounded porticoes, and fluted pillars. Whereas the lower story contained reception rooms, a parlor, a library, a dining hall, and a kitchen, the upper level had 50 bedrooms for a maximum of 125 occupants. Interior hallways connecting each room converged at the center of the building. The home also included an engine room, equipped with steam furnace and boilers, and laundry facilities, located in the basement, while a 10,000-gallon cistern set astride the roof provided "running" water, as well as a means for fire protection and waste disposal. The home resembled a cross between a rest home and a large country hotel, although an imposing raised-letter board stretched across its central facade announced that it was the "Confederate Soldiers' Home."[4] The original building of the Arkansas home was likewise a two-story brick structure. Described as "neat, comfortable and attractive," it measured some 60 by 115 feet, with two long galleries running the length of the building, which could accommodate as many as sixty-four persons. Neither the Tennessee nor the Arkansas home was inexpensive to build, each costing its respective state legislature $10,000–$25,000 in the early 1890s.

No matter how much it cost, home administrators had one specific goal: to supply practically everything within the bounds of reason for the happiness and comfort of the veteran. "Our whole aim here," remarked Arkansas superintendent Rufus McDaniel, "is to make the last days of the dear old veterans just as happy and peaceful as it is [possible] for humans to be." Peace, quiet, comfort, convenience, and a nourishing diet were all fundamental components of the homes' paternalistic vision of what they were to provide. Yet for those earnest men who bore legal and financial responsibility for them, the institutions also had to be maintained in due order. Hopes for effective and efficient care could not become realities without an appropriately hierarchical control of every person within the home and every aspect of its administration. As one South Carolina home official admitted: "We cannot expect to have a real home unless order is maintained." Superintendent McDaniel agreed: "Some discipline must be administered."[5] Thus, trustees sought not only to "shield" veterans from the tempestuous "outer world"; they also struggled to impose a desired order within the home walls.[6]

Toward this end, trustees prescribed work for veterans under their charge. In fact, the managers of the Falkner Home in Alabama, for example, required each veteran to pledge in writing that he would work as long as he was able. The Falkner board could not have been more pleased to find, during one of its initial inspections, that the veterans were engaged in a variety of "light" employment: one was digging up a stump; another was tilling a flower garden: a third took immense pride in a woodshed he and his fellow inmates had constructed; and still others were chopping wood to fill the shed for the coming winter. Physical, emotional, and moral benefits abounded in labor, so it was contended, even for the poor and aging. The North Carolina board of directors required residents to labor "for their [own] comfort and happiness," while Louisiana's Camp Nicholls put men to work in order to avoid inactivity and its "pernicious consequences." The "bitter monotony of enforced idleness" would "naturally cause men to become dissatisfied with their surroundings," warned the board of visitors for Virginia's Lee Camp. Therefore, some form of "light and congenial employment" to help "dissipate the spirit [of self-pity]" seemed appropriate. Apparently it was difficult for persons, especially those approaching retirement themselves—as many home trustees were—to accept the idea that a formerly industrious and prudent laborer would no longer be able to provide for himself. With adequate supervision and discipline, they seemed to feel, an inmate might become independent. And at least one man expressed the hope that if an old and disabled veteran entered a home, perhaps he could be made "almost self-supporting."[7]

Both Henry Grady and John Gordon, two key spokesmen for Confederate soldiers' homes, stressed that a veteran who remained active retained his self-worth. When the *Constitution* launched its fund-raising drive in April 1889, Governor Gordon recommended that Georgians consider establishing a "Confederate Co-operative Industrial Home," essentially a workhouse. The plan featured a number of "advantages," Gordon asserted, for veterans and their families would work at manufacturing clothing, shoes, baskets, or canned fruits. By supporting themselves, he argued, inmates would maintain their self-respect and self-reliance and develop bodily strength. In addition, a self-sufficient home would relieve the Georgia legislature of the burden of taxation. Such a plan, Gordon boasted, is "effective philanthropy." Even though Grady envisioned a farming community inhabited by soldiers and their families rather than a manufacturing community, he, like Gordon, expected residents to work, either on individual five-acre plots or collectively. There should be, he said, an abundance of "home cultivation": gardens, orchards, dairies, and pastures that would allow the veteran to feel that he was "helping at least to earn his daily bread."[8]

Both Grady and Gordon believed that a model soldiers' home had room for the veterans' spouses and dependent children, and others shared their thinking. For example, during the planning stages for the Mississippi home, veterans envisioned an "industrial farm" for ex-soldiers and their families. In August 1890 John P. Murphy assured his fellow delegates at the second annual meeting of the Ex-Confederate Association of Arkansas, that their home would not only be a place where his poor comrades could "spend their declining years in peace and quiet" but also "where the widow of the old soldier can find rest and shelter, and . . . the soldier's orphan can obtain a manual training school."[9] When the Arkansas home finally opened two years later, only veterans were admitted, but an annex for women was constructed in the early twentieth century. Nothing came of the school, however. Several of the homes that eventually barred wives and children from entering—those in Florida and Tennessee, for example—permitted families to occupy the home until it became evident that such an arrangement was neither practical nor cost effective. And, although Jeff Falkner invited veterans and their families to dwell in his cottages, relatively few ever did, as most of the veterans who came to live there occupied the home's dormitories instead.[10]

Although embracing neither Gordon's nor Grady's plan, Georgia home trustees decided to incorporate labor for ex-Confederates as a means of "recreation." Before the home finally opened, the board mandated "light work" for convalescing and ambulatory residents. Duties ranged from waiting on tables,

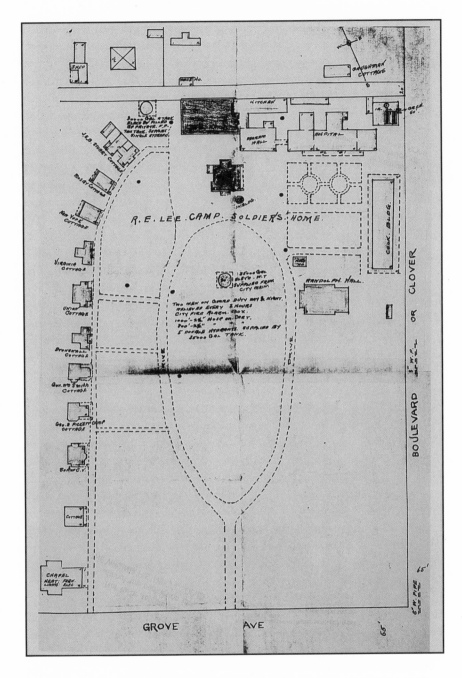

Plat of the Lee Camp Home, showing that the Virginia home was much more than
a single building and was indeed a veritable community.
(courtesy of Virginia Historical Society)

night patrol, and building maintenance to cleaning rooms, scouring hallways, cooking, dishwashing, and disposing of waste. Some men also repaired shoes and clothing and toiled in the home garden.[11] Other soldiers' home administrators, too, prescribed work for their residents. Texas managers, for example, required each able-bodied inmate to perform his portion of work with alacrity and "good faith." The superintendent could assign any "reasonable labor" beyond the mandatory duties of keeping quarters clean and neat. Refusal to obey an officer's orders, the rules read, would result in "prompt dismissal" from the home. Veterans at the Texas home mended fences, hung shingles, pitched hay, patched clothing, and resoled footwear, in exchange for "tobacco money," that is, a few dollars with which an inmate could purchase small items, including chewing or smoking tobacco.[12] Lee Camp veterans had to clean their rooms "properly" and "beautify the home" as directed by the commandant, as well as "do such work as their physical ability will allow, without remuneration." In 1892 William A. Shiplett reported that, in the two years he had resided at the Virginia home, he had been detailed to nurse sick inmates and bury deceased ones and to build a barn. During the same period another man had worked in the office as a file clerk; a third had grazed horses and minded cows, while a fourth had shoveled coal. The alternative to working, the board of visitors allegedly informed the inmates, was "the gate— do the work or go out of the gate."[13]

Camp Nicholls's directors also demanded "strict obedience" to the rule governing inmate duties. They held each man responsible for his own clothing, bedding, and quarters, enjoining him to keep them "properly cleaned and in good order." The same rule applied to the grounds and buildings, while another rule prohibited the practice of hiring substitutes. At the Louisiana home during the 1890s veterans painted cisterns, repaired buildings, whitewashed trees, pulled weeds, and cleaned privies. In 1900 the board appointed a dozen "suitable" inmates to form a home fire brigade, responsible for manning extinguishers and drilling regularly. Beginning in 1888, directors even permitted inmates, by written request, to labor outside the home, but when they became convinced that outside labor contributed to lapses in discipline, they rescinded the rule eight years later.[14]

Home founders assumed that residents would want to work anyway, basing their assumption on old notions of social responsibility and on the persistent popular image of Johnny Reb. Fundamental to the founding of Confederate soldiers' homes was an unquestioned distinction between the worthy and unworthy poor, between the prudent and industrious objects of a benign stewardship and the lazy and self-indulgent paupers who had no claim upon public benevolence. And, for home advocates and administrators, there was no doubt into which category Johnny Reb fell. Though battle scars may have rendered him unfit to earn a livelihood and old age and poverty may have overtaken him, the common southern warrior still remained a shining model of honor, valor, and manliness—too proud, therefore, to accept pity. It would not be considered charity if men worked in the home. Thus, it was only natural that administrators expected inmates to work when given an opportunity, in order to prevent the loss of self-esteem.

Veterans like A. B. Carter reinforced such beliefs. Having lost his right arm at Spotsylvania, he was unable to perform "hard labor." But the Shelby County, Tennessee, farmer requested that board president Fitzhugh Lee give him "something to do" in the Virginia home to enable him to support his wife and daughter. In fact, they too would do "anything that came in their line," he averred. Impressed by the old man's determination, Lee forwarded Carter's application to the board, concluding that his seemed to be a "deserving case." Other applicants manifested a similar desire to remain active. Former North Carolina sergeant Daniel C. Hill claimed that he would "gladly" work in the Virginia institution. One Nashville ex-Confederate obviously delighted in telling trustees about his vast experience in growing sweet potatoes. Equipped with this knowledge, he boasted, "I can be of much benefit to our home." A fellow Tennessean, aged seventy-one, fancying himself a "very competent" veterinarian, believed he would also be of "great service out there [at the home] in looking after the horses, cows and other stock." Another veteran put it simply: "I want to come," but "I do not want to be idle."[15]

The process of distinguishing between deserving and improvident veterans began with admission applications. Formal entrance criteria were similar in all early soldiers' homes. Potential inmates had to meet several basic standards, and trustees had to be convinced that a veteran's indigence was caused by a war-related disability or other events beyond his control, and certainly not by idleness or other personal failings. For starters, trustees required applicants to furnish evidence of their military service (no imposters were wanted). Only an honorable discharge or imprisonment by the enemy excused a soldier from the fighting; therefore deserters need not apply. Furthermore, men who had renounced the southern cause by swearing an oath of allegiance to the United States were ineligible. A case in point was W. T. Vick, who had been a soldier in the Fortieth Mississippi Infantry but who, according to a report by the Adjutant General's Office in Washington, took an oath on April 10, 1865, before enlisting in the Fifth U.S. Infantry. Vick was denied admission to the Arkansas home because, as Superintendent Clarence P. Newton explained, he had sworn the oath before Lee's formal surrender on April 12, which the board considered the official end of the war.[16]

The application form for the Jefferson Davis Memorial Home consisted of nearly fifty questions, most of which dealt with the ex-Confederate's military service. The form asked the veteran where he had enlisted, in which regiment, and what the name of his commanding officer was, as well as inquiring about the date of, reasons for, and terms of his discharge, transfer, reenlistment, or surrender. Was he ever wounded? if so, when and where? Was he ever absent from his command? how long and why? Three signatures by "creditable" references or approval of the commander or adjutant of a UCV camp, as well as a physician's certificate, were also required. A Camp Nicholls applicant had to provide two vouchers that bore the names and ranks of former comrades. In light of these questions and requirements, it seems clear that a faulty memory could jeopardize approval of a veteran's application. What if an applicant could no longer accurately recall the details of his enlistment? In such cases, advised Alexander S. Salley, Jr., secretary of the South Carolina Historical Commission, who routinely verified applications for admission to the home in Columbia, officials should ask the veteran the name of his captain, explaining: "If he does not know that, then you may be sure that he is not what he claims to be. . . . Every soldier should know the name of his captain." In addition, Alabama veterans were expected to remember every one of their commanders, from corps and division level down to their company's second lieutenant and adjutant. Virginia trustees insisted on notarized affidavits (preferably signed by two men who had served in the same regiment) accompanied by a judge's certificate. If two "reputable" witnesses could not be found, Texas applicants had the option of submitting their old discharge papers. The soldiers' home should be a home for "Worthy Disabled Ex-Confederate Soldiers," exclaimed Camp Nicholls board member Fred A. Ober, "not an asylum for tramps" who cannot verify that they performed honorable service.[17]

The form employed by the South Carolina Confederate Infirmary at Columbia enabled the board of commissioners to determine effectively whether an applicant's military service had indeed been honorable. When Amos O. Banks of Lexington County applied for admission, for example, he indicated that he had enlisted in Company F, Fifth South Carolina Cavalry, at Lexington Court House, on December 26, 1861. He had served throughout the war except for a period of about six weeks, until, after having been been wounded in June 1864 at Cold Harbor and losing the use of his right wrist, he spent the rest of the war confined in a hospital bed in Richmond. He also stated that he had fought honorably and faithfully and that he had remained loyal to the Confederate government to the bitter end. Banks was eighty years old when he applied to the infirmary, unmarried, 5'11", a farmer, and his nearest relatives were nieces and nephews at Columbia and in Lexington County. By signing the application, he claimed not only that he suffered from a wartime disability but also that he had no relative "upon whom he [could] rely" for help. Moreover, he declared that he was a "person of good character and habits," and if admitted, he promised "upon pain of expulsion," not only to abide by and obey the rules and regulations but to "perform such duties as may be required" of him, as well as to "obey all lawful orders." Banks signed the application on May 19, 1909, in the presence of two witnesses. Certifying the application, the Lexington Board of Pensions also vouched for Banks's record, before forwarding the file to the home. After checking that Banks had satisfactorily answered each question, David Cardwell, president of the board of commissioners, approved his application and admitted Banks to the home. There he died less than two years later.[18]

Home authorities also required confirmation that a veteran truly lacked the physical ability and means to reside on the outside. Admission procedures at the Texas home incorporated a series of physical examinations. By law, an applicant had to be checked first by a private physician and then by a home examining panel of three, who determined whether the prospective inmate was disabled to the extent that he could no longer earn a living. If by periodic evaluation the home surgeon concluded that the inmate's condition had improved, the managers reserved the right to issue an honorable discharge to any man having "sufficient ability . . . to support himself." Such action was necessary, according to the law establishing the Texas home, in order to prevent the institution from becoming a refuge for "lazy, able-bodied men." As one inmate informed a trustee of the Falkner Home, "the Home is a good thing for feeble and Sick men, but I don't think that great big powerful Strong men who are able to tote a crosstie, ought to be allowed to stay here." In Hardee Cottage, where he resided, there were two Irishmen who looked like "prizefighters," he said, and ought to be dismissed. Although required to labor, a Texas inmate, paradoxically, risked forfeiture of his right to reside at the home when he exhibited physical well-being by working too diligently. No wonder the "majority do nothing," growled the Texas home physician, "but make up beds, attend meals and sleep."[19] At the same time, none of the homes admitted patients suffering from chronic or contagious diseases. The former undermined the institution's limited ability to provide beds for curable inmates, while the latter endangered its population and staff.

Administrators appeared equally concerned about a veteran's financial fitness but lacked effective methods for confirming it. Each home sought to admit only the indigent and disabled, generally interpreted as those unable to provide for themselves and their families. The interpretation of "indigency" varied from state to state over time. In Mississippi in 1916 a so-called indigent veteran was one who owned property worth less than $2,500. In Texas in 1917 it meant owning property valued at not more than $1,000. In Arkansas as late as 1923 the law prohibited inmates from possessing money or real estate worth in excess of $500.[20] In Louisiana even the paltry sum derived from a Confederate pension ($8.00 per month in 1900) was enough to disqualify an applicant; in fact, many states prohibited their Confederate veterans from drawing a pension while residing in the home. In most states, however, prospective inmates did not have to document their claim of poverty.[21] In Georgia, Virginia, Arkansas, and North Carolina, applicants simply swore or affirmed their economic status before a public official. In Tennessee, respondents merely had to answer in a satisfactory manner such questions as "In what business are you now engaged, if any, and what do you earn?" or "What estate have you in your own right, real and personal, and what is its value?" Admission boards rarely investigated responses, for they understandably viewed applicants as genuinely needy. After all, none but the poor and desperate would willingly seek the dubious comforts of an institution, no matter how well managed.[22]

However poor he might be, an applicant still had to be morally worthy. The Lee Camp board of visitors insisted that, no matter how good a man's war record might be, if his disability had been caused by his own "bad habits and character," he would not be admitted. Henry E. Shelley, president of the Texas home board of managers, did not believe that the state intended to support "any . . . insubordinate, vicious, . . . obnoxious and disagreeable . . . characters." Rather, added Superintendent James Q. Chenoweth, inmates should be "worthy" men who "cheerfully" conduct themselves according to the "high standard" represented by the "true" and "honorable" Confederate veteran.[23] Although discipline among inmates was a common concern for administrators of all nineteenth-century almshouses and other charitable institutions, one factor that set Confederate soldiers' homes apart from other homes—including other veterans' homes—was the chief requirement that applicants not only were bona fide Confederate veterans but also conformed to a preconceived idea of what a Confederate veteran ought to be. Before a veteran could be admitted to a home, he had to pledge to conduct himself as any *real* Confederate soldier would.[24] Officials required an applicant for the South Carolina Confederate Infirmary to declare that he was a person of "good character and habits," and to promise that, if admitted, he would obey all rules and "lawful orders" and perform such duties as might be required of him. Moreover, by signing the application, he was doing so, as the application specifically stated, with "FULL KNOWLEDGE THAT ANY VIOLATION OF THE RULES WILL SUBJECT HIM TO DISMISSAL, AT THE DISCRETION OF THE BOARD OF COMMISSIONERS." In applying for admission to the Arkansas home, veterans were warned that no "drunkard or deadbeat or a man of bad character" need apply, and anyone signing affidavits on behalf of a veteran was advised to "bear this [policy] in mind" and to "remember [that] you are under oath!" All Alabama inmates were required to promise not only that they would observe all the rules and regulations but also that they would obey the commandant and other officers, as well as be courteous to and respect their fellow residents.

Precoded application forms, in which answers had to fall within some acceptable range of responses, also screened out undesirables. Some "closed" questions read: "Do you use intoxicants to any extent?"; "Is your mind ever unbalanced?"; "Has applicant opium, chloral or any other drug habit?" Home authorities, of course, automatically rejected anyone who answered in the affirmative to such queries. "Insane persons and habitual drunkards," both demoralizing elements in a home, would be excluded and left to the alms-house. After all, or so it was believed, a *true* ex-Confederate was the model of sobriety. Only those who had borne since the war a "good moral character" and "good habits" would be granted a safe haven. Thus, endorsements attesting to the moral worth of a veteran were expected to accompany his application. A typical endorsement by the pension board in South Carolina read:

> This old man W. G. Parker is a native of York County S.C. He was in Georgia in 1861 plying his avocation as a Machinist and enlisted and entered the Confederate Service from that State. He lost his leg at the battle of Chancellorsville Va in 1863 which disabled him for further service in the war. He married his wife in York County who died about 15 Years ago. He has one son who is married but is not able to support his own family and take care of his father. Mr Parker has always been an industrious, lawabiding good citizen and we commend him to your care.[25]

Home officials also demanded that each prospective inmate agree to "abide by and obey all rules," to conduct himself as a "soldier & gentleman," and, most of all, to remain orderly.[26] "Order" was a word held most sacred by those gentlemen who sat on the boards of Confederate soldiers' homes and wrote the bylaws. Order meant discipline and routine; it implied centralized control over inmates, as well as staff. An "authorized authority," recommended Camp Nicholls president George Lord, "should be at all times ready to preserve good order and discipline at the Home." Rules governing the proper conduct and management of the home were "absolutely necessary," and for the "best interests of all concerned," avowed Texas board members in 1892. Our institution cannot be maintained without "reasonable discipline," stressed Georgia board president Lowndes Calhoun a decade later. Twelve years afterward, Horatio W. Bell, Calhoun's successor, claimed that rules not only protected the rights of inmates to enjoy the "advantages of the[ir] home" but also were necessary to "reform and improve the[ir] behavior and deportment." Without discipline, another trustee insisted, "you might as well give up. You could not manage a Soldiers' Home or anything else. . . . You have got to have it." Therefore, from the outset, home administrators expected their charges to

Admission to the Confederate Infirmary is made on the recommendation of the Pension Boards of the respective Counties. But it is necessary that the application be first submitted to the Board of Commissioners of the Infirmary in order to ascertain if there is a vacancy. Two Veterans may be admitted from each County.

Form of Application for Admission to the Infirmary for Confederate Veterans at Columbia, S. C.

BOARD OF COMMISSIONERS

DAVID CARDWELL, - - - COLUMBIA, S. C.
E. B. CANTEY, - - - CAMDEN, S. C.
J. W. REED, - - - CHESTER, S. C.
WILIE JONES, - - - COLUMBIA, S. C.
M. L. BONHAM, - - - ANDERSON, S. C.

OFFICERS OF THE INFIRMARY

CAPT. W. D. STARLING, *Commandant.*
B. F. DAY, - - - *Adjutant.*
Da. WILLIAM WESTON, *Surgeon.*

To the Pension Board of _____ **County.**

1. The application of _____
of the County of _____ , shows:

When and Where Enlisted	Company and Regiment Mustered In	Date, Place and Cause of Discharge

2. Where wounded? _____ When? _____
Give name of engagement _____
3. Were you confined to any Hospital? _____
When? _____ Which Hospital? _____
How long confined? _____ Cause of confinement? _____
4. Were you confined in Prison? _____ Where? _____
How long? _____ Where were you captured? _____

5. Applicant states that he served honorably and faithfully during the War in the Confederate Army (or Navy), and was loyal to the Government of the Confederate States to the end of the War; that he is _____ years of age; that he is unmarried (or married); that he is _____ in height, and is by occupation a _____ ; that his nearest relative is _____ , whose postoffice address is _____ ; that because of old age, infirmity, which arises from _____ , and from poverty, he is unable to provide for and support himself, and has no relative upon whom he can rely for such support; that by reason of his age and bodily infirmities he is unable to work. For these reasons he applies for admission to the Confederate Infirmary. And applicant declares that he is a person of good character and habits, and if admitted to the Confederate Infirmary as an inmate, he agrees and faithfully promises, upon pain of expulsion, to abide by and obey the rules and regulations made for the governance of the Infirmary; and that he will perform such duties as may be required of him, and obey all lawful orders of the officers of said home. AND HE SIGNS THIS APPLICATION WITH FULL KNOWLEDGE THAT ANY VIOLATION OF THE RULES WILL SUBJECT HIM TO DISMISSAL, AT THE DISCRETION OF THE BOARD OF COMMISSIONERS.

IN WITNESS WHEREOF, Said applicant has hereunto set his hand this _____ day of _____ , 19___
IN PRESENCE OF

6. STATE OF SOUTH CAROLINA,
COUNTY OF
Before me came _____ , who being sworn, says: He is the person who signed the above application, that he knows the contents of the same, and the same is true of his own knowledge.

SWORN to before me, this _____ day of _____ A. D. 19___

7. CERTIFICATE OF WITNESSES:
We _____
of _____ and
of _____ , do hereby certify that we know of our own knowledge that _____ the within named applicant, was duly enlisted and served honorably and faithfully in the War between the States, and we believe the statements contained in his application are true.

SWORN to before me, this _____ day of _____ A. D. 19___

---

abide by the rules, to be passive, temperate, quietly spoken, and deferential. To be an inmate was to exchange independence for security, to subject oneself to the physical and moral authority of trustees and superintendents, as well as to the special diets and rigid schedules of attending physicians, or risk being labeled unruly or senile and, on that account, dismissed.[27]

The desire to impose an ordered discipline in soldiers' homes was not merely rhetorical. Administrators followed through to make the internal functioning of homes as paternalistic and orderly as possible, which in practice meant drawing up a system of regulations providing for semimilitary routines and disciplinary codes, and then enforcing them. Unless sick or excused, inmates would stand in formation at roll call, twice a day, answering to their names. The commanding officer would inspect each man's dress and appearance to ensure that institutional policies mandating weekly baths, "trimmed hair and beards," and "clean and neat" home uniforms were observed. Regulation uniforms—including official shirts, pants, hats, suspenders, shoelaces, underwear, even buttons—had to be worn whenever an inmate left the home on a pass or stayed around the home on Sundays and holidays, times when outsiders would most likely visit. Written passes were required to leave the home grounds—fully enclosed by a "substantial fence"

8. CERTIFICATE COUNTY BOARD OF PENSIONS:

This is to certify that the County Board of Pensions of_____
County, in the State of South Carolina, has carefully considered the application of_____
_____to be admitted as an inmate of the Confederate In-
firmary at Columbia, S. C., from_____County, and the Board
recommends that the same be granted.

_____
Chairman Board of Pensions.

Attest:_____ _____County.
Secretary.

9. ORDER OF ADMISSION:

The within applicant,_____, having been recommended by the County Board of Pensions for_____County,
and approved by the Board of Commissioners of the Confederate Infirmary:

IT IS ORDERED, That the applicant be admitted to the Confederate Infirmary at
Columbia, S. C.

_____
Chairman Board of Commissioners Confederate Infirmary.

The Infirmary will open about May 10th, 1909

The admission form used to screen applicants to the South Carolina Confederate Infirmary. (courtesy of South Carolina Department of Archives and History)

and guarded by a night watchman—so as "to protect the inmate and preserve order and discipline." Inmates were, in some cases, almost literally incarcerated. The grounds, barracks, and quarters were subject to careful inspection, "daily if necessary." Bells dictated daily activities: to rise at 6 A.M., to extinguish lights at 9 P.M., to assemble for dress parade, and especially to eat. At the Texas home, a bell sounded precisely fifteen minutes before each meal; a second bell twelve minutes later signaled when inmates should "congregate around" the mess hall; a third bell rang when it was time for the men finally to enter the room and seat themselves. In addition, the rules specified that each inmate "always occupy the same seat . . . and his hat must be hung upon a rack for that purpose."[28]

Every aspect of the inmate's life thus would be subjected to the institution's paternal oversight. The Florida trustees, for example, "demanded" of their inmates "cleanliness, manliness, [and] purity of language." Swearing, gambling, boisterous conduct, expectorating on the floors, defacing the premises, carrying or concealing weapons, fighting, panhandling, or exhibiting impertinence were all grounds for punishment. Admittedly, some prohibitions seemed frivolous. For example, Texas trustees warned residents against reclining on their beds with their boots on, going to the superintendent's home in their shirt sleeves, or committing any "nuisance" on or "about the buildings." And at Camp Nicholls, no "old soldier"—"no matter how many battles he [had] fought"—would be "allowed to smoke or chew [tobacco] in bed." Managers in every home fought a ceaseless battle against alcohol. Inmates could not frequent any saloon or barroom within a mile radius of the home, and those found intoxicated faced prompt "restraint" or dismissal. Moreover, inmates were expected to conduct themselves in a "gentlemanly and orderly" manner, one that was becoming to a true Confederate soldier or sailor, so as not to "annoy or inconvenience [their] comrades," and to "yield respect and obedience" to all officers "appointed over them."[29]

Imposing order also meant selecting a strong executive to oversee daily management. Trustees envisioned the home as a family writ large, presided over by a superintendent or steward, the father of this extended family, through whom the board exerted its legal authority. In that family the roles of authority and deference would be carefully acted out; home staff were expected to be "faithful" and "earnest," the residents "contented" and "grateful." When trustees sought to fill vacant superintendent positions, they solicited recommendations for the wife of the applicant as well as the applicant himself, for she too bore an appropriate responsibility for maintaining the institution's moral health. Serving as matron or stewardess, she resided with her husband on the grounds of the institution they managed. Superintendents possessed no special training and claimed none. Most often, like trustees, they were Confederate veterans. For example, William Bullitt became Camp Nicholls's first superintendent owing to his "soldierly qualities and excellent administrative abilities," while the Lee Camp's second superintendent, Captain Charles P. Bigger formerly headed the Richmond City Almshouse. From 1921 to 1926, the superintendent of the South Carolina Infirmary was Confederate veteran W. H. Stewart, a farmer, Davidson College graduate, and former member of the state legislature as well as of the Klan. In many cases, home boards preferred a man who previously had exhibited some measure of responsibility and executive and financial ability. His key attributes would be honesty, sobriety, industry, prudence, intelligence, piety, and kindness coupled with "enough firmness to command respect." Such virtues were deemed indispensable if he was to manage the home as the head of a family.[30]

Whatever his background—farmer, gentleman, bookkeeper, merchant, policeman, prison guard, or hotelkeeper—a superintendent learned inevitably that his was a "troublesome undertaking." To say the least, confided Georgia superintendent George N. Saussey in 1917, it was "no bed of roses." His was an almost impossible task; the demands of the position were extraordinarily diverse and consuming. In partial testimony to the job's many demands, turnover rates for superintendents were alarming. For example, over a ten-year period, the Florida home had six different superintendents. In addition to enforcing all rules and regulations and maintaining good order, cleanliness, and economy, his responsibilities involved purchasing, hiring and firing, and shuffling mounds of paperwork—invoices, ledgers, reports, admittance records. In short, he controlled both people and things. When asked to describe his duties as superintendent of the Texas home, Dr. John C. Loggins replied that he simply took "care of the old men, seeing that they have three meals a day, and see[ing] that their bedding is all right and they are supplied the things they need." Moreover, Loggins reported, "I try to keep them clean." Like a good father, the superintendent also assumed personal responsibility for the physical and moral condition of his children. Ironically, the more earnestly he functioned as patriarch, the more intrusive he must have seemed to inmates and staff.[31]

By superintendents and administrators' own reckoning, the most disagreeable and unpleasant duty they had to contend with was disciplining inmates. It is indeed "a pity," Georgia trustees lamented, to have to "correct these fathers and grandfathers . . . with bleached and bald heads, but we must, however much we may revere them as heroes." Ideally, no self-respecting Confederate veteran would require reform. Yet, contended administrators, exacting "moderate" or "reasonable" punishment on "disobedient and refractory" inmates served, regretfully, as another method of winnowing out the undeserving. Our home is intended for the "worthy and not the unworthy," that is, not for "those who violate rules," remarked Camp Nicholls's co-founder, Judge Walter Rogers. "The good and true soldier on the firing line," claimed Louisiana superintendent H. H. Ward in 1908, "can readily be distinguished whenever found. . . . Real soldiers to the end obey the rules and regulations." Texas superintendent Chenoweth obviously shared the same sentiment. "The rules are no burden upon a large majority of the inmates who were faithful soldiers and good citizens," he declared, but they are for a "few who demonstrate they were neither good soldiers nor good citizens." The metaphor of the family applied here, too. When children disturb the peace of a home, so the argument went, they are disciplined, sometimes "even to disinheritance." So, when old men are "childish and hard to control," advised Georgia officials, use the rod, "seeking always to be just," as well as "forbearing."[32]

Punishments prescribed for those who violated or refused to conform to the regulations varied. Depending upon the particular infraction, penalties ranged from caution to expulsion; in between were reprimand (either privately or publicly at morning roll call), restraint or "quarantine" to the grounds or quarters, suspension of passes or privileges for one to four weeks, and extra "fatigue" or guard duty. Trustees guaranteed an inmate "under arrest" or "on charges" a "fair opportunity" to be heard and to present "testimonies" in his behalf, along with the right of appeal. Senior members of the board or a specially appointed investigating committee would be both judge and jury. The superintendent or one of his subalterns functioned as prosecuting attorney, while counsel was either the inmate himself or another inmate acting for him during the "court-martial" proceedings.[33] For inmates found guilty, administrators sought to impose penalties in accordance with the seriousness of violations. For example, the Lee Camp stipulated that "conduct unbecoming a Confederate veteran," particularly behavior "calculated to incite insubordination and subvert discipline"—the equivalent of mutiny as defined by the Confederate Articles of War—would result first in a severe public reprimand by the board president, or two to four hours of extra work per day, plus from one to six months confinement. A repeat offense would be met with a dishonorable discharge. Habitual drunks as well could expect rough treatment. An inmate who imbibed too freely too frequently could be sentenced to ninety days confinement, for one-third of which he would be locked in a punishment room equipped with iron bars and fed bread and water every third day. If deemed "drunk and disorderly," "abusive," or "incapable of proper behavior," an inmate in the Texas home was placed under arrest by the superintendent, who would then summon a policeman "to take him to the calaboose to be dealt with as other offenders against the law." In the eyes of those who wrote the bylaws, disrespectful language and conduct toward home officers or visitors, disobedience and the refusal to work, "outrageous behavior," and being absent without official leave all constituted "just cause" for dismissal. Expulsion was necessary in such cases, warned one Georgia trustee. "If you don't have something like that . . . very soon you will have pandemonium."[34]

If expelled, an inmate carried with him a taint of humiliation and disgrace. His uniform would be confiscated and replaced with a "citizen's suit." All personal effects he had entrusted to the superintendent's iron safe would be returned. And he would be furnished transportation back to his former place of residence. Branded a "person unfit," he would be barred from the grounds and denied the opportunity to apply for reinstatement for as long as twelve months—maybe longer, if he failed to prove to the board that he intended to amend his ways.[35]

As oppressive as this energetic and overbearing stewardship appeared, officials genuinely preferred to "keep a man in the Home" rather than to "turn him out," for they believed there truly was no other place like a home (in the broadest sense of the word) for impoverished men to find rejuvenation and nurture. Soldiers' home founders shared the assumption, held by many nineteenth-century Americans, that home was a sacred, even redeeming, place, where inhabitants could find solicitude amid sheltered abundance.[36]

R. E. Lee Camp Soldiers' Home

Oct 5th ___ 190_9_

Captain J. E. GRAVES,
   Commandant R. E. Lee Camp Soldiers' Home:

Captain:

I respectfully ask an Honorable Discharge from this Home _The South Carolina Home having officially notified me that it is ready to receive me —_

Francis Douglas Walker
Veteran R. E. Lee Camp Soldiers' Home.

Approved: _Graves_
Commandant.

James Emery
Chairman Executive Committee.

Inmates who behaved themselves could expect to receive an honorable discharge, which entitled them to a transfer to another home. This discharge paper was issued by the Lee Camp Home to Francis Douglas Walker, who, a few months after transferring to the South Carolina home, was expelled by the commandant for allegedly using the word "damn" at the breakfast table.

(courtesy of South Carolina Department of Archives and History)

"There are, of course, gradations of worth and deserving among the inmates," the Texas board of managers conceded, "but it may be safely said that the lowest on the list has fully earned exemption from subsistence as a common pauper." The dismissal of an old Confederate soldier from the home is a "punishment not to be inflicted except in extreme cases, when it is absolutely necessary for the preservation of peace, order and discipline," concluded trustee Charles D. Phillips of Georgia. No veteran ought to be forced "out upon the cold charity of the world, destitute and helpless," vowed Georgia board president Bell in 1915, except as a last resort. Acknowledging that it was natural for age and disease to "cause men to become dissatisfied" in an institution, the Lee Camp warned, however, that once "their expression of dissatisfaction" becomes "malicious, add[s] calamity and attribute[s] dishonorable motives to the Board," then "it becomes a matter of public concern" and the inmate must be rebuked.[37]

Were the trustees taking their responsibilities too seriously? Were they being too harsh and uncharitable? Home officials invariably thought not, pointing out that only a "handful" of intractable inmates posed disciplinary problems, while a "large proportion" honorably conformed and cheerfully submitted to a "few simple" rules and seemed to appreciate the "advantages . . . bestowed upon them." In the Georgia home, explained Clement Evans, discipline was redemptive, not punitive: "the good would be made better, and the bad would be reclaimed through the influences about them." The boards invited visitors to see for themselves that the veterans were constantly under as "proper [a] moral condition" as a mother would "provide for her children." Superintendents encouraged inmates to attend on a regular basis gospel services conducted by a home chaplain or visiting local minister, who was charged with taking an active interest in all that relates to "good discipline and the moral and spiritual welfare of the inmates." Offered for a resident's "amusement and entertainment" were biweekly prayer meetings, old-fashioned singings, memorial observances, Sunday school lessons, reading clubs, temperance rallies, and Easter egg hunts. Recognizing that there must be "food for the mind and heart, as well as the body," the Lee Camp established a home library filled with nearly 1,000 volumes, about one-third of which were religious works. The Tennessee trustees supplied their home library with "good [w]hol[e]some reading matter, religious and secular," not "yellow back" literature. In 1915 the North Carolina board appealed for contributions to purchase a phonograph for its residents, to "brighten up idle hours with stirring martial music, sweet ballads of the Old South and the infectious music of to-day." In sum, each board aimed to make its home a secluded, "comfortable, peaceful, delightful, and orderly abiding place" for worthy old Confederate veterans.[38]

In gratitude for their sacrifices, homeless heroes were afforded more than a roof. Spared the pauper's cruel fate, destitute Confederate veterans residing in a soldiers' home would have every need supplied by those who understood best their "infirmities and idiosyncrasies." Institutional care would entail much more than just escape from a depressing and demeaning environment. The best foods, clothing, tobacco, medical care, and "respectable" companionship would all be cheerfully provided by former comrades. In the Georgia home, reported Lowndes Calhoun, aged, infirm, and "worn out" men received the kindest attention. Similarly, Governor James Hogg of Texas envisioned the home as an "elysian retreat," where the wounds of a southern soldier would be "soothed by gentle hands." The inmates' "table is supplied with the best the market affords," asserted one official, "nor are they lacking in clothing." Residents received uniforms "to suit the season," shoes, and underwear, while a first-class laundry kept them looking like they had "just stepped out of a bandbox." With such amenities as steam heat, electric lights, hot and cold running water, and showers and tubs, the Georgia home provided "more comfort and conveniences than ninety percent of the inmates ever enjoyed before," boasted one of its superintendents. "Our Soldiers Home is a model of comfort, neatness and convenience," beamed the UDC of North Carolina in 1916.[39]

The locations chosen for the various homes attest to their important and noble functions. According to Bromfield L. Ridley of Murfreesboro, no better site could have been found for the Tennessee institution than the Hermitage grounds: "It is known as 'Clover Bottom,'" with "bluegrass covered with majestic hickories, towering poplars and strong-armed oaks," seemingly a "sacred place." Visitors to the home could not help being impressed by the "handsome" and "comfortable" facility, fully equipped to provide solicitude and compassion to old and disabled men who might otherwise have lived out the remainder of their lives alone, uncared for, and forgotten. One woman visiting Camp Nicholls during its early days of operation was pleased by its proximity to Bayou Bridge, at the end of a streetcar line and within easy access to downtown New Orleans. "Upon entering the gate," she remarked, "the first thought is 'how pleasant, how peaceful, how homelike.'" The home was shaded by live oaks, the grass was neatly manicured, and the rooms were "delightfully situated," "perfectly ventilated," and amply furnished. Camp Nicholls was indeed "an ideal place for a Home. An air of cleanliness is found everywhere," exclaimed its superintendent in 1908. "The grounds are well kept and shaded by large water oaks with moss hanging from each branch. . . . A man who would 'kick' here would not be satisfied in paradise—if he should get there." In fact, it seemed that every home was ideally located, something to be bragged about. The Texas home, according to that state's governor in 1911, is situated upon one of the "most interesting and attractive sites in the vicinity of Austin." Georgia's home stood on a "beautiful, healthful site, with good water, fresh air, pleasant surroundings . . . ample for gardens and orchards." The climate, pure water, and "refreshing breezes" found in the "pretty woods" of Mountain Creek, Alabama, located about 600 hundred feet above sea level, were "unsurpassed" and surely the "healthiest in the state." Florida's home commanded "one of the prettiest views" along the Saint Johns river, while one of Mississippi's governors boasted that "no more beautiful spot can be found in Dixeland than Beauvoir by the Sea."[40]

Southerners could indeed take great pride in all that was being done on behalf of needy Confederate veterans. At least that was the opinion of many soldiers' home apologists. The South was fulfilling an obligation held sacred among all civilized nations to provide for her sons, "who in the full vigor of their manhood, offered their lives in response to her call." In leaving nothing to spare, soldiers' home administrators also created a place that exerted control over the lives of those believed incapable of taking care of themselves. Many of the elements that define a "total institution" could be found in the soldiers' homes of the New South.[41] Home officials obviously thought it necessary to adopt disciplinary methods in order to define proper behavior and normalize activity. Their emphasis on order and inspection reflected a desire not only to prevent disturbances but also to transform individuals. Moreover, physical exertion was seen as eliminating the hidden dangers of idle time. Institutional architecture revealed these same basic attitudes. Rooms distributed along interior hallways within a main edifice with a pair of symmetrical wings permitted an internal supervision of inmate movement. High wooden, stone, or even barbed-wire fences, ostensibly constructed for guarding home property, actually confined "captive" residents to the grounds and thereby isolated them from the wider society. Removed from the demoralizing influence of the poorhouse, aging ex-Confederates were enclosed behind protective walls, where they could be venerated, preserved, and reformed.

"It has been the purpose of the Board," read the Camp Nicholls report to the Louisiana legislature in 1886, "to establish a home, and in all respects to make the inmates feel that it is their home."[42] In spite of this assertion, basic human needs—comfort, solicitude, compassion—fell unavoidably under bureaucratic control. Residents reaped the ambiguous benefits of an energetic paternalism; and the more they recognized this, the more they grew to resent it.

CHAPTER SIX

Inside the Walls

o you will see," Confederate veteran Benjamin J. Rogers wrote to one of his former comrades, "we have a home in the true sense of the word for the old boys." Rogers, sixty-five years old himself, was referring to the Lee Camp Soldiers' Home, where he had resided less than a month in 1904. "I like the place so far," he admitted, for the accommodations provided him could not have been more comfortable. His room, located in Joe Johnston Hall, near the main building on the thirty-six-acre complex, was equipped with electricity, steam heat, and hot and cold water, and it was completely furnished. In addition, home officials had issued him all the clothing he needed: a full uniform, including hat, overcoat, shoes, underwear, socks, and colored handkerchiefs. On Mondays, his clothes were taken to the laundry room; they were washed and returned in paper bundles by the end of the week. On Fridays, soap and tobacco were dispensed freely. He enjoyed "good wholesome food," and "plenty of it," as well as medical care by a pair of physicians and trained nurses who were available around the clock. In return for this benevolent treatment, all he and his fellow inmates had to do at the home, he said, was "to fall too . . . and behave themselves." The superintendent was always there to make sure that the rules were strictly obeyed. Mandatory labor was minimal: each resident was required only to clean his room every morning and perform guard duty on a rotating basis. "Taken all in all," Rogers concluded, it was "an ideal spot for an old Confed to spend his declining years."[1]

Normally, inhabitants of such institutions were not the sort who kept journals or diaries, or who wrote to concerned family members or friends who carefully preserved their letters or postcards. For this reason, personal accounts such as Rogers's provide an all too rare glimpse of life inside the walls from an inmate's perspective. W. L. Griffing, too, could not have been more pleased with his treatment at Beauvoir, exclaiming, "if there is a place on earth nearer Heaven I haven't been able to find it." Griffing had nothing but kind words for the staff, particularly the matron, whom he referred to as the "beloved Mother of the Home," and the women in charge of the hospital, who supposedly could "nurse the dead back to life." According to John Haps, an octogenarian and native of Holland, who enjoyed keeping a formal garden at the Mississippi home, with every kind of tree imaginable—peach, fig, pomegranate, cherry, orange, crape myrtle, magnolia, and more—"life here is as pleasant to me as it can be made on earth. It resembles Heaven to me." Other veterans were just as pleased with their home. A newspaper edited by and for Texas inmates, but also intended for "old vets on the outside," praised the Texas institution. "At all times," the newspaper bragged, it was a "good place," where any "reasonable man can feel happy and contented, if he so desires." J. O. Bradfield, a Texas inmate, passionately rejected the inference that the home in Austin was some kind of "poor farm" where the old men suffered "all sorts of troubles and inconveniences." F. Hymel of Camp Nicholls confessed that, although he had first thought of the home as a place of "exile" where he would spend his last days, he soon came to appreciate its every comfort and convenience, especially the large library, the number of UDC-sponsored entertainments, the weekly Catholic mass, and the theaters and racetracks nearby. John H. Owens informed his cousin that the thing he enjoyed most about being at Beauvoir was that he was able to "fish every day if I wish and catch some nice fish and crabs," while fellow inmate Marcus D. Herring, who spent more than six years at Beauvoir, enjoyed being able to swim in the Gulf of Mexico before breakfast and take a walk between breakfast and dinner. Mississippians, Herring asserted, should "be proud of this Home."[2]

In the public mind, as well as in the thoughts of the great majority of founders, the Confederate soldiers' homes of the New South were exactly as Herring and Rogers and the other inmates portrayed them: peaceful places where inhabitants could indeed find rest, comfort, and satisfaction. Nell B. Lewis, inspecting the North Carolina Soldiers' Home on behalf of a Raleigh newspaper, witnessed the inmates obviously enjoying their leisurely lifestyle, spending most of their time seated about the place alone or in groups, reading the Bible or magazines, or whittling canes or toys, but mostly "dozing in the sun" and chewing "Apple Tobacco." The establishment seemed a fitting location, the reporter noted, for elderly men to sit and think or "jest sit," and "idly watch the days pass by." Will Branum, a *Daily Picayune* correspondent touring Camp Nicholls, witnessed basically the same scene: veterans sunning themselves on benches, leading lives almost "monastic in . . . quietude." At the South Carolina Confederate Infirmary, according to one report, the "old veterans don't have one thing to do but eat, sleep, chew tobacco and smoke— that's all." They were supplied with free clothing, plus $10.00 a month in spending money and fresh vegetables from the home garden. Moreover, the three "brothers in black" (i.e., the attendants at the home), who are "kind and polite" to the veterans at all times, did practically everything for them. James C. Dozier, secretary for the South Carolina board of public welfare, agreed that the veterans were "happy and contented" just sitting in large chairs, reading, playing checkers, and generally amusing themselves. Visitors to the Alabama home, too, could not help being impressed with its "homelike surroundings." "The cackling and singing of the hens, the shrill crow of the cocks, . . . the grunting, squealing pigs . . . the sunny, cheerful greetings of the Commandant to his comrades, the inmates, the assiduous and kindly attentions of his good wife to the 'old boys' "—everything about the institution indicated that it was a "pleasant and comfortable" place to live. A report in the Montgomery *Advertiser* described the place simply as a "beautiful village," where veterans "find peace, home, and happiness." According to one UDC member, inmates at the Arkansas home had "no rules and restrictions" whatsoever; the veterans "go and come as they please, go to bed and get up when they please." In fact, the old soldiers had "more comforts, pleasures, and luxuries . . . than they receive at home!"[3]

But the establishments were not so idyllic and serene as they appeared or as administrators and sympathizers pretended they were. There were some depressing, monotonous realities that aging veterans had to accept. For it was in these homes that men marked time, and waited to die, "like soldiers, with their boots on."[4] Taylor Thompson, an inmate in the Texas home for more than fourteen years, knew that fact all too well, as reflected in a poem he composed and titled "Waiting For Death." The poem began:

> Just sitting 'round, waiting for death—
> That's what we are doing, my boys;
> Just waiting to draw the last breath,
> For long since we have done with life's joys.[5]

No one except those men who were least enterprising and most lacking in self-respect really wanted to enter a home in the first place, or so it was believed. William G. Roberts of Bristol, Tennessee, did not want to go to the soldiers' home in Nashville and almost had to be forced to go. Irishman John Huffernan of Memphis opposed public relief "as a general thing" and hesitated to apply for admission to the soldiers' home on account of its "*public* character."[6] Along with the sunnier sentiments noted above, Benjamin Rogers expressed similar concerns about biding time in an institution. He worried about "seeing a lot of old men in all conditions of decrepitude day after day," which he feared would grow "monstorous" to him. Within the short period he had resided in

the Lee Camp Home, Rogers had learned that the institution was an environment in which an inmate paid a price in dignity. For example, as he observed,
each man was assigned a seat at long tables in the large mess hall, while home
officers and employees ate a better meal in a private dining room. Rogers also
disliked the rigid practice of assigning passes, wherein an inmate would be
permitted to leave the grounds only up to three times a week, provided that
there were no charges against him.[7]

The soldiers' home was an object of fear and an asylum for the dependent
and socially isolated, or so it seemed, especially to men as sensitive as Asa Wall of
Frederick County, Virginia. An assistant surgeon in the U.S. Army before
casting his lot with the Confederacy, Wall objected to the selection criteria
employed by the Lee Camp Home on its application forms and felt particularly
incensed about the policy barring habitual drunkards, lunatics, and traitors.
Unlike one applicant to the Arkansas home who said that he desired to learn
whether he was regarded "as worthy as any of the Boys there," and therefore
had no objection to the admittance board investigating his record, Wall was
made to "feel a little *queer* to say the least" by such "interrogations." First of all,
"the line of demarcation between sanity & insanity has never been satisfactorily
determined," he argued. Secondly, home administrators had no right whatsoever to investigate his "morals" in this manner, Wall protested. Were it not for
his advanced age of sixty-five years, the fact that he had never married, and the
fact that he was impoverished and in poor health, he would not have applied for
admission.[8] Other applicants for admission feared governing boards would
attribute their poor physical condition and low economic status to some moral
incapacity or personal weakness. H. O. Bass of Powhatan County, Virginia,
wrote the commandant of the Lee Camp Home in 1905 that, although he was a
widower, without money, and had "no place to go," his request to enter the
home was not "*on* account of any dissipation from drink or otherwise," but "just
my misfortune in some way I hardly know what." Thomas Bullock—a sixty-
nine-year-old ex-Confederate from Spotsylvania County, Virginia, three times
wounded, partially paralyzed, and though not "altogether helpless," in "destitute circumstances"—wrote: "[If] I could provide for myself even in the poorest
way I would not ask for entrance." Another veteran, J. B. Hodgkin, informed the
Virginia governor that many of his former comrades had a "great aversion" to
entering the state's soldiers' home, for they viewed it as "the last step, the next
service being that of the undertaker."[9]

Annoyed, hesitant, desperate, and fearful, Wall, Bass, Bullock, and Hodgkin,
all eventually wound up as inmates of the Lee Camp Home. Admitted in 1896,
Wall soon earned a reputation as a "hard drinker" and was dishonorably
discharged four years later, having "abused, and assailed the Home on all
occasions." Bass, apparently still uneasy about his dependency on charity, was

The mess hall of the Lee Camp Home, Richmond, as shown in a postcard, c. 1910.
(courtesy of Virginia State Library)

granted at least two furloughs, so that he could make his "own living," before being readmitted to the home a third time in January 1906. He died at the home five years later. Bullock, on the other hand, survived only four weeks in the home. Doctor Hodgkin, after only a few months, left the institution in July 1913, allegedly for "health reasons." For these men, conditions inside the walls were apparently less satisfying than those prescribed in bylaws or envisaged by founders or represented by newspaper reporters and members of the UDC.[10]

According to inmate complaints, the homes were too impersonal and bureaucratic, trustees were crooked and apathetic, and superintendents were overbearing incompetents, who hardly endeared themselves to the objects of their paternal concern. The cooking was bad, the water was undrinkable, uniforms were shoddy, and the female employees were cold and crabby. Moreover, grown men were treated like children; they resented asking for passes, sleeping in overcrowded wards, doing without enough spending money, and being lectured because of their occasional misdeeds. Even worse, the staff and fellow inmates physically and emotionally abused them.[11] Inmates C. M. Hooper and Emmett F. Ruffin painted a bleak picture of conditions in the Confederate Soldiers' and Sailors' Home of Florida, where less than a dozen veterans resided. Hooper complained to the board that the institution was in a terrible state of disarray, owing to the outrageous conduct of some of his fellow inmates. C. C. Hays reportedly had been "very bad for many weeks," but Julius C. Bridges, Hooper charged, was undoubtedly "the most emphatic nuisance on the place, a liar, a mischief maker, breeder of discord, . . . whose loud talking, disorderly conduct at the table and in the House prevents any decorous conversation, or rational enjoyment wherever he chooses to go." In the dining room Hooper had witnessed Bridges using "foul and obscene words" and frequently sitting at the table "and blow[ing] off his gas to the disgust of all." In addition, another inmate was taking quinine and drinking whiskey to such an extent as to "incapacitate him from any intelligent thought or statement," and still another was "a feeble weak minded man, an opium eater," and a drunk. Finally, Hooper complained that one of his fellow residents—"whose *nose* and face publish his vice and his disgrace, without other witnesses"—had been forcibly ejected from city hotels and barrooms.[12]

Ruffin also criticized the "inner workings" of the institution and delineated its problems. First, he said, there was simply no discipline. Second, the home's sanitary conditions left something to be desired, for there was "debris of all kinds laying around the yard and under the main building." Third, some inmates lacked "dignity or decorum" and acted "more like a lot of hogs and wild animals" than like gentlemen. Fourth, there was entirely too much drinking and frequenting of the barrooms in Jacksonville, sometimes as often as twice a day, and coming home in a "maudlin condition." Fifth, the home had some seven to eight tillable acres, but "not one furrow of it [was] under cultivation," and what tools were available were not properly stored. Sixth, there were some inmates who had the means and property and family to provide for themselves. And, seventh, many seemed physically able to do at least four hours of light work a day, but did nothing. In sum, Ruffin pointed out, Mr. Daniels, the steward in charge of the home, was much too lenient and lacked "determination enough about him to enforce the rules." If the rules of the home were actually enforced and respected, he declared, then "everything would run along Smoothly and the inmates would be as one Happy Family."[13]

Administrators were quick to acknowledge that problems did exist; in their view, however, that the problems were with some of the men residing in the home rather than the home itself. Throughout the late nineteenth and early twentieth centuries, authorities of every Confederate home—ranging from trustees, superintendents, and physicians, down to matrons and chaplains—complained again and again of failures in discipline. Most of these were relatively minor, though they were potentially detrimental to the homes' hygiene and moral standards. For example, inmates spat where they were not supposed to, emptied slop jars out their room windows with insouciance, stuffed towels down commodes, or misused sinks as urinals. Some inmates refused to take baths, appropriated food from the mess halls, or kept pets in their rooms. As a result of the residents' often filthy habits, home administrators and staff were continually confronted with dirt, foul odors compounded by food and feces, and the presence of vermin, roaches, and flies.[14]

South Carolina legislators who inspected the home in Columbia reported in 1915 that, though they had "a great reverence for the Confederate soldiers" and disliked having to speak of the "filthy conditions of most of the rooms," the plain fact was that having "to manage the men is a problem, for many of them will not clean their rooms" and "this is a menace to health."[15] Other infractions, however, could be even more serious. Some inmates created disturbances, vandalized home property, brawled with other inmates and staff members, begged from strangers and visitors, smuggled in forbidden drink, and scaled the home walls for evenings of carousing. On one occasion four Camp Nicholls inmates stole away on a "fishing frolic," and one fell into nearby Bayou Saint John and drowned. Alarmed and concerned, managers decided to erect more substantial fences and hire night guards to help foil future escapades. Female employees occasionally complained of rude assaults and the vilest language. Bell Reid, stewardess of the Georgia home, claimed that the men acted so disorderly and unruly in the mess hall that she kept a pistol for her own protection. In 1917 one Virginia inmate, apparently irate over food quality and service, stormed into the mess hall, yelling and cursing and brandishing a pistol in each hand, and chased Sue Hill, the stewardess, out of the building.[16] Authorities also suspected that a well-understood and intractable underground dominated home life. Theft and dissimulation were everywhere; things were constantly disappearing, in spite of the personal oversight that the home managers always exerted. A black market in whiskey and tobacco flourished in every home, despite the best efforts of superintendents and governing boards to end it. In particularly egregious cases, uniforms, furniture, bedding, food, and even the drug supplies of the home itself could serve as trading goods for the more entrepreneurial inmates. To complicate matters further, one Virginia inmate charged in 1908, what the inmates "did not steal, the employees did."[17]

In addition, despite the assertion that veterans yielded "willing assistance" whenever asked and took "delight in keeping things in order," some men clearly refused to work at the home, or failed to perform their duties without "growling" that "they didn't think they ought to," while others labored outside the home, in what administrators construed as a blatant attempt to avoid labor details.[18] One Lee Camp inmate poked fun at his comrades' work avoidance in doggerel:

> We have a shoe-maker,
> a fellow minus a leg,
> who, if we ask politely,
> will sometimes drive in a peg,
> But sometimes he is so afraid

that he won't get his pay,
He manages to close his shop
and just goes off for the day.[19]

There were, of course, less direct means of defying home authorities. One was to desert or emigrate voluntarily without permission, as many inmates apparently did. Normally, an honorable discharge from a home served as a veteran's ticket for readmission or the basis for his transfer to another home at some future date. For example, W. L. Griffing's discharge papers, as issued by the Arkansas superintendent, indicated that he had been a "good inmate, Giving no trouble to this administration." Less than a year following his discharge, Griffing gained admittance to Beauvoir, where he again earned the reputation of being a "good man," before his death five years later.[20]

By leaving without his official discharge papers in hand, however, a veteran practically forfeited his right to readmission or to admission to another veterans' institution. In other words, for the veteran to make an unauthorized departure was tantamount to going AWOL in the Confederate army. The homes' official annual statistical compilations accounted for inmates under the categories of "admitted," "died," "expelled," and a special category for those who "left," "escaped," "disappeared," or were either "furloughed," or "absent." Records indicate that inmates left homes in larger numbers during the temperate months of March through May and September through October, while proportionately more inmates died during the winter and mid-summer months. Incidentally, December, followed by March and January, was the peak month for in-migration. In fact, there appears to have been a seasonal pattern to the admittance of veterans who were farmers by trade. For example, of the 219 farmers in a sample of the residents of the Texas home (see the Appendix), 91 (41.6 percent) were admitted to the Confederate Home for Men during the months of January through March, the ebb of the agricultural cycle. The lowest percentage of in-migration by Texas farmers occurred during the months of July through September, usually when surplus workers were able to find temporary employment. Virtually the same pattern has been detected among the 101 farmers in a South Carolina sample. Proportionately fewer veterans who claimed farming as their occupation applied for admission to the Confederate Infirmary in Columbia during any of the four months from June to September than did so in either April, May, October, or November. In cases involving voluntary out-migration and in-migration, season and climate may have been key demographic factors in both Texas and South Carolina. Sometimes the homes' statistical reports also had to account for veterans who adopted another passive, albeit final, mode of resistance: suicide, a problem that persisted among inmates well into the twentieth century.[21]

Ninety-one-year-old Charles Allen, a former Confederate artilleryman, chose to deal with life in the Lee Camp Home by leaving, though without bothering to obtain an official furlough. Once he had reached his home near Raleigh, West Virginia, in early February 1912, after residing less than a year in the institution, he angrily notified the commandant: "I am not comin back any more[.] I had as well goe to . . . the asylum as to come back and doe nothing. You may rock me out of my weight on erth but you cant take my rights from me!" The wife of another Virginia inmate informed a Lee Camp official that her husband had returned home in late September 1893 "very dissatisfied" and that she did not believe he would "ever be satisfied out there." Wesley Givens was highly displeased with the Arkansas home and attempted to leave several times. "Yesterday we found him down at the gate with his suitcase," reported Superintendent Rufus McDaniel. "We persuaded him to come back and today we found him back down there with his suitcase" again.[22] Several years earlier McDaniel had attempted to dissuade another Arkansas inmate from leaving the home. He had talked to him, as had other employees, and tried to get him to stay, but, McDaniel concluded, the veteran seemed to have had "the wanderlust."[23]

Although acknowledging that he and his fellow inmates were well taken care of at Beauvoir, J. E. Roebuck said that he simply had to leave, since "any man, regardless of age, who has always worked for his living, or who has any manhood, ambition or energy left, just to stay there and read, sleep, eat, and brood over the sad fact that he is only waiting there to die in idleness, will soon rust out and die with sheer inactivity." Roebuck continued: "I really believe now that, had I been forced to remain there in the same condition . . . I would either be dead or confined in a lunatic asylum." So, while still an inmate, the Marshall County, Mississippi, native borrowed some money to purchase paper and pen and write a novel that would sell over 11,000 copies in the four years following his departure from the home.[24]

But not everyone fared as well outside the walls as Roebuck. After having refused to accept the disciplinary measures imposed on him for bootlegging, sixty-two-year-old David G. Boisseau left the Lee Camp Home in January 1912 and subsisted on charity for more than a year. "You must remember," Boisseau pleaded to the board in his appeal for reinstatement, "that there is none of us but what makes mistakes. . . . I have always Regreated my mistake." He urged the board to try to forgive him and allow him to return.[25] John W. Meeks, an attorney from Pocahontas, Arkansas, and a former member of the state board of charitable institutions, described the sad plight of three former inmates who wandered into his town. One, he said, had since been abandoned by his well-to-do nephews, who refused to take an interest in the "poor old fellow" on account of his senility; another had died some two or three months after leaving the home; and the third, Robert Burrow, who had formerly grown dissatisfied with conditions in the Missouri home and left there too, now desperately desired readmission. Burrow, at age eighty-six, was soon permitted to reenter the Arkansas facility. Some six months later, however, he was granted a second discharge, and he died shortly thereafter.[26]

Many other ex-Confederates remained in a soldiers' home only temporarily before leaving, as Burrow, Roebuck, and Allen did. For example, James M. Hughes, the first veteran admitted to the South Carolina Infirmary in April 1909, received a discharge after only two months and was never heard from again. Hughes was not alone. Although an analysis of inmate data (see the Appendix, Table 14) reveals that the "average" time a veteran resided in a home ranged anywhere from 4.31 to 5.23 years, depending upon his age and when he was admitted, slightly more than one-third of all inmates "left" after only one year or less (see the Appendix, Table 15). One reason for such a short "tenure" (time in residence) is that, no matter how stalwart they once may have been, Confederate veterans probably were not immune to "relocation mortality effect"—an observable increase in death rates due to various stress factors following mobility.[27] In other words, it appears that some veterans, owing perhaps to chronic health problems or the recent death of a spouse, were too physically and emotionally unstable to survive for long after the ordeal of being admitted to the home and attempting to acclimate to its surroundings. The inmate registers of the various homes contain numerous entries that reveal such a trend. For example, the first inmate admitted to the Georgia home, Mendel Levy, age seventy, formerly a private in the Fifty-Ninth Georgia Infantry, entered in June 1901 in a "dying condition" and drew his last breath the following month. Among the first admitted to Beauvoir was Captain Prentiss Ingraham, who after the war had been a soldier of fortune before gaining renown as a dime novelist and poet. After leaving Chicago in 1903, he applied for admission from his native Adams County, Mississippi, and entered the home at age sixty, on August 12, 1904, only to die four days later and be laid to rest in the home cemetery.[28]

The roughly two out of every three men who resided in the homes for more than a year lived there, on average, for about four to five years, and a few for considerably longer.[29] Some ex-Confederates were on the rolls of their respective institutions for as many as ten, fifteen, or even twenty to twenty-five years. For example, when J. D. Morgan, formerly of the Sixty-Third Alabama Infantry, was admitted to the Mountain Creek facility in April 1914, there were about eighty other veterans in the home. Twenty years later, however, Morgan was the sole surviving inmate. Among the earliest of Georgia inmates, James M. "Uncle Jim" Mills was admitted in September 1901, at age fifty-nine. A veteran of the battle of Missionary Ridge (1863), he died at the home

Inmates George L. Cathey (standing), a former captain in the Georgia Legion, Rusk's Brigade, and G. F. Beavers, a veteran of the Twenty-Ninth North Carolina Infantry, in front of their cottage at the North Carolina home, on the occasion of Cathey's one hundredth birthday in November 1922. Joining in the birthday celebration were the UDC state president, students from nearby Meredith College, and a local chapter of the Children of the Confederacy. Cathey died at the home the following year. (author's collection)

hospital in 1927. Perhaps the longest tenure was that of G. C. Cline, a farmer from Cabarrus County, North Carolina, who entered the home at Raleigh in February 1901 and died there thirty-one years later.

There is no reason to imagine, however, that Mills or Cline or Morgan remained institutionalized for the entire period of their tenures without once setting foot outside the walls, since inmates in good standing were promised, and in fact usually received upon demand, passes, furloughs, or honorary discharges. Such was the case for Charles M. Speer, originally of Monroe

County, Georgia. First admitted in June 1911, Speer was discharged from the Georgia home on at least two separate occasions prior to his death there in December 1933. Another Georgia veteran, Z. M. Rogers, who had served in an artillery unit at Second Manassas and Sharpsburg, was admitted to the home in Atlanta in 1901, discharged at his own request in 1907, readmitted in 1914, and transferred six years later to the state insane asylum in Milledgeville, where he died shortly afterward. But more "typical" were the tenures of Joe Boatright of Richland, South Carolina, who entered the Confederate Infirmary in October 1909 and "left" (as home records indicate, without any further explanation) in July 1911; or Captain A. J. Herod of Yazoo, Mississippi, who came to Beauvoir in January 1905 and was discharged in April 1909; or Robert W. Allen, a farmer from Palestine, Texas, who was admitted to the Confederate Home for Men in December 1905 and died in October 1911.[30]

What became of the majority of inmates who preferred not to risk encountering the outside world, had nowhere else to go, or were prevented from leaving for health or other personal reasons, and were willing to stay put at least for the time being? Were there no other means available for coping with the institutional environment than just "waiting for death"? A veteran could always do as he was told, obey all the rules, mind his own business, enjoy life within the limits as defined by those in authority over him, and aspire to become a "model" inmate, as did John Haps, who for fourteen consecutive years tended the gardens at Beauvoir before his death in 1924. Apparently many inmates followed the example of Haps and others, either causing no trouble for their administrators or at least doing nothing serious enough to be noted by whoever kept the records. Home records are not comprehensive, often revealing little of inmates beyond the bare essentials of name, age, occupation, and time in residence. The records do (more often than not), however, indicate when a veteran stepped out of line: perhaps when he took out his frustrations on the fellow inmate who irritated him every time he tapped his cane, the one with whom he had cross words the day before, or the obnoxious lout down the hall who snored too loudly, was always the first in line for meals, or refused to take a bath.

Although admonished by home authorities to respect each other, many inmates evidently did not do so for a variety of reasons. The Texas home board observed, for example, that some "spry old bucks" often quarreled and fought "like youngsters" over any "trivial thing," including dominoes or a "friendly" card game, and were known to scrap over newspapers, magazines, and even food. Tip Harrison, the Georgia home board secretary and Grady protégé, testified in 1906 that a pair of inmates had a "little slapping spell" in their room over the different forms of baptism. Horatio Bell reported five years later on an incident that had occurred in the Georgia home mess hall, in which a few inmates fought, using cookery and tin serving pitchers as weapons, and turned over tables, creating "much excitement." Some veterans, literally, fought "the war all over again," remarked the *Carolina Free Press*. Henry G. Lamar, a seventy-year-old veteran of the Wilderness campaign and Petersburg, died in December 1917 after his roommate in the Georgia home struck him with an iron poker. Determined insane and dangerous, the assailant was committed to the sanitarium in Milledgeville. The son of a former superintendent of the Alabama home recalled many years later that the veterans were a "rowdy bunch," often getting into fights with each other; on one occasion a "Yankee" came to stay at the home, but the old Rebs raised such a fuss that he was forced to leave.[31] Politics also served as a source of dissension and disorder, thus dispelling the stereotype that the aged are relatively uninterested in such matters. For example, in 1914 Superintendent H. W. Richardson reported "considerable friction among inmates over politics" at the South Carolina Confederate Infirmary. Upon hearing from Superintendent Elnathan Tartt that President Woodrow Wilson had been reelected in 1916, veterans at Beauvoir reportedly held a "demonstration" lasting "fully an hour." Bells pealed and the soldiers "shouted and made merry," refusing to go to bed "until a late hour."[32]

Inmates lashed out not only at one another but also at their keepers—and vice versa. To hear home officials tell it, the inmates were the aggressors; yet, by the same token, inmates saw themselves as innocent victims. As one Virginia veteran put it: "Some of us Poor-Inmates [are] made fish off and others made fowl off." The homes' official records also contain several isolated examples indicative of the mutual animosity. One particularly "bloody fight" occurred at the Georgia home in December 1911, when an inmate and the superintendent "engaged in combat," according to the bystanders who had to separate them. After making a full investigation, summoning witnesses, and taking testimony, the board suspended both men. Afterward, the superintendent was indicted and arraigned by a grand jury but was subsequently acquitted and released. That same year sixty-four-year-old inmate Robert S. Saffold, a self-confessed "doper" and "morphine fiend," who had spent nearly a decade in a state sanitarium battling his drug dependency prior to his admission to the Georgia home in 1906, entered the superintendent's office, struck him with a pair of brass knuckles, and began choking him with his bare hands, before finally being restrained. A similar episode had taken place at the home some nine years earlier, when the acting superintendent had been charged with assault with intent to murder an inmate. After hearing the testimony offered by a number of inmate witnesses, a joint committee of legislators and board members found the officer not guilty and unanimously commended his conduct. In 1913 a Texas inmate, whom the board had recently exonerated for having criticized the home's administration, caned the superintendent on the steps of the Travis County Court House. Four years later Taylor Thompson told a special investigating committee that one of his comrades in the Texas home, "a man who knew that his own end was rapidly approaching," had it in for the home physician and would have killed him with a pistol he had hidden if he had been given half a chance. Similarly, Georgia Superintendent John A. Thompson testified in 1906 that the inmates seemed to "plot against" him, because he "tried to enforce the rules."[33]

Sociologist Erving Goffman has suggested that among the several adaptive techniques employed by inmates in coping with institutional life, violence and other flagrant refusals to cooperate were but initial and temporary reactions. Indeed, it stands to reason that if an old and cantankerous ex-Confederate was dissatisfied with home conditions, rather than lashing out with fury, he could leave. The walls, or fences in most cases, were by no means impassable. But for some inmates it was not so simple as that, as Doctor John C. Loggins testified before a legislative committee in 1917. He did not believe that some men would "go out . . . unless you forced them out. They cannot live with their children," he asserted, "or anyone else" for that matter. Mary E. Smith implored the Lee Camp board to readmit her brother, who, though "sick, weak & nervous" and "utterly unfitted for work of any kind," had been dismissed from the home. Please "take him again," she urged, for he has "no other home open to him."[34]

Once a veteran had resigned himself to remaining in the home for an indefinite period of time and making the best of it, he might still have recourse to another, less direct, defense or coping mechanism, namely reminiscing. Studies have indicated that living in the past, recalling earlier achievements and enlarging upon them, not only may enable individuals within an institutional setting to confront stress situations with dignity and courage but may also enhance their self-esteem and forestall a decline in mental health. In other words, the need for "life review" springs out of an emotional need to feel secure, accepted, and important—strong medicine for men who might otherwise be more inclined to withdraw into a sullen shell or to succumb to fear and self-pity.[35] Although more research remains to be done before the importance and implications of reminiscing are fully known, it is certain that inmates of Confederate veterans' homes engaged in it, almost to excess. Will Branum, inspecting Camp Nicholls in 1913, reportedly came across an inmate who was sitting alone on the veranda of one of the home pavilions. To Branum's query if the veteran knew the whereabouts of a particular private, the old soldier replied: "I don't think there is nary private in this place—ceptin' me. That's why I'm so lonesome. All the rest of 'em is generals and colonels and captains—mostly captains!" Although the overwhelming majority of inmates in all the ex-Confederate homes had actually fought in the enlisted ranks, as they advanced in age, apparently, many had overlooked that minor detail.

Studies have shown that the process of reminiscence is enhanced in an environment where past and present are interchangeable and the past is dramatized. In the postwar South, there were fewer places where past and present more often merged than in the Confederate soldiers' homes. As Branum and other visitors noted, the inmates had many opportunities to sit and talk, to reminisce about which colonel led what attack, and to recount the specific contribution each had made during the war some forty or fifty years in the past. After all, no matter how diverse their previous life experiences may have been, soldiers' home inmates—from Virginia to Texas, and from Florida to Arkansas—shared a single vital event, a common watershed that had drawn them together: the war itself, with which they all identified and to which, ultimately, they all owed their presence in the institutions. As a favorite hymn sung by veterans at reunions aptly put it: "We're old-Time Confederates," and "that's good enough for me."[36]

It is paradoxical that the very activities that increased group consciousness and even encouraged collective behavior among Confederate inmates, actions that posed a threat to the desired order in the home, were in fact cultivated and promoted by home administrators. Director Julian Levy pleaded with his fellow AANV members to visit the Camp Nicholls Home, where they would see their former comrades and converse with them about "old scenes, old times, old friends."[37] And visitors came by the droves—not just other veterans but also women and children, curiosity seekers, vaudeville acts, touring brass bands, and souvenir collectors, especially on weekends and holidays or for special events. Confederate soldiers' homes were gathering places where people could congregate and reaffirm their devotion to the dear principles of the Lost Cause. They were people places, important places to visit and be seen in on Election Day or Confederate Memorial Day, appropriate places to celebrate Robert E. Lee's and Jefferson Davis's birthdays, and perhaps somewhat ironic places to hold Fourth of July barbecues, featuring plenty of speeches and an odd mix of watermelons and Rebel flags, war songs and flowers. Among the more typical entertainments held at the South Carolina Infirmary during the 1920s were Sunday afternoon preachings and singings, Secession Day (December 20) speeches and essay contests, and sacred numbers performed by a boys' vocal quartet; Saturday afternoons were reserved for visits from the young women of Chicora College and Columbia College. In her charming book, *The Making of a Southerner*, Katherine DuPre Lumpkin recalls a time when, as a young girl growing up in Columbia, she proudly presented to the inmates a rocking chair that she herself had purchased with money raised for the home. Another woman who lived in the community of

Officials and staff of the Jefferson M. Falkner Soldiers' Home, Mountain Creek, Alabama, c. 1910. (courtesy of Confederate Memorial Park, Marbury, Alabama)

Mountain Creek remembers when she and other girls used to dress up and go to the Alabama home and put on "shows," during which a few veterans played the piano or fiddle while others just sat around, whittled, or smoked pipes and patiently listened or dozed. Sometimes out of sheer curiosity people waiting to catch a train to Birmingham or Montgomery visited the veterans' home since it was near the railway station in Mountain Creek.

And the inmates usually were quite happy to see the outsiders come, no matter what their motivations. Upon arriving at the Alabama institution, one man said, he was nearly mobbed by the inmates who gathered around him, "being eager to hear and to learn what is going on in the world." During his visit, one old man in particular made "strange signs . . . trying to attract [his]

attention." As it turned out, the visitor recalled, the veteran had seen him wearing a Masonic pin and was gesturing in an effort to convince him that he too was a brother Mason. In the afternoon following a meeting of the UDC national convention in New Orleans, some of the ladies went out on chartered street cars to Camp Nicholls to have a picnic on the grounds. Upon reaching the entrance to the home, they saw the veterans—all seventy-five in number—dressed in their Confederate gray uniforms, standing at attention in double columns. It was quite an impressive and inspiring sight, according to one woman, who, observing her companions as she and they greeted and shook hands with each veteran, witnessed "many a gray haired woman of the Confederacy exchang[ing] a word and a tear."[38]

By the same token, home officials actively encouraged participation in all kinds of outings—parades, ceremonies, dedications, celebrations, concerts—to the delight of ambulatory inmates. Several homes procured free transportation to and from annual veterans' reunions and arranged for outside room and board at reduced rates. Delegations of Confederate soldiers' home inmates, invariably accompanied by their nurses and some "colored orderlies," turned up at almost any public gathering, from political rallies, public funerals, and lotteries to motion picture debuts, cross burnings, and battlefield tours. In March 1929 approximately twenty Beauvoir veterans ranging in ages from eighty-one to ninety traveled free of charge in private Pullmans from the Gulf Coast to Washington, D.C., in order to attend Herbert Hoover's inauguration. Once the veterans were there, arrangements were made for them to ride in new Packard limousines in the inaugural parade down Pennsylvania Avenue. Movie cameras captured the event on film, as the veterans passed in front of the reviewing stand where the Hoovers and other dignitaries were seated. Before returning to Mississippi, the group also paid a visit to Arlington Cemetery to see General Lee's home and made a special side trip to Mount Vernon.[39] Several years earlier about one hundred veterans from the same institution had met Warren G. Harding and his wife at the White House, each one being introduced by the home's superintendent. When President Harding uttered something about the "united country, no North or South" in a short speech he had prepared, the veterans cheered respectfully.[40] Wherever they went, when displayed in their Confederate gray cloth uniforms, aged and limbless inmates represented more than their home. In the public's mind they served as living monuments from a mythic past to be admired, indeed some would say revered, in spite of whatever took place inside the walls.

CHAPTER SEVEN

Twice a Child

As the editor of the Biloxi *Daily Herald* astutely perceived, there was "more truth than poetry" in a ditty contributed by a veteran who had recently returned from an outing to New Orleans with his fellow inmates, "The Beauvoir boys in gray—The J.D. Club of ancient rakes." The clever verse ended with the stanza:

> Never had stood before such enticing bars,
>> Where ten cents could get a treat,
> But none got on a drunk,
>> Except—but I will not tell,
> All returned safely to their bunk—,
>> And will glad[l]y answer the dinner bell.[1]

A breakdown in discipline of the sort the poem suggests was no laughing matter, however, to home authorities, who were often at a loss to explain why virtuous Confederate heroes sometimes behaved so badly. "A visit to a soldiers' home, anywhere, is rather sad," remarked one observer, "for it is hard on these old men to be separated from the refining influences of home life" and not give in to "temptations of various kinds." Not everyone caused trouble, of course. In every home only a handful of "high strung" "evil minded characters" consistently fell into the categories of "chronic growlers," "malcontents," or "unreasonable, ungrateful refractory men." Virginia board members believed the physical maladies and advanced ages of the veterans were the immediate causes of their intransigence. Longtime Georgia home president Horatio Bell agreed. "It is very difficult," he lamented, "to deal with . . . old men in their dotage . . . on account of the wear and tear of age, and it's hard to keep them in good humor." Old men are fickle, remarked the Texas home quartermaster: you "cannot tell what" they "will wish from day to time any more than you can fly!" Georgia trustee Charles Phillips put it bluntly: "Old Confederate Soldiers are just like children." But a Lee Camp bard advanced a different theory:

Old soldiers like old maids,
　　are often prudish and hard to please,
They like to lie about in the sun,
　　to smoke and take their ease.
And some, in certain times of the moon,
　　seem to get very cranky,
Which we all think is owing
　　to their meetings with the Yankee.[2]

If unacceptable behavior had one root cause that everyone could agree upon, it was a penchant for strong drink. In 1907 Fred Ober of the Camp Nicholls board observed the Louisiana institution was more of an "asylum for Inebriates" than a home for Confederate veterans. Commandant Terry of the Lee Camp Home reported that his men were made "almost wild" by their fondness for liquor. According to an inmate of the Virginia institution, any veteran who wanted a drink could go to downtown Richmond and "get all the whiskey he wishes," even if he had been denied a pass. "The whiskey drinking habit has been the source of more disagreeable trouble than any other," moaned Judge Bell of the Georgia home. Another Georgia trustee declared the home "almost like a barroom," citing more than two dozen cases of drunkenness and related instances over a three-month period. Inmates afflicted with this "annoying, disgusting" habit, one report noted, had "invade[d]" the premises, acted unruly, sung too loudly, insulted chambermaids and nurses, and generally refused to cooperate. Inmate James M. Mills testified before a Georgia legislative committee that, after several of his comrades frequented saloons in Atlanta, they would usually return to the home, "raise a row and go to their rooms and sleep it off."[3] But the sprees were less innocuous than Mills made them sound. One home physician attributed ten deaths—one a suicide—to whiskey or other stimulants. While conducting routine physical examinations of Texas inmates in 1900, Dr. L. D. Hill discovered at least a dozen morphine addicts and two more inmates with an opium dependency. The South Carolina home surgeon's report of 1913 indicated that most of the inmates had a drug habit. Ten years later a report revealed that a majority of inmates took medicine daily for "different diseases and complaints," while a Georgia physician's report of 1904 had warned that the number of habitual users of patent medicines in the home had indeed become a "problem."[4]

From the inmates' point of view, reliance upon drugs and alcohol provided a justifiable escape from everyday realities. Administrators who were sympathetic to such realities urged leniency in dealing with veterans who had substance dependencies. "Let's be [more] patient with the old men," board president Julian Carr advised the superintendent of the North Carolina home.

"They are old and childish and we have got to bear with them." Close personal surveillance should be maintained, advised the Georgia internal investigating committee, but at the same time home officials should try to "temper justice with mercy."[5] One way to deal with the drug or drinking problem, administrators reasoned, was to improve morale, thereby removing an inmate's original motive for turning to the bottle. If inmates believed that there was something wrong with the way that they were being treated, they could complain to those officials who were responsible for responding to such criticisms. Committees periodically and rigorously inspected the home to ensure that a proper economy was observed, the floors were scrubbed, the walls were whitewashed, the bedding and blankets were plentiful and clean, and the staff treated inmates with kindness. Home administrators set up rotating committees and conducted internal investigations to check the truthfulness of inmate accusations. No complaint was too trivial. The committees encouraged inmates to appear before them, to offer suggestions for improvement, and to express their grievances. Inmates could speak their minds, committee members advised, for the superintendent was not in the room. How often are you fed? Is the bread molded and crusty? Are you pleased with your quarters? Do you have any knowledge of those able to work yet who do not? Is there anyone residing here who is not a Confederate veteran? These were the sorts of questions inspection teams asked.[6]

Home officials also found moral suasion an effective preventative weapon in the battle against alcohol. Several of the governing boards, for example, required all prospective inmates to subscribe to a pledge of obedience to the rules, especially the proscription against the consumption and possession of whiskey on the grounds. To remind inmates of their promises, several of the homes had copies of the rules printed in plain, large type, framed, and posted in conspicuous places. To help inmates keep their word, trustees also adopted the practice of having the men convene in the home chapel. More than just a place for interdenominational religious services and home meetings, the chapel also served as a morality stage. Here before the inmates the president and other trustees would publicly commend (or reprimand) men for their proper (or improper) conduct. Here the home chaplain sometimes preached to the audience against the awful temptations of strong drink and the necessity and rewards of following rules and regulations. Here interspersed among the life-size portraits of President Davis and Generals Lee, Johnston, and Jackson were placards reading "Be ye not drunk with wine," or "Surely the Lord is in this place," or "Be ye kind to one another." And it was here that the temperance ladies lectured on the virtues of remaining sober and the terrible consequences of insobriety, and that UDC representatives pinned crosses of honor on the lapels of inmates whose lives best measured up to the moral standards prescribed for them.[7]

In spite of all these admonitions and inducements, some inmates persisted in drinking. One veteran's doggerel, in addition to addressing his fellow inmates' intemperance, reflected the determined intransigence of some of the men in the Lee Camp Home.

> We . . . are good Teetotalers,
> and we have signed the pledge,
> Rather than a drink of whiskey,
> we would swallow an iron wedge.
>
> . . . .
>
> As we consider it poison,
> we keep our bottles hid,
> For fear some one might take it,
> not knowing what he did;
> And as it is often we get sick,
> we just slip and take a smile,
> Keeping a sharp look-out, indeed,
> with our eyes "skinned" all the while.[8]

From the perspective of those in charge, such unruly behavior represented an unnecessary but real threat to the desired good order and well-being of the home. "A man who habitually gets drunk," argued Texas superintendent Rufus King, "is able to support himself if he would keep sober" and should be expelled from the home for this "disgraceful conduct." But, short of expulsion, there were less severe sentences available for punishing those who got out of line too often. To help counter the spread of alcohol abuse inside the walls of the Virginia home, for example, the board appealed to Richmond merchants and citizens to refrain from selling or giving whiskey to inmates with passes. "We know that there is a temptation to treat these old men when in the city," wrote President Norman V. Randolph, "but as a general rule it is disastrous to them." In 1912 Tennessee administrators made a similar call to prevent political candidates from sending "election whiskey" to the home. The Texas board went one step further by having a law enacted to prohibit any person from selling or giving intoxicants to inmates. When it was learned that Herbert Wananaker had brought whiskey onto the premises of the South Carolina Infirmary and given it to one of the inmates, the superintendent confronted him, warning that if the offense was repeated, he would be reported to the proper authorities. The Virginia board issued a circular to all known Confederate veterans' camps in the state, asking them to exercise "close scrutiny" and to "inquire diligently" into a prospective inmate's "moral character" before endorsing his application for admission to the home. Too often, the circular read, the home had been imposed upon by veterans whose

Interior view of the hospital chapel at Beauvoir in the 1920s. Such places often served as a morality stage, where right behavior was rewarded and improper conduct publicly scorned. (courtesy of Beauvoir, the Jefferson Davis Shrine)

service record was flawless but whose "dissipated dispositions" made them "unfit members" of the institution.[9]

The constant need to battle alcohol abuse led Camp Nicholls administrators to reconsider their home's routine therapeutic practice of prescribing whiskey as a stimulant and tonic. In 1891 home surgeon Yves R. LeMonnier had recommended two rations of whiskey per day, in order to help the "old and decripid" men "keep up animal heat," and the board adopted the motion. Yet by 1907 board member Fred Ober believed that whiskey consumption had reached a point at which some restraint should be placed upon it. If alcohol was so destructive to man's health, he argued, how could it help restore that health once impaired? Economic considerations more than temperance qualms, however, had led Ober to raise the question. Each day, according to his calculations, the dispensary doled out anywhere from eight to nine pints of whiskey (in individual doses ranging from about one to two ounces per inmate) at an annual cost of $800. In the end, rather than abolish the practice altogether, the board decided to regulate more closely the amount of whiskey each inmate imbibed, since the home rations, so some board members argued, helped deter inmates from leaving the home grounds for a drink.[10] An even more effective deterrent, however, was to withhold the one dollar "gratuity" or pension allocated each month to Louisiana inmates. Originally intended to provide indigent Camp Nicholls residents with spending money, the stipend, to the dismay of home officials, invariably went toward the purchase of whiskey that was either brought back into the home or consumed on the spot where it was bought. Explaining that the money was intended for "the worthy and not the unworthy," the board petitioned the legislature for, and was granted, the right to deny the allowance to those who violated the rules. Punishments were meted out to fit the crime. For example, intoxicated inmates could expect to receive, in addition to a period of confinement, a fine ranging from $1.00 to $5.00; repeat offenders received longer sentences and larger fines. This policy resembled the one established by the South Carolina board, which prescribed one week of confinement to the grounds for first-time offenders, a thirty-day furlough for an inmate reported inebriated on a second occasion, and a dishonorable discharge from the home if a veteran appeared wholly incapable of controlling himself. Finally, some homes set aside a specially designed room or building where "chronic violators" could sleep off their "indiscretion[s]." Board members considered such a facility preferable to turning out a veteran.[11]

On the other hand, gross insubordination was a grievous act that home administrators could not afford to tolerate. More often than not in such cases trustees adopted a hard-line policy, recommending firm discipline and strict enforcement of the rules. Failure to enforce the rules, many contended, would deny the "good and orderly" inmates their rights. A state legislative committee that visited the South Carolina Infirmary in 1913 held this view. Although admitting that the question of disciplining a Confederate veteran was a "difficult one," the committee believed that discipline should be maintained, even to the extent of expelling an inmate. During the eight years that John K. Mosby served as superintendent of Beauvoir, he attempted to hold "the scales of justice at an equal balance." On a few occasions, he admitted, he was "compelled to dismiss rebellious and insubordinate inmates, but never in a single instance, until [all] persuasive powers had been exhausted . . . and all authority defied." And there was no more serious breach of discipline than an outright challenge to the board's authority. In such cases, expulsion was the only possible solution. When asked whether he thought the penalty of ejection was too severe for refractory old men, Georgia trustee W. S. Thompson responded frankly: "I think [not], so far as my knowledge goes and my observation of men and specially *that* class of men" [emphasis added]. Besides, he warned, "there might be a very great danger of really defeating the object of the Home if the idea ever gets out that the men are not amenable to discipline." Although punishment may appear harsh, asserted Fred Ober, the good name of the home must be maintained "at all hazards."[12]

Trustees took their work seriously and were quite assiduous in dealing with "discordant and rebellious" inmates. When a veteran called the Virginia commandant a "Damn Son of a Bitch" and threatened to "Blow his damn Brains out," the inmate was court-martialed and ordered immediately expelled from the home, after having resided there less than six months. In 1910 a seventy-three-year-old Georgia inmate who called the matron a "damned bitch" was eventually committed to the state insane asylum, as was a drunken Tennessee inmate who detonated a stick of dynamite, wrecking his room and ripping a ten-foot-square hole in the main building's roof. Asked by a group of veterans whether he would readmit a former Arkansas inmate who had been given a "forced" furlough owing to some "misconduct," Superintendent Rufus McDaniel responded in the negative: "I have tried so hard to treat each man and woman as if he or she were my own father or mother." Yet, while a "great majority of the Inmates . . . are thoroughly happy and contented, . . when one persists in violating the rules . . . some discipline must be administered." The inmate in question had engaged in a number of fights and threats, McDaniel continued, and, despite the superintendent's having "cautioned him and remonstrated with him, and remonstrated yet again," he did not cease.[13]

To speak disparagingly of the home, especially when outside the walls, also met with resolute disapprobation and extreme punishment. So did a host of other "intolerable" offenses, including indecent exposure, begging, using profane language, aggravated assaults against fellow inmates or employees, habitual drunkenness, chronic kicking, "cohabitating with negro wenches," disturbing religious services, and propositioning female servants.[14] J. T. Johnson from Newberry, among the first veterans admitted to the South Carolina Infirmary in June 1909, was "so bad," reported board president David Cardwell, that "we had to furlough him." The board considered him not only offensive to the other inmates but also dangerous, owing to his "vicious behavior." Even some of his fellow inmates had petitioned on at least two separate occasions for his discharge. Included in his file is one petition signed by six inmates who charged Johnson with "conduct unbecoming a Soldier & a Gentleman at the Breakfast table" and another stating that he had drawn a knife on an inmate and struck him. Superintendent W. D. Starling verified that the charges were true and that he had indeed broken the rules. Therefore, on advice of the home physician, the board voted to expel Johnson and send him on the next train back to Newberry. Similarly, the board expelled E. B. Blackfoot, whose drinking had gotten so out of control that the city recorder had ordered him off the streets of Columbia. Some thirty-two of his fellow inmates requested his dismissal, and Blackfoot was committed to the State Hospital for the Insane, which was directly across the street from the Confederate Infirmary.[15]

Once expelled, a former inmate could petition for readmission. And most often board members were willing to forgive the veteran and give him a second chance, provided he would amend his ways. For example, J. M. Hughey of Abbeville resided at the South Carolina Infirmary until he imbibed whiskey and the commandant, as Hughey phased it, "turned me out and told me to go." In his appeal to return to the home, Hughey promised "not to indulge too freely any more" and to "try to comply with the rules and regulations." Moreover, he vowed, "I will only leave the Home to attend church," so there will be "no chance for me to go astray."[16] After being disciplined, others like Hughey found it difficult to adjust to life outside the walls and consequently applied for readmission. A Georgia veteran appealed for reinstatement in 1911, several months after he had been dismissed for insobriety and "immoral conduct." In the meantime, according to a public poor relief agency that had assisted him, he was "absolutely in want, strolling about Atlanta, sleeping wherever he could . . . and living in filth and rags." When the board met to discuss his case, the trustees agreed to allow him to return, provided he promised to follow the rules and keep sober, which terms he gladly accepted. Former inmate Pleasant Wood was dealt with in a similar fashion. Suspended from the Georgia home in 1912 for intoxication and calling the stewardess, Avarilla T. Clayton, a liar, the seventy-year-old was summoned before the board. It ordered him to apologize to Miss Clayton, which he did, explaining that, when drunk, he had forgotten "the respect due a lady," for which offense he now had the utmost regret. Satisfied, the board then admonished Wood to be more careful, excused the charges against him, and reinstated him. A former Tennessee Soldiers' Home inmate who was temporarily residing in the Rutherford County poorhouse promised the home board president that, if admitted, he would be "an obedient Ex-Confederate and act as becomes a *gentleman. . . .* I shall say nor do anything against the Home nor its inmates. I will do anything that I am asked to do unless it is *hard work.*"[17]

G. W. Thompson's appeal for reinstatement to the Arkansas home was just as straightforward. "After due consideration," he wrote:

I am sattisfied that I violated the rules & regulations of the Soldiers Home & am willing to make all amends and beg pardon & offer any apology you may deem necessary, & I further promise that I will abide by the rules & regulations as adopted by the Board of the home. I am phisically unable to perform any manuel labor.

hoping that this will meet with your approval, I beg to remain
Yours &c. . . .[18]

Thompson signed the petition and then had his local UCV commander
endorse it before forwarding it to the home. After reviewing the letter,
Superintendent Felix G. Swaim noted that the veteran owed him no apology,
explaining "I only did *my duty*," but he now was willing to give Thompson a
second chance, provided he would live up to his word. Thompson was readmitted, but less than two years later he again ran afoul of the home authorities.
What followed was a remarkable series of exchanges between Swaim and the
Adjutant General's Office in Washington. Swaim could "hardly believe" that
"such a man," who had "given the Home so much trouble," had "made an
honorable soldier," and he asked that Thompson's Confederate service record
be reinvestigated. "If his statements prove true," Swaim promised, Thompson
would remain in the home. Apparently it was easier to order an inmate's
removal from the home on the grounds that he was a deserter than on some
other charges. An assistant to the adjutant general replied that Thompson had
been a prisoner at Fort Delaware as he claimed, but the records did not show
whether or when he was paroled or exchanged. Swaim requested that the
veteran's file be searched again, and yet a third time, with these specific
instructions: "*See how he got out of Fort Delaware!*" But there was simply no
hard evidence.[19]

Soldiers' home administrators were understandably cautious about pardon-
ing former inmates whose conduct in the institution had been considerably
less than ideal. Some veterans' applications for forgiveness and reinstatement
were refused outright. Such was the case for Camp Nicholls veteran Malachi
Whittle, who petitioned the Louisiana board for repeal of his three-month
confinement to the grounds for intoxication and reinstatement of his full
privileges as an inmate. Whittle asserted that, when he was first admitted to
the home, he had already suffered from fainting spells. As a result, a "drink of
any kind" aggravated his condition; nevertheless, it would not happen again,
he pledged. "I never fail in my work, taking care of the storerooms and the
benches on the grounds," he claimed, and others would attest that he was
usually a "quiet peaceable man." Unmoved by his explanation, the board
denied the request. Other appeals for readmission were also greeted somewhat
coolly. M. L. Bonham, an attorney at Anderson, South Carolina, and a member
of the Confederate Infirmary's board of commissioners, informed the superintendent in writing that "Old man Riley Rowland" would be coming to the
home seeking readmittance, upon the condition that he "obeys orders and
behaves himself." Knowing that Rowland had had "a pretty hard time since he

left," that he had been sick and quite feeble and now could hardly walk, Bonham thought that Rowland would be in a "proper state of mind" upon his return. Board president Cardwell, upon seeing the letter, gave Rowland a less than enthusiastic endorsement, conceding: "I suppose we will have to try him again." But probably few inmates received more reprieves than did William J. Delbridge. On three separate occasions he had been discharged from the Georgia home on account of his "liquor habit," and each time he had applied for and received reinstatement. After losing his fourth bout with the "deceptive stuff," Delbridge once again applied for permission to reenter the home. If readmitted, he promised to work on the farm, free of charge if necessary, and not to break another rule "forever." The superintendent of the Fulton County almshouse endorsed his application, vouching that the sixty-two-year-old infantry veteran had conducted himself "splendidly" during his four-month stay in that establishment. Delbridge won his appeal and continued to reside in the Georgia home, apparently with no further incident, until his death some two years later.[20]

Disciplinary boards disliked having to reconsider their own decisions. A Camp Nicholls veteran, Rufus Houston, was "mortified" by the sentence imposed on him for brawling with a fellow inmate. Although as punishment he had been deprived of a pass for six months, his opponent had lost pass privileges for only two months. "If I had been sentenced to the penitentiary, I do not believe it would have injured my reputation more," Houston declared. Upon reconsideration, the board did not reverse itself but did see fit to reduce his sentence by one-third. Andrew J. Rogers had even less good fortune. Found guilty of drunkenness and disorderly conduct, the Virginian had been confined to the Lee Camp Home grounds for nearly four months before he applied for permission to leave the institution "for good." The board, however, choosing not to reopen the case, rejected Rogers's petition, thereby forcing him to remain at the home against his will.[21]

Ordinarily such matters remained hidden from the public, but some veterans refused to accept a board's decision as final and appealed to outsiders for intervention. After Thomas O'Donnell had confessed to having smuggled whiskey into Camp Nicholls and had been ordered dismissed in 1895, he subsequently sued to gain readmittance and won the legal proceedings on the grounds that he had been a victim of discrimination. At least two other inmates openly challenged through legal means the right of home boards to impose discipline. Sixty-seven-year-old Louis Soraparu, accused of circulating derogatory reports against Camp Nicholls and its directors, claimed the governing board could not lawfully expel an inmate. Another veteran, who had been suspended a year for fighting at the Texas home in 1912, sought to have an injunction served against the superintendent to prevent his sentence from being executed. In both cases the courts decided in favor of the administration, ruling that the home did, in fact, possess full disciplinary power.[22]

Such was not the case for the South Carolina home. The first sign of trouble there came in 1912, when Superintendent J. P. Caldwell began enforcing the rule prohibiting gambling, intoxication, quarreling, fighting, obscene language, and any other conduct "whatsoever unbecoming a soldier and a gentleman." After one of the inmates who had been suspended succeeded in getting himself reinstated by court order, a dangerous precedent had been set. The court ruled that the home board lacked the legal authority to expel inmates. Although the law establishing the institution had empowered the governing board to devise rules and regulations regarding inmate admissions and deportment, no direct authority had been bestowed upon home officials that would allow them to send a veteran away. Nearly every dismissal subsequent to the court-order reinstatement was challenged and ended in the same manner, with inmates ultimately prevailing in their discrimination suits and the home having to pay for "useless and expensive litigation."

In one case, for example, readmission was won by inmates N. W. Jones, J. W. James, and W. C. Cameron after they were dismissed because they had "promoted strife and mischief." Another case involved C. C. Horton, a man whose "quarrelsome disposition" rendered him "dangerous" and "unfit to be an inmate." Even his fellow veterans all feared him. As Superintendent J. L. Wardlaw explained in a letter to the governor, Horton, who cultivated a plot of ground near the main building, often criticized the other inmates as they passed by him on their way to the superintendent's office for their weekly tobacco allotment, calling them "beggars" and saying that they were no better than "decent negroes." Wardlaw talked with Horton and warned him that he would be sent away from the home if he persisted. After Horton was involved in a scuffle with one of the other inmates and was suspended for thirty days, a group of inmates asked that he be dismissed for their protection. But Wardlaw, wanting to be merciful, allowed him to return to the home. A few months later Horton fought again and was dismissed, but this sentence was also suspended, on the condition that he behave himself. But when he threatened to "brain and cut the throat" of another inmate, Wardlaw declared this the last straw. Horton was summarily dismissed, as he had been on two previous occasions. Nevertheless, after careful and exhaustive hearing of the case, a judge ordered that Horton be readmitted. When appealed to for a decision, the state attorney general's office ruled that the board had no authority to expel men, even the likes of Horton, though it could make such rules for "*managing* disorderly men, as the head of a family had to manage and control his family." In other words, it could make rules and enforce them, but not to the extent of dismissing an inmate.[23]

Boy Scouts, like the one shown here with a group of old soldiers in the 1930s, occasionally visited the Mississippi home, where they spent the weekend camping on the grounds and visiting with the veterans.
(courtesy of Beauvoir, the Jefferson Davis Shrine).

As a result of the Horton case, remarked one disgruntled administrator, rebellious inmates were now free to foster all kinds of "disturbances and dissensions," while home officials were rendered powerless. Therefore, as another superintendent later put it, once a veteran had entered the home, he was there "to stay unless he fights or otherwise violates the law of the State." Moreover, he could "complain every day" without fear of being disciplined. That was his right. However, the board had other means of dealing with recalcitrant inmates, ranging from cautions and reprimands to restrictions to the grounds or confinement to the "special annex," so as to protect the safety and welfare of the others. And if a veteran was found to be mentally ill, or particularly troublesome, he could be sent across the street to the State Hospital for the Insane or, worse yet, transferred to a county poorhouse.[24]

Thomas J. Severn of Alexandria, Louisiana, knew firsthand of the "diabolical" discipline wielded by the Camp Nicholls board of directors. Although possessing a good war record, and "never in the habit of drinking or gambling," Severn had been placed under arrest by Superintendent John J. Aubertin for refusing to work. "He has endeavored to escape all exertion," Aubertin insisted in a letter to the board president, "except a showing of great activity and capacity at meals." After looking into the case, the investigating committee reported that in the three years since 1897 while Severn resided at the home, he had been brought up on the same charges on at least three previous occasions. If there ever was a shirker, here was one who surely deserved to be punished, board members must have thought. Yet, before being sentenced, Severn left the home, relinquishing its "supposed benefits." After promptly informing his state senator of his side of the story, he then had his own sensational account of "persecution" in the home published in a local newspaper.[25]

Apparently nothing came of Severn's appeal, but the obstinacy of another Camp Nicholls inmate six years earlier had had more far-reaching results. In an open letter to the home's two founding veterans' associations, the AANV and AAT, W. B. Ripley accused the soldiers' home administrators of "infamous mismanagement." Among other things, Ripley charged, the superintendent was not only incompetent, mendacious, peculative, and brutal but also a deserter from the Confederate army! Worse still, the home—"a rare combination of convict camp and pauper asylum," as Ripley preferred to view it—had degenerated into "a place of penance, humiliation and degradation," where some inhabitants had been "hounded to premature graves," while others who had resisted had been expelled "to die of privation and exposure." Considering Ripley's charges too serious to ignore, the home board countered by first investigating and then rejecting the stinging indictments. Completely exonerating the superintendent, the board instructed Ripley to "keep quiet." Furthermore, the board sought to impugn Ripley's accusations publicly by calling into question the recalcitrant veteran's own war record and character. Ripley retaliated by having his letter published in local newspapers. Then, astounding no one, he left the home, not to be heard from again. Soon Louisiana lawmakers announced a "thorough and searching" investigation of their own. Inmates would be interrogated under oath, and none of the "gentlemen" (home authorities) would be called upon to serve as witnesses or to cross-examine them. It is impossible to state whether Ripley's charges received a fair hearing, since the testimony is no longer extant. It is known, however, that after compiling a "large mass of evidence," the special legislative committee dismissed Ripley's complaints as outlandish and "imagined." The *Picayune*, controlled by a home director, was hardly surprised by the decision. Here was yet another case, the newspaper commented, of how men who believe they "should have all the whiskey" they want break the rules and raise a fuss.[26]

Ripley had dared to buck the system and had lost, but not altogether, for his controversy evidently accentuated a persistent public debate among home sympathizers and critics. It was a debate that embraced the central dilemma of whether providing benevolent care instilled a pauper mentality in its recipients. In Ripley's instance, the administration was upheld, but administrators were not always supported by other committees that were specially appointed from time to time to respond to cries of "charity abuse." Legislative investigations touched practically every Confederate soldiers' home in the New South. Perhaps the most remarkable investigation was one in 1906, occasioned by charges brought by some twenty-two residents of the Georgia home, including several men who had been disciplined for various offenses. The inmates signed a petition complaining of a host of improprieties, ranging from fiscal mismanagement to a shortage of heat and good food. Fearing that the charges could "do great harm to this great institution," state legislators established a joint committee empowered to summon witnesses, enforce attendance, and take evidence during public meetings, which were held in the Senate's chambers as well as the home chapel. Among those representing the plaintiffs was an Atlanta attorney who had seen better days, Hugh H. Colquitt, a former officer of the Fulton County Veterans Association and the brother of U.S. Senator Alfred Colquitt. Colquitt was also an inmate; in fact, he was the very inmate who had drafted the petition. Judge Frank Freeman, a trustee, served as counsel for the home. During the four days—and nearly 500 pages—of exhaustive testimony, inmates voiced familiar criticisms: the clothing was inadequate; trustees were out of touch; discipline was too stringent; the staff was too harsh and rude. The superintendent "simply [ran] a convict camp," one veteran charged, "to keep the men in embarrassment all the time." The stewardess, claimed another inmate, was absolutely "the devil in petticoats." In short, argued Colquitt, he and his comrades were not being treated as the people of Georgia "expect[ed] their Confederate Veterans to be treated." After interviewing dozens of inmates and home authorities, the committee agreed and directed that the problems cited receive immediate attention.[27]

An investigation of the Texas institution in 1917 had similar results. Progressive-minded legislators were appalled by the facility's poor sanitary conditions, the inefficient bookkeeping and inventory control methods, unusually large liquor purchases, and—during a time when Americans were overly concerned about national security matters—the fact that several German natives were employed at the Texas Confederate Home for Men. They also heard numerous complaints of abusive staff officers; the home physician was a drunk, they were told, and Dr. John C. Loggins, the superintendent, could not care less about the inmates. In the end, the committee strongly urged the replacement of both men, as well as the home quartermaster, who had inadequately managed the institution's appropriations.[28] To recommend was about all the committees could do, however, as they lacked the legal power to effect changes outright. Still, administrators could hardly afford to ignore the feelings of the body that provided biennial funding for the home and would eventually vote on extending the home's charter. And certainly neither side desired a public scandal. Yet not all suggestions were routinely followed, as evidenced by the fact that Doctor Loggins retained his position as Texas superintendent for more than two years following the investigation.

Legislative inspectors more often than not ended up siding with management, dismissing most inmate charges as elaborate and imaginary. Regarding criticism of the South Carolina Infirmary, one committee concluded: "Of course there are some complaints, but would it be possible to run an institution of this kind *without any complaint?*" Another report made by a special legislative committee appointed several years later to investigate the same institution had "nothing but praise" for the administration. The only real complaint was the lack of heating, the committee determined. Otherwise, the old men are "somewhat childish, and their grumblings can easily be overlooked." When home officials were asked to conduct their own investigations, results were similar. For example, after an inmate's letter to Governor Martin Ansel appeared in a Columbia newspaper, the South Carolina Infirmary announced an internal investigation into all allegations against the home. The board met at the home and called all residents who had anything to say to come forward. Unsurprisingly, "no one made any complaint," the board reported to the governor, not even the letter writer who before the meeting had left the home and the city. The inmates "prized the management," the report continued; they regarded the superintendent as "kind and considerate" and the food as "good and abundant," and they were "comfortable and contented." Apparently the complaints had emanated from a few men who "chafed under the mild but necessary discipline." One incident had occurred a week earlier, when an inmate attacked the superintendent with a knife. The assailant was to blame, however, since the superintendent was alleged to have acted only in self-defense, and the inmate was allowed to leave. Upon receiving a copy of the report, the governor thanked the board for its "thorough" investigation.[29]

It is doubtful whether the inmates had received a fair hearing. Committee members could hardly prevent the backlash of repression some men apparently experienced after testifying against their homes. Dr. John B. Hodgkin, an inmate, informed the Virginia governor that veterans were generally "shy of making complaints," fearing they would "lose prestige with the officers." Others upheld Hodgkin's avowal. A special committee inspecting the Tennessee Soldiers' Home in 1897 noted that many inmates appeared timid when questioned, "lest they should meet the disapprobation, censure and perhaps dismissal" of home authorities. When asked during the investigative proceedings of the Lee Camp Home in 1892 why no complaints had been made earlier, J. M. Bromson, a four-year resident, responded: "For the simple reason we have been afraid of that gate. It has been thrown up to us by the negroes!" Another Lee Camp inmate testified that one of the "darkies" in the hospital had informed him that, if he did not like the institution, "the gate was open." Sixty-six-year-old George W. Killen, a Georgia inmate for nearly three years, alleged that if any of the men complained, trustees would dub them "chronic kickers" and deal with them as with any other annoyance or nuisance. Judge Freeman, the Georgia home attorney, commented to H. H. Liggin, an inmate for eighteen months, "You have been told time and time again, if you had any complaints to make [they] would be investigated." Liggin, who had also spent time in a Yankee prison camp during the war, responded: "Yes, and I have been told by inmates that we would not be heard and it would go hard with us if we complained. . . . If a man ever signs his name to charges it is just [as] well as being gone."[30] On the other hand, there were also several known cases of reverse intimidation. Lee Camp board president Norman V. Randolph complained to the chairman of a legislative investigation in progress in 1898 that three witnesses had warned individual inmates not to testify in favor of the administration or risk being ostracized by the other men.[31]

Such a report merely confirmed and reinforced the dominant notion held by administrators and the general public that some men did not belong in a home in the first place. Dr. A. R. Holderby, the Georgia home chaplain for nearly twenty years, asserted that a certain class of inmates was "very thoughtless and reckless" and would say or do almost anything to bring reproach upon the institution, when in fact there was much more to commend than to condemn. In 1911, the Georgia superintendent described his charges this way:

Scene in front of Camp Hardee cottage, one of the largest dormitories at the Alabama home in Mountain Creek. Only the foundations of the building remain today. (courtesy of Confederate Memorial Park, Marbury, Alabama)

There is such a conglomeration of characters & temperaments that it would be an impossibility to define. The old Veterans display much dissatisfaction as to the environment & surroundings. Many of them have fair common sense and are disposed to look on the bright side . . . while a number [are] demented . . . troublesome and exacting; their wants are never satisfied, and it is a problem.[32]

Rather than denounce the home, according to one Camp Nicholls director, inmates "should bow down and thank God for the many kindnesses and considerations given them!" Since the homes were supposedly well managed, and the inmates were on the whole treated kindly, there was no real need for reform. Even so, managers had to be diligent enough to prevent criticism, official or otherwise, by investigating all complaints and rumors of mistreatment. In exchange for this personal solicitude, committee members anticipated satisfactory answers and appropriate deference. Residents were also expected at all times to abide by their superiors' decisions and to yield power and control over their own lives or risk being considered uncooperative, ungrateful, and disorderly. For it fell within the purview of the investigating committees to discipline individual inmates and to report any disobedience and punishment to the full board. In effect, the same hand that supposedly safeguarded inmates chastened them as well.

As a reminder of the institution's ultimate control over the veteran and the desire for order and impersonality, residents in all the homes were appropriately referred to as "inmates." A late sixteenth-century word in origin, meaning, literally, "inn mate," nothing better symbolized the gap that separated the home's population from the genteel presumptions of those who administered the institution than did this term. Although three centuries later it remained fashionable to consider residents of various public institutions as inmates, the term also carried with it a distasteful stigma. Nevertheless, in the governing boards' minutes, as well as in most official correspondence and transactions, veterans domiciled in Confederate soldiers' homes were continuously designated as inmates, and sometimes as "old boys," well into the 1920s. At the same time individual board members were always called "comrade" or otherwise had functional titles (president, secretary, treasurer, etc.) appended to their surnames; this, despite formal protests by both groups in at least four homes to amend the practice. When, in 1905, six veterans boldly presented a handwritten petition requesting that inmates residing in the "Confederate Veterans Home (Prison) of Georgia" be henceforth termed "guests," the board president "lectured" these men, informing them that their actions were insubordinate, and then invited them to leave.[33]

The fact that some men may have felt degraded by being labeled as inmates and the fact that governing boards stubbornly refused to relinquish use of the term further illustrate the complex realities that both groups faced. If they gave in to veterans' demands, administrators would risk the appearance of losing all discipline and control. Yet treating veterans in a dehumanizing manner would violate the founding tenets of the soldiers' homes. At bottom, what was at issue here was but another principle that neither a soldiers' home resident nor his keepers could ultimately escape. Sooner or later, no matter how independent and proud a man may have struggled through all his life to become, he invariably reaches a point where he is no longer capable of exercising control over himself. As commentators as diverse as Cicero and Shakespeare have observed, an old man is twice a child. The laws of nature had foreordained it, and there was really nothing much that anyone could do to prevent it.

CHAPTER EIGHT

Patterns of Change and Decline

In *Ghosts of the Confederacy*, Gaines Foster explains how the "central institutions" of the Lost Cause ceased to thrive after 1913. At that time, major organizations, such as the UCV, that had long embraced and exploited the Confederate heritage began to disintegrate as membership rolls diminished. Reunions, which had formerly served as the "central ritual" of the ex-Confederate celebration, became trivialized and commercialized. Moreover, memorial associations, monument building, and ceremonial unveilings decreased in number and importance. In sum, Foster argues, by the end of the first decade of the twentieth century, "little institutional structure survived to sustain the memory of the war."[1] But what of the soldiers' home, which also symbolized and embodied, literally, the Confederate past? How and why did that institution change over time? When did its significance in southern society begin to diminish? Regrettably, Foster and others have ignored the homes, some of which continued to provide shelter and care for living relics of the Confederacy well into the 1930s.

Long before then the average inmate's experience had come to be something very different from that of his predecessors decades earlier. One source of change was the same multifaceted scientific and technological innovation that was reshaping society generally, and urban areas specifically. Electric lights, indoor plumbing, metal bed frames, inexpensive textiles, telephones, mechanized fire extinguishers, and easy-to-clean composition floors had all become part of the homes. The introduction of refrigerators and freezers meant a more varied and inexpensive food supply, as well as a more adequate diet. More effective modes of heating and ventilation also affected inmate experience: no more could some complain that beds placed near a central stove were too hot while those in more remote corners of a ward were too cold. A new awareness of pathogenic microorganisms, and the adoption of health practices shaped by that awareness, helped curb outbreaks of infectious ailments. Death too had been removed from the wards and rooms of the home and systematically transferred to a hospital located on the grounds or in the city.

Over the years the hospital gradually played a more prominent role in the lives of inmates.[2] This trend is best illustrated in Louisiana's home. In the beginning, when a Camp Nicholls inmate became sick and required daily nursing, he would be transferred across town to Charity Hospital. Providing diagnoses, writing prescriptions, and making referrals were the primary functions of the home physician, who rarely made more than two rounds through the wards each week. In the mid-1890s, however, administrators added a home infirmary, consisting of a small, one-room structure equipped with only half a dozen beds and a dispensary. This "very poor excuse" for a hospital served only those with "trivial" ailments, not terminally ill patients. For example, of the twenty-one Camp Nicholls inmates whose deaths were reported from 1896 to 1898, only one actually died at the home.[3] That ratio would change dramatically over the next decade, after a bona fide hospital was constructed on the grounds. In 1904–6, for instance, thirty-one of thirty-nine inmate deaths took place at the home, and over the next two years twenty-nine of thirty-three deceased inmates died there. In his report for the 1912–14 period, home surgeon James I. Richard stated that it had not been necessary to transfer any of his patients to Charity Hospital for treatment. Instead, inmates had spent their last days in the home's modern and expanded medical facility, where they had been cared for around the clock by resident nurses and as many as three staff physicians, who customarily performed surgeries and often used an X-ray device to diagnose and treat certain disorders. By 1931 the Confederate home at Beauvoir had one large seventy-bed hospital, built at a cost of over $70,000, as well as three auxiliary hospitals—one for the treatment of cancer, another for paralyzed veterans, and a third for patients with pneumonia and influenza—staffed by as many as fifty employees: a surgeon, seven nurses, fifteen orderlies, four cooks, eight servants, eight laundrymen, a carpenter, a watchman, a bookkeeper, a maid, and a yardman.[4]

The quality of treatment that was available in home hospitals is difficult to evaluate. Although suspicions arose and rumors frequently surfaced, there is no reason to conclude that overcrowding, understaffing, and unsanitary conditions were as prevalent as critics alleged. Predictably, home physicians boasted that their services greatly enhanced the health of "broken and suffering" Confederate veterans. Texas home surgeon T. F. Moore cited as proof a comparatively low death rate of 12.7 percent for the years 1911–12. This figure, he pointed out, fell much below the then-acceptable federal standard of 16 percent for persons between the ages of sixty-five and eighty-five.[5] When asked by a prospective inmate residing in Vivian, Louisiana, about the treatment veterans received in the Arkansas home, Superintendent Clarence P.

Newton assured him: "it is humane and accaptible to them. The death rate is about half that on the outside."[6] Another possible treatment quality index may be found in admission-discharge ratios. For example, of the one hundred Lee Camp inmates admitted to the home's hospital in 1905, seventy-five obtained a discharge. Over the next decade and a half, the ratios stayed relatively stable. Only one-third of those who had been admitted sometime during 1918 remained hospitalized by the end of the year. Dr. H. M. Folkes reported an even more successful rate at the Mississippi home. Out of a total of 1,548 patient admissions recorded by that institution's hospital staff during 1912–13, only 53 (3 percent) ended in death—even in the face of a considerable malaria epidemic that visited the home in 1912.[7]

Inmates probably enjoyed greater access to medical treatment than most homeless indigents—especially those residing in rural areas—could ever have hoped to receive. Even so, home physicians held few illusions about their abilities to forestall the inevitable. The brave new weapons of medical science were of little use in treating biological realities. "Our aim," conceded Camp Nicholls surgeon Yves R. LeMonnier, is merely "of a prophylactic nature, i.e., prevention instead of cure." Another surgeon added: "Our subjects are all old [and] we cannot expect among them . . . the usual low death-rate." In an effort to account for a "distressing" death rate in the Georgia home in 1906, trustees rationalized that, after five years of operation, the 180 reported deaths out of 330 total enrollments were not unusually high, given the fact that most of the old soldiers had been "practically . . . bedridden, paralyzed, [and] helpless" when they had first been admitted. From the administrators' perspective, a hospital that provided dignified and cost-efficient custodial care was a credit to its institution.[8]

At several homes, a hospital was but one of many new additions established in part to meet the demands of a rising inmate population. When the state first assumed financial control in 1891, the Texas Home for Men consisted of 15½ acres, five buildings (nearly all wood frame cottages), and a barn. By 1905 the establishment had expanded to include two dozen separate (predominantly brick) structures distributed over a 24½-acre complex. The grounds of the North Carolina home were originally only one-fourth as large as the Texas plat, but by 1915 as many as fifteen different edifices sat upon it. Camp Nicholls, occupying approximately the same total acreage as the home in Raleigh, boasted eighteen buildings—a veritable community composed of dormitories, library, mess hall, laundry, barbershop and baths, infirmary, and "dead house" (morgue). Home administrators seemingly had tried to antici-pate any inmate need by constructing an annex of some kind or remodeling a building. As a result, by the period of the First World War the homes had become far more elaborate institutions than the modest and crude facilities first utilized some three decades earlier.[9]

At the same time the homes had become increasingly bureaucratic. As inmate population multiplied (see the Appendix, Figure 2)—and aged (Appendix, Table 16)—the staff was augmented (Appendix, Figure 3). Gone were the days when a home could be operated adequately and safely by a superintendent and his family, assisted by a handful of "faithful" servants. The Texas institution (which housed the largest number of ex-Confederates at any one time) claimed by far the most paid employees in one year—fifty-three, or about one employee for every seven inmates. By comparison, in the same year, 1917, the Georgia home, with only 103 veterans enrolled, had a 3:1 inmate-employee ratio. At the same time South Carolina's fifty-five inmates were cared for by a staff of eleven officers and employees, namely, the superintendent, matron, steward, surgeon, and seven "Negro help[ers]."[10] By the 1910s workers performed some of the very tasks that younger and more robust inmates had formerly done. This change too had been the by-product of technological and scientific progress. With the improvement in medical facilities came also the need for additional specialized personnel: a whole cadre of hospital matrons, cooks, laundresses, waiters, and orderlies, not to mention nurses and aides for both day and night shifts.

Enhanced staffs, larger physical plants, more advanced medical care: all of these changes entailed a much more complex and demanding financial structure. Initially, prior to receiving state monies, none of the homes possessed substantial funding. Administrators pieced together annual budgets with an eclectic mix of contributions from local government, the proceeds of community fund-raisings, and other private sources. Veterans' associations and ladies' committees were organized to devote special collections to the homes. Annual budget deficits had to be met by board members out of their own funds and through appeals to the wealthy and benevolent—men like entrepreneur Walter M. Lampton of Magnolia, Mississippi, who, though neither a veteran nor the son of a veteran, earned the sobriquet "financial Gibraltar of [the] Jefferson Davis Soldiers' Home" for his largess, which included thousands of dollars in cash donations, as well as such sundry items as blankets and quilts, tobacco, chickens, ice cream, a fountain of gold fish, and a Victrola.[11] Even though budgets remained small and at most institutions the cost per inmate per month remained under twelve dollars, the homes in the 1880s and 1890s were hard put to balance their books at the end of each year.[12]

And this situation would only deteriorate. Even after state appropriations finally began coming in, administrators encountered obstacles in meeting their daily financial obligations. The plan was for some of the homes to be

As the ranks of Confederate veterans thinned, sometimes ex–body servants were admitted as inmates of the homes. Seated on the steps of their cabin at Beauvoir in this 1936 WPA photo are Frank Childress (left), an eighty-five-year-old former dispatch carrier, and Nathan Best, age ninety-two, who had returned from the war minus an arm. (courtesy of Mississippi Department of Archives and History)

almost self-sufficient, but it never seemed to work out that way. The Arkansas board of managers, for example, found themselves with a deficit of more than $12,000 for 1915–16, despite income generated through the sale of a variety of items: block ice, hogs, garden produce, junk, even a crippled mare. They were in a quandary as to how to balance the budget, for the money they brought in simply could not keep pace with what they had to expend: the roof leaked, the bathroom floors needed repairing, a teamster and two others charged an exorbitant weekly fee for hauling coal from the railroad station to the home, and the price had risen on tobacco and shoes. Some aspects of the problem were diffuse and gradual, reflecting general economic and technological change. By the turn of the century, appropriate alterations and upgrading had to be performed when home administrators and physicians expected to have telephone service, electric power, and central steam plants, as well as modern dishwashing and laundry devices or a new Ford truck. Meanwhile, construction costs and the cost of constantly maintaining larger physical plants climbed steadily, as did the number of repairs needed. After nearly twenty years of continuous service, in 1911 the entire main building of the Arkansas home had to undergo a complete overhaul. It was by all accounts a major undertaking. The inmates were moved into tents, the interior walls were replastered and finished "in light colors," and new plumbing and indoor bathrooms were installed; a modern power plant supplying steam heat, hot and cold water, and electric lights was also included in the package, which carried a total price tag of $10,000.[13] Costs relating to medical care remained a relatively small part of home budgets, while food, fuel, and wages consumed the lion's share of available funds.[14] Aggregate inmate expenditures also rose regularly. For example, in 1904 the Texas home spent an average of 35 cents per inmate every day. Fourteen years later the outlay had grown to 84 cents per diem. Even with inmate laborers, no home could escape the inexorable pressure of rising costs.[15]

In order to meet those costs, some home and state officials originally worked out a formula fixing public support on a per capita basis. In 1891, for example, for every inmate the Tennessee home admitted, the institution received a state appropriation of $50 per year.[16] The arrangement worked fine, as long as supply costs, staple crop prices, employee wages, average inmate population and age, and numerous other variables remained constant, which, not surprisingly, they seldom did. Therefore, once every two years, beginning as early as 1893, sympathetic Tennessee lawmakers augmented the home's per capita allowance anywhere from 5 to 50 percent. By 1914, when for the first time in fifteen years the average inmate population had dipped to well below one hundred (while the average inmate's age approached eighty), per capita funding swelled to $200. By 1920 it had increased another 40 percent. From

1899 to 1914, Tennesseans paid an estimated quarter of a million dollars in per capita allowances alone.[17]

Although consistently caring for the smallest number of veterans, the Florida institution also experienced a significant increase in appropriations over the years. At its inception in 1893, the home received by law $100 per inmate per year—provided the sum did not exceed $2,500—and not a penny more. Therefore, during its first decade of operation, when inmate enrollment averaged less than one dozen, total state appropriations to the Florida home rarely surpassed $1,200 per year. Because there was simply no way the men could be adequately cared for on such a shoestring budget, in 1909 the legislature decided to put the home on a more secure base, increasing the annual maintenance fund to $120 per capita; in addition, it now allowed nearly $1,000 for hospital costs (staff salaries, medicines, and "disinfectants" and the like), over $600 for compensating the superintendent and matron, a $500 contingent fund (earmarked for insurance, repairs, furniture, etc.), $50 in burial expenses for each inmate, and $2,000 for the enlargement of the hospital, as needed. In other words, beginning in 1909, annual governmental outlays were multiplied threefold. When enrollment at the Florida home reached twenty-five in 1915 and four years later peaked at thirty-four, state funding likewise increased in corresponding increments.

In spite of these hefty cumulative appropriations, bills sometimes began piling up, and invoices periodically went unpaid. Debt retirement payments for the Tennessee home during the 1899–1914 period totaled just over $11,000. In addition, the homes faced miscellaneous expenses that were the products of someone's sympathy or reforming zeal, such as annual payments for half-time religious services, special subsidies to offset the costs of inmate funerals and uniforms, marble headstones to replace wooden boards used in the home cemetery, property insurance, reimbursements for the executive board's travel expenses, and occasional employee raises. The state of Louisiana set aside several thousand dollars each year for the treatment of Camp Nicholls inmates at a local eye, ear, and nose clinic. In 1917 the Texas home employed an oculist and audiologist of its own, as well as a pharmacist to serve on the staff. In 1919 Mississippi home superintendent Elnathan Tartt boldly submitted to the state's lawmakers not only a request for a 65 percent increase in the per capita allotment but also an itemized list detailing over $37,000 worth of repairs and improvements for Beauvoir, including a new bakery, a wharf, a barbershop, hot baths, and a complete supply of new mattresses. In regard to the last item, he declared, "I am sure that no member of the Legislature would want their aged mother or father to sleep on an uncomfortable, insanitary mattress." Although giving only $17,500 for repairs, the legislature responded generously to his appeal and doubled the annual appropriation to $100,000, as well as granting $2,000 for new mattresses and establishing a $600 "amusement" fund. Caring for elderly and poor ex-Confederates proved to be an elaborately expensive enterprise.[18]

From time to time the financial burden was eased considerably by women volunteers. Energetic ladies throughout the South organized musicales, theatricals, and raffles, catered teas and sponsored lectures, all in an effort to supplement limited home budgets. Their goals were often quite specific: purchasing needed medical supplies, rocking chairs, spittoons, fly swatters, or croquet sets or outfitting an entire reading room and amusement hall.[19] The many contributions made by a ladies' auxiliary to the Tennessee home typify the efforts made by such groups. In March 1890 over one hundred wives, widows, and daughters of ex-Confederates of Davidson County, Tennessee, organized in order to raise "moneys, goods, chattels, provisions, livestock and all other needed articles" to assist indigent veterans and their families domiciled at the institution. In 1892, when cost overruns incurred in construction of the home's main building resulted in an indebtedness of nearly $7,000, the Nashville auxiliary sponsored a series of "old fiddler's concerts" at the downtown Union Gospel Tabernacle and enabled trustees to pay off pressing liabilities. By 1899 the group, now part of the United Daughters of the Confederacy, completed a memorial campaign drive that succeeded in procuring furnishings for the entire home. During the next two decades the several UDC chapters of Nashville, like scores of other "ladies of charity" groups all over the South, could be counted on to provide emergency funds or to help defray the spiraling costs of dependent veteran care by paying the salaries of needed workers.[20]

In addition to raising funds, various UDC chapters appointed "home committees" to ensure that the old soldiers were properly cared for in their remaining years. Such delegations of lady visitors (often accompanied by children), constituting in effect a secondary bureaucracy, became standard features of home life. The pious women, girls, and boys read to inmates, pinned badges of honor or flowers on their lapels, held ice cream festivals and watermelon cuttings, supplied Christmas trees and Easter hams, and helped celebrate Lee's birthday, Valentine's Day, or other special occasions. From time to time wives of renowned ex-Confederate leaders—Mrs. Jefferson Davis, Mrs. Albert Sidney Johnston, Mrs. Thomas J. "Stonewall" Jackson, and Mrs. Edmund Kirby Smith, for example—joined the committees in paying homage to even the lowliest of old veterans. Mrs. Bradley T. Johnson served as president of the Board of Lady Visitors, which conducted weekly inspections of the Maryland Confederate Home. From all accounts inmates enjoyed the visits, which sometimes included the singing of a number of favorite songs of the South. As one contemporary noted wryly: "almost any woman who visits them, unless she be unmistakenly cock-eyed or obviously disfigured, is to them 'a durn handsome gal,' whom they greet gladly, and escort with pleasure where she will." The visits could be poignant as well; witness the scene as veterans bid adieu to their guests at the conclusion of a visit to the Tennessee home in 1906, as described by one of the ladies. "As the long line of crippled, enfeebled and tottering old men passed and shook hands with me," she wrote, "I thought of what they were forty years ago: youthful, vigorous, able to cope with the world . . . now the beneficiaries of the State."[21]

Although the ladies' committees could become something of a nuisance if their evangelism grew too enthusiastic or they interfered with the staff, on the whole, most homes welcomed female help in fund-raising and in furnishing rooms and wards. In fact, women were viewed as ideally suited to maintaining a watchful eye over home housekeeping. When they attempted to play a more prominent role as policymakers, however, male staff members and administrators frequently objected. Women had certainly planned and supported the homes, but their worthy contributions did not necessarily mean they were regarded as capable of managing the institutions. The Daughters of the Confederacy in Missouri, for example, raised nearly $75,000 and planned, built, and equipped their state's home. They also provided for inmates' uniforms, prompting the division president to remark proudly: "Now, instead of the motley crowd assembled on the galleries of the Home, one finds a genteel array of old soldiers clothed in the uniform of gray." But when time came to decide who would compose the board of managers for the Missouri home, only veterans were invited to serve. In 1910 the Tennessee governing board announced that it would henceforth restrict the number of visits made by members of the UDC, because of the latter's mistaken belief that they had the "right to employ and dismiss attendants." Not willing to become a "mere puppet or figurehead," Ben S. Williams in 1921 resigned his position as superintendent of the South Carolina Infirmary, owing to constant "interference and assumption of authority" on the part of a female member of the board of control. Also resigning were the chairman of the board, General W. A. Clark, and another veteran, both of whom were said to be "utterly disgusted." Mary H. Southwood Kimbrough of Greenwood, Mississippi, a long-standing and influential member of the UDC and a friend of Varina Davis, who made it a practice to visit the Mississippi home at least once a year, infuriated the board at Beauvoir by charging administrators with fiscal mismanagement, accusing the superintendent of being inept, and going around the state telling everyone that the home was broke and "in need of necessities of life." Attending physicians in some homes fought running battles with ladies' visiting committees, while some superintendents saw women as annoying presences in their homes' wards and corridors.[22]

Although men who administered the homes and women who took an interest in them often could not see eye to eye, women gradually became more involved in the homes as caregivers and eventually succeeded Confederate veterans as administrators. Developments within Camp Nicholls reflected this changing pattern. In 1903 the Louisiana home board first decided to try the "innovation" of hiring female hospital nurses. Fifteen years later fully three-quarters of the home's staff members were women. All held minor positions, however, and not until 1920 did women serve as directors "to advise with and assist the Board." Two more years would pass before women were officially appointed by the governor and allowed to exert the same authority as their male counterparts on the board. From the outset, the Alabama UDC supported Jeff Falkner's soldiers' home endeavor; they created the Mountain Creek Fund in 1903 and a few years later formed the Mountain Creek Soldiers' Home Hospital Relief Committee. At the committee's request, the legislature appropriated funds to provide the home with a trained nurse as matron and two orderlies. The committee also arranged for many "conveniences and necessities" to be donated to the home, including fruits, chickens, eggs, and other foodstuffs, as well as ice blocks and hammocks for use in the summer and pocket money and handkerchiefs at Christmas. In 1910, at the ladies' insistence, the state board of control for charities incorporated the UDC committee as an auxiliary to the all-male home executive board and gave it charge of the linen department, hospital furnishings, and the cemetery; the matron was also required to make monthly reports to the UDC. Some years later the UDC was involved in having the legislature change the law under which the home operated so that wives of veterans could remain in the home after their husbands died, and finally in 1927 the chair of the committee became a full member of the state board of control.[23] Meanwhile, beginning in the early 1920s, UDC officers served as ex-officio members of the Georgia home board and as full-fledged members of the board for the South Carolina Infirmary and the Kentucky home. Mary Kimbrough and another woman were appointed to the board of directors at Beauvoir, and in North Carolina a woman served as chair of the board of trustees. In time, policies barring wives and widows (in some cases, daughters and nieces) of Confederate veterans from enrolling as inmates would be reversed as well.[24]

No one could deny that the scale and enterprise of the homes had expanded and changed by the middle of the second decade of the twentieth century. Yet the years immediately following 1913 were not marked by the institutional breakup and rapid decline that Foster has implied. Of course, the most striking challenge to Foster's thesis lies in the fact that, by 1913, several of the homes were only a few years old. The ones in Alabama, Mississippi, Kentucky, and (technically speaking) Georgia were just embarking on their second decade of operations, and the South Carolina home was barely into its fourth year. Furthermore, in July 1911 the state-supported Oklahoma Confederate Home at Ardmore officially opened (making it the fifteenth home founded nation-wide) after more than two years of organizing, fund-raising, and lobbying by the state's veterans' association.[25] It is difficult to imagine how these homes could have lost their viability so soon after being started. Rather, they and the others generally experienced growth or remained stable, occupying an endur-ing and crucial position within society for several more years.

These conclusions can be substantiated in part through an analysis of home enrollment data. Overall, inmate populations did decline somewhat in the years following 1913 (see the Appendix, Figure 2). For example, Georgia's inmate enrollment peaked at 136 in 1914, but five years later the average number of inmates residing in the home had diminished to only 94, a reduction of more than 30 percent. Camp Nicholls experienced an even greater drop during the same period, from 131 to 75, more than a 42 percent net decrease. But such changes were erratic. Until 1918 the Louisiana home's population average dipped in only 5 to 8 percent annual increments. Moreover, from 1922 to 1925 Georgia's average inmate population expanded slightly, nearly matching its level of the previous decade. In addition, in the years following 1913, three of the institutions under investigation actually witnessed population growth. Alabama's veteran enrollment did not reach its peak of 91 until 1918. By the end of 1920 total enrollment in the Texas home reached its zenith of 441, representing a rise of more than 22 percent over the figure officials had reported some six years earlier. Between 1914 and 1920, the North Carolina home also experienced a slight increase in numbers, while the inmate population of the Lee Camp Home in Virginia remained fairly con-stant, at least during the period of World War I. Viewed as a whole, the aggregate inmate population for the six largest homes in 1914 stood at 1,143. By 1920 the total had decreased by only seventy-six, a reduction of less than 7 percent.

One reason why home populations remained basically stable during the period after 1913 is that the number of veterans admitted to each home continued to offset the number of those who left, either voluntarily or involun-tarily. An examination of admittance and out-migration data for the Lee Camp Home from 1907 to 1911, reveals that the inmate population grew from 275 to 289 (see the Appendix, Table 17). In three of the five years in this period, about a dozen more veterans entered the institution than died or were dismissed, resulting in a marginal net gain. The reverse was true during the five-year period from 1913 to 1917, when slightly more inmates left the home than were admitted. Yet the differences were minuscule (perhaps even hardly noticeable at the time), considering that between 1913 and 1917 annual inmate admissions averaged only about two fewer (79.5 versus 77.4) than in the 1907–11 period.

Another indicator that the homes remained intact as institutions for several years after 1913 can be found in their finances. Without exception, funding for the homes had either stabilized or increased by 1915 (see the Appendix, Figure 4). According to the available data, the same pattern holds true (except for the Louisiana home) for the following years until 1920. In that year total appropriations to the Alabama home ($30,130) were nearly twice as high as they had been in 1910 ($16,061), though population remained essentially the same (eighty-five veterans). When funding figures are paired with enrollment data, it appears that homes experiencing a noticeable decline in population soon after 1913 (those in Virginia, Georgia, Louisiana, and Tennessee) escaped a corresponding decrease in funding. This pattern reflects the rising costs each home encountered during the period. For example, in 1920 the Georgia home received fully 50 percent more money from the state than it had in 1913, even though enrollment figures had plummeted more than 30 percent during the same period. On the other hand, as the number of Texas inmates rose between 1917 and 1920, the amount of appropriations likewise expanded; this, during a period marked by a rapid growth in Texas government expenditures.[26]

Even as the broadening scale of their activities and the rising costs of their operations transformed the soldiers' homes of the New South between the 1880s and the 1920s, some fundamental aspects of the homes remained tenaciously unchanged by 1920. For one thing, paternalism survived. The vision of the superintendent as prudent father and the home as his home writ large had not been discarded, in spite of a more complex set of responsibilities and an enlarged staff. Most home officials still professed a personal relationship with, as well as a commitment to the comfort and welfare of, the inmates. And most officials remained conscientious about outsiders' perceptions of their performance, even to the point of worrying whether inmates on furloughs presented a "creditable appearance" in public. The investigating committee still served both as a critic of everyday home realities and as a disciplinary body. Inmates were still expected to show proper deference and, as always, to be amenable to discipline.

It has been suggested that as Confederate inmates grew older (and presumably less active), the number, frequency, and severity of rule infractions decreased.[27] But there is little to support such a claim. For example, the Georgia home, though opening some seventeen years after the Lee Camp Home, experienced just as many (if not more) breaches in discipline during its first decade of operation as the latter did during the same period. And able-bodied octogenarians could be and apparently were at times just as uncooperative, ornery, and offensive to those in charge as relatively younger inmates. In fact, the last known disciplinary action in the Georgia home occurred in 1926, when the average age of the sixty-nine inmates exceeded eighty-four years. Trustees expelled R. C. Pressley, a bootlegger, whose room Atlanta police had raided several times before. From the available evidence, it appears that there were more recorded instances of inmate violence and physical assaults against staff members during the first two decades of the twentieth century than in any other period of the homes' combined existence.

One explanation for this phenomenon may be that these were the peak population years in the homes, when the accommodation of proportionately more inmates created a potentially more volatile environment. Be that as it may, governing boards found it increasingly difficult to undertake the personal oversight that had long characterized the institutions. The superintendent could no longer realistically be expected to visit each ward or room; nor could trustees, who were destined to play an increasingly passive and distant role. Although remaining concerned with their financial responsibilities, governing boards (whose original ranks had gradually thinned over time, too) had become less and less involved with each institution's day-to-day routines.[28]

To those residing outside the walls, the homes continued to serve the same purposes for which they had been founded. The institutions provided a safe refuge, a comfortable community, and a better alternative than almshouses for needy and worthy ex-Confederate soldiers. People still talked about fulfilling their "sacred duty" by keeping the old men "happy," and southern politicians still decried the terrible injustice of how little government agencies were doing for their veterans. In December 1898, again in 1902, and still again in 1904, Congressman John F. Rixey of Virginia introduced legislation calling not only for the government to allow ex-Confederates to be admitted to the national soldiers' homes but also for the Confederate homes to receive the "same financial assistance" as those in the North and West. "We do not suggest or ask this as a charity," Rixey maintained, "but as an act of justice, equality and right, just as we insisted, when the South re-entered the Union, that the Confederate soldier should have the ballot, with the right to hold office. In this light I, as a Southern Representative, not only suggest, but demand it." Representatives from various northern states endorsed the proposal. Washington Gardner of Michigan, for example, declared that it was "better to feed the hungry and shelter the living Confederate than to care for the graves of the immortal dead." Yet certain southern members of Congress blocked the move and kept it bottled up in committee. Bolstered by letters of protest from their angry constituents, the southerners argued that acceptance of such a gift would undermine the poor Confederate soldiers' "pride and self-esteem" and especially his sense of honor.[29]

In August 1916, on the eve of America's participation in yet another war, the

Senate Committee on Military Affairs held a hearing in Washington on a bill that would provide homes for Confederate veterans. This time the legislation was introduced by Union veteran and California senator John D. Works, and the hearings were presided over by Duncan U. Fletcher of Florida, an SCV member who had strongly supported the creation of the Confederate home in Jacksonville. Once again conservative members of Congress opposed the measure, fearing that if passed it would lead to further demands for extending federal pensions to ex-Confederates and their widows. Earlier that summer the House Committee on Invalid Pensions had held a hearing on a measure intended to do just that, as introduced by John H. Tillman of Arkansas, who, invoking an oft-repeated claim, called for the return of an estimated $100 million illegally collected by the federal government through the confiscation and sale of captured and abandoned property and the collection of taxes placed on cotton and sugar cane.[30] In the end, neither of the bills emerged from committee. Nevertheless, in a June 1917 address, before a large delegation of UCV members convening in the nation's capital, President Woodrow Wilson assured his audience of "the passion of admiration" all Americans "still entertain for the heroic figures" of the Confederacy.[31]

As shrines containing living symbols of the Confederate past, soldiers' homes continued to have a beneficial function for society as a whole. In its rituals the Confederate home remained as it had to be: a microcosm of the values of social solidarity and deference to authority. To those too young to remember the war—the many children's groups who visited and entertained the veterans on countless occasions—the homes continued to serve as places of instruction in the old ways of southern honor and manhood. According to one woman who attended a barbecue at the Arkansas home in 1922, "It gave a warm feeling about the heart to look upon the gentle, kindly old warriors as they bowed courtly bows to the ladies, greeted everyone they passed with a cheery smile and pleasant word and made all feel glad to be there." Among the many organized groups that visited the Georgia home from time to time were the Children of the Confederacy, the Georgia Tech Glee Club, and young ladies of the Washington Seminary. The purpose of their monthly visits, according to the chairman of the Georgia home committee, was to bring "the young people into touch with the veterans, thus inspiring them with patriotic Southern sentiments." As one member of the Mississippi SCV phrased it, the home was "but a . . . sacred sentiment, that links us with the past."[32] And, if need be, the homes provided a place where southerners of all ages could congregate on any given day to celebrate and relive once more the achievements of Johnny Reb. In 1910 people came "from near and far, from farm and store, [from] office, shop, bank, courthouse, schoolroom, [and] ball grounds," to the Kentucky home near Louisville. There,

Many young people were interested in the lives of ex-Confederate soldiers and corresponded with them. This postcard, dated April 27, 1939, was addressed to J. C. Bradford, an inmate of the Arkansas Confederate Home. (author's collection) the soldiers in gray, the band boys in military array, the Sons of Veterans in admiring groups, the lovely girls wearing Confederate colors, their glorious mothers with flags and badges and Chapter pins, the rosy-faced children with wide-open eyes, the sober sires approving and sometimes applauding and waving, and above all the glorious stars and bars with our beloved blood-red battle banner under which so many gallant Southern sires and sons had bled and died—all these made a scene and called out a shout such as no other people ever exhibited! The heroes of the fight— the veterans, weary and worn, sick and wounded—seemed to forget their pains and poverty, their cares and sorrows amidst their friends and in the peace, plenty, and honor they enjoyed.[33]

As the Confederate soldiers' homes prepared to enter their fifth decade of collective operation, radical and penetrating changes began to alter these traditional functions. In Texas, dramatic change first occurred on January 1, 1920, when a public corporate organization replaced the Confederate board of managers as the primary instrument for implementing care and social control. Under the enabling legislation enacted at the time, all of the state's eleemosynary institutions, including the Texas Home for Men, were to be administered by a more centrally directed and capital-intensive regulatory agency.[34] Since the founding of the Florida home in 1891, the board had refused to allow a member of the UDC to sit on the board (except in an advisory capacity) because the charter had specifically stated that only veterans could serve. This arrangement changed in April 1921, when the old board was dissolved and the management of the institution was transferred to a new board of five commissioners, consisting of the UDC division president, the UCV and SCV state commanders, the state comptroller, and one other person nominated by the board.[35] A similar reform would affect the Georgia home much later, in 1931. In all three cases, the state would ultimately succeed Confederate veterans and UDC committees as official and ex-officio preservers and protectors of the homes' aging populations. After the state officially took control of the homes, widows and daughters of veterans were usually permitted to enroll as inmates, and the superintendent's and matron's positions were amalgamated and given to a female nurse-superintendent appointed by the governor. Meanwhile, population figures in all the homes gradually declined. By 1920, more than three-fourths of all the veterans who would ever be enrolled in the homes had already been admitted. As a result, in the following decade, when inmates died or were dismissed, there were considerably fewer comrades to take their places. By 1930 only about five dozen inmates (all males) resided in the Lee Camp Home. That institution too had also undergone radical changes, beginning in March 1921, when a grandson of a Confederate veteran assumed the position of commandant. Biological realities took their toll on commandants no less than on the ex-soldiers who were in their charge. By 1936, for both symbolic and economic reasons, the board of visitors permitted women to enroll as inmates. Five years later the last veteran died and the home closed.[36]

By this time, several more Confederate homes had ceased operating. Although in 1926 there was talk of closing the Maryland home at Pikesville and moving the remaining veterans to an old men's home in Baltimore, the institution remained open for several more years. In 1933 six veterans were transferred from the Tennessee Soldiers' Home to what had been the girls' infirmary of the Tennessee Industrial School, which in turn assumed control of the home's buildings, furnishings, and 230-acre farm. In 1937, when the North Carolina General Assembly authorized the closure of the Raleigh home, ninety-two-year-old T. S. Arthur, one of only a handful of surviving inmates, protested the decision. In his much publicized petition addressed to the legislature Arthur pleaded: "Our home . . . is the last resort we have to end our days in peace. . . . Please pause before kicking us out!" The following year, after the last veteran left the home, the institution shut down, and its buildings were occupied by a New Deal agency and a city recreation agency. Four years later, in the midst of another war, the state of Louisiana converted Camp Nicholls, the oldest of the Confederate soldiers' homes, into a military installation. Following the death of the last veteran in 1938, the Florida home was closed and the property converted into cash, which General Frank M. Ironmonger, state UCV commander, proudly turned over to the state comptroller to be used to establish a home endowment fund, the proceeds of which to this day fund scholarships for students within the University of Florida system.[37]

Before the last veteran had passed away at the South Carolina Confederate Infirmary in 1944, it was rumored that the home would be closed and converted into an institute for the blind. But the state's 350 veterans opposed the move. "They are all upset about it," averred E. M. Yarborough, the division commander, explaining: "To them, the mere discussion of using this spot for other than Confederate purposes is sacrilege—the embodyment of discouragement, lack of appreciation and an effort to shove them aside." Thanks to a liberal admissions policy, which gradually allowed widows, daughters, sisters and ultimately nieces of veterans to reside in the home, it was possible to keep the facility open for twenty more years.[38] Finally, with only twenty-nine elderly women as inmates, the board opted in February 1957 to close the home. With passage of an act by the legislature, the remaining inmates were placed under the care of the State Department of Public Welfare and then transferred to boardinghouses or private homes, and the institution, which critics had originally thought would not last more than a decade, officially closed on June 29, 1957, after over forty-eight years of continuous operation.

Talk again surfaced of finding another use for the property, perhaps making it into a rehabilitation center for alcoholics, but that plan too was resisted. Finally the home "fell victim to [the] hammers of progress," when it was razed in June 1963.[39]

In many states, one may today visit the places where former Confederates resided, though the surroundings have changed. The home for veterans in Raleigh, for example, is now the North Carolina Motor Vehicles Division building. A New Orleans police station now occupies the land at 1700 Moss Street, where Camp Nicholls had been located. Only the main front steps that led into the South Carolina Infirmary on the corner of Bull Street and Confederate Avenue in Columbia are extant, and a small plaque noting the historical significance of the site has been erected. The Tennessee home has been leveled (only the rusted shells of the former pumphouse and morgue remain), and the home property is once again part of the Hermitage, Andrew Jackson's former estate. The Florida home has been torn down, and a municipal waste water treatment plant now occupies what had been its site on Talleyrand Avenue, across the street from the Jacksonville Port Authority. The Texas Home for Men has been demolished and replaced by housing for married students at the University of Texas. An asphalt parking lot for the Atlanta Police Academy now marks the spot where once stood the home that Grady built, which, ironically, was among the last of the homes to close its doors. Scattered remnants of the R. E. Lee Camp Home in Richmond have been preserved—Robinson's farmhouse (the administration building), the chapel, and part of the kitchen. Where a half dozen cottages had stood was constructed the Virginia Confederate Women's Home, in which several elderly descendants of veterans lingered for years, until a circuit court judge in the late 1980s ordered them evicted and transferred to a nursing care center, so that bulldozers could begin to do their massive work (although, in fact, the vacant building has yet to be torn down).

Among all the Confederate soldiers' homes, only two function, though in a limited sense, today. There were so few inmates (three men and nine women) remaining in the Alabama home in 1930 that the UDC decided, in lieu of observing Confederate Memorial Day at the institution, to drive the inmates to the observance in Montgomery, where they rode in the parade, sat on the speakers' platform at the cemetery, and ate lunch at the Jefferson Davis Hotel. After the last veteran died in 1934, the home hospital was converted into apartments for the last seven widows. Five years later the legislature ordered the home closed, the few women inmates were entrusted to the care of the State Welfare Department, the home's two cemeteries were handed over for safekeeping to the Soil Conservation Service, and extant buildings were abandoned and dismantled or were removed in tact, except for the mess hall, which stood until the 1960s. But the UDC rekindled interest in the home in the 1950s, memorial services were resumed on site during the following decade, and since 1975 the maintenance and administration of the more than one-hundred-acre site, which is now known as Confederate Memorial Park, has been provided by the Alabama Historical Commission.

Beauvoir, too, remains open to the public and is as much a tourist attraction today as when President Franklin Roosevelt visited the home on April 29, 1937. Three years after Roosevelt's visit the legislature voted to restore the original Davis property—including the Beauvoir Mansion proper and the Library Cottage, in which President Davis composed his memoirs—to the SCV, eventually giving birth to the Jefferson Davis Memorial Shrine. All buildings lying east of the cottage were reserved for the soldiers' home and its inmates, who were transferred to the hospital and remained under the control and management of the state. Syndicated advice columnist Elizabeth Meriwether Gilmer ("Dorothy Dix"), a daughter of a veteran, who lived and worked in New York City but kept a Gulf Coast residence, happened to pass by the home in 1940 and spy "two long rows of worn and shabby rocking chairs" behind a "For Sale" sign. The home was closed now, she thought to herself, its "doors barred, [its] windows shuttered." The sight disturbed her. Then it grew dark, as she recounted in her letter to the editor of the New Orleans *Times-Picayune*, and

> A wind came up from the Gulf and gently swayed the rockers back and forth, and I swear to you they were no longer empty. They were filled with gray ghosts of old men who bent their heads together and thrashed over, as they had done a thousand times before, the stories of the battlefields on which they had fought—Shiloh and Bull Run and Chickamauga and Vicksburg and Gettysburg and Appomattox—and they spoke in cracked voices of great adventures and told tales of heroism and suffering and sacrifice beyond belief.[40]

Even though there were no longer veterans residing in the home after 1947, people still looked to Beauvoir for answers. J. L. Peete of Memphis, Tennessee, apparently found what he was looking for. Writing to Mrs. Josie C. Rankin, the superintendent, about a relative who had entered the home in August 1910 from Warren County, Mississippi, Peete informed her: "After I left you that day I went to the Confederate Cemetary and found the marker to Mr. Peete's grave." A young English instructor at the University of Texas was interested in obtaining information for a forthcoming work on the poet Prentiss Ingraham, who had died at Beauvoir. Mrs. Emile Joffrion of Baton Rouge, desiring to become a member of the UDC, needed proof of the army record of her father, Thomas W. McNamara, of the Twenty-First Mississippi Infantry, who had entered the home in 1906.[41] There were only a few souls remaining in 1955

Young women often visited the homes and had their photographs taken with the veterans, as in this scene from the 1930s at Richmond's Lee Camp Home. (courtesy of Virginia State Library)

when the legislature approved the transfer of the soldiers' home to the control of the SCV, thereby ending an era that had lasted more than half a century. In 1957 the two remaining widows were placed in nursing homes, and the process of demolishing soldiers' home property that had begun some two years earlier continued. The home hospital, however, was preserved and turned into a museum, souvenir shop, and administration complex for the Davis Shrine that draws thousands of visitors, curiosity seekers, and Civil War buffs and reenactors to Beauvoir every year.[42]

An estimated 20,000 indigent and disabled ex-Confederates entered the veterans' homes over the years. There they were given food, medicine, and shelter, furnished with uniforms of cadet-gray cloth, regimented, publicly exhibited, and told again to follow orders. Some refused to follow orders and were summarily dismissed. Others left after only a few days and never looked back. Many more, however, remained in residence for months or years, determined that they had found what they wanted. Old sorrows were forgotten, former comradeships were rekindled, new friendships were made. Moreover, pretty girls and other visitors from the "outside" came to mingle, to entertain, to preach, to listen sympathetically to tall tales, or to have their photographs taken beside the Rebel "heroes."

Among the veterans were men who had witnessed the shelling of Fort Sumter, who had ridden with Stuart or Forrest, who had charged with Pickett, or who had stacked their guns at Appomattox. A few were as well known as Arkansas's Major Harold Borland, the son of U.S. senator and Confederate general Solon Borland and a West Point graduate. And three grandsons of Francis Scott Key resided at the home in Maryland. Most inmates, however, were obscure individuals; men like Jasper Ferguson, who had fought with the Fifth Arkansas Infantry at Shiloh, Missionary Ridge, and Chickamauga and was wounded six different times; or James M. and Wesley J. Brown, father and son in the Georgia Reserves, who had served together as Andersonville prison guards; or one Thomas J. Thomasson of York County, South Carolina, who in April 1911, paralyzed and helpless, had been hauled in a wagon to the South Carolina Confederate Infirmary and placed on its front steps by his children, who left him there to die all alone three months later.[43]

"We are old. We are going fast," an inmate at the Maryland home warned a visitor on Confederate Memorial Day in 1921. They are all gone now. When an inmate died, he was neatly dressed in his home uniform, given a gun salute, and provided with an honorable burial. Sometimes a bell tolled, heard throughout the neighborhoods in the vicinity of the home. The last bell has long since tolled, and only a few photographs of the old soldiers survive. With the passing of each inmate, southerners lost not only a participant in the struggles of the 1860s but also a tangible link, indeed their most tangible link, with their Confederate heritage.

EPILOGUE

On February 19, 1929, along San Gabriel Boulevard in Los Angeles, Dixie Manor, the last Confederate soldiers' home to be founded, opened its doors. The lovely old "southern-type" cottage surrounded by orange trees on "spacious grounds" boasted some twelve rooms, one of which served as the infirmary. California's home for Johnny Reb was an anomaly in a number of ways. For one, it was the first such institution established and managed from the outset exclusively by the UDC. Every detail was under the control of the ladies, from the home's finances to its day-to-day management. A few years earlier as many as six veterans residing on a county poor farm near Hondo had been cared for by the ladies' committees of the twelve chapters that made up the UDC in southern California. But "that was not a pleasing thought to those of Southern sentiment," commented Mrs. Gertrude Montgomery, corresponding secretary of the UDC, California Division. So UDC members established Dixie Manor and brought the men to this new facility, where they were made to feel "happy and [as] well cared for" as possible in a "real" home, the word "institution" never being used to refer to it. "Every loyal Daughter rejoices that the last days of these veterans, so far from their native Southland, are being made comfortable," reported Mrs. Erna Grabe, publicity director for the state UDC.

In addition, the California home originated at a time when the other homes were in a state of general decline. On the whole, Confederate veterans were at least in their eighties, and the nine or so inmates who claimed Dixie Manor as their home in 1929 would be gone within a few short years. Yet people still came to catch one final glimpse of the "boys" who wore the gray, even as far away as California. When the home was officially dedicated on April 14, 1929, as many as 500 people witnessed the ceremonies. In 1930 alone, an estimated fifty visitors a month, from as many as twelve different states, stopped by Dixie Manor. To the casual observer, such homage paid to ancient warriors was a natural and proper act for a civilized people. But to people who saw the veterans as they, and many of the things they stood for, neared their end, like those who were present when a quartet from the Georgia home showed up at the premiere of *Gone with the Wind*, it was an experience they would not likely forget.[1]

APPENDIX

The various quantitative analyses that appear throughout this study are based on the files of 2,296 selected ex-Confederates who actually resided in the soldiers' homes. I derived information on each veteran of each home from different sources, depending upon the factors of availability and accessibility. For example, the microfilmed applications to the Tennessee home provide the best source for raw, quantifiable inmate data. On the other hand, an extremely high percentage of the applications to the Georgia, Arkansas, and Texas homes are, unfortunately, missing or presumed destroyed. And there are only a few existing applications for admission to the Mississippi, South Carolina, Florida, and Alabama homes. Nevertheless, I compiled vital statistics on hundreds of veterans by gleaning information from several bound rosters that have been preserved in the state archives in Atlanta, Austin, and Jackson. I relied upon a similar volume for North Carolina veterans who were admitted to that state's home after, roughly, 1910. Applications to the Virginia home are extant, though they have not been microfilmed and each of the hundreds of case files has been assigned its own folder, making expeditious research impossible. Biennial reports issued by the Camp Nicholls Board of Directors supplement the data that I drew from the handful of applications to the Louisiana home.

In order to reach my predetermined sample size for a particular home, I chose every other name from the lists of veterans or gathered as much data as the sources would allow. I excluded from consideration applications or roster entries that were so incomplete as to be useless or that were highly illegible, as well as those that the board rejected. For the most part, I also overlooked veterans who, though entitled, decided not to enter a home or who died before being admitted. For each of the 2,296 veterans selected, I created a file, encoding pertinent information, including birthplace, residence, age, occupation, military service, disability, marital status, and month and year of admission. Only the Texas and North Carolina homes' rosters yielded a veteran's religious affiliation, although, unlike the records of other homes, these same records omitted his military rank. Application forms and roster entries contained (at least, potentially) identical information, but the amount and quality of quantifiable data in fact varied between the two sources. I then entered each file into a simple, public-domain database program that automatically computes frequency distributions of categorized variables.

A Confederate soldiers' home is known to have existed in all of the eleven states that comprised the Confederacy, as well as in Maryland, Missouri, Kentucky, Oklahoma, and California. My primary focus has been on the veteran inmate population of the eleven homes in former Confederate states. The sample of 2,296 veterans equals approximately 20 percent of the total number believed to have resided in those eleven homes through 1920. Exactly how many Confederate veterans actually lived in these homes during this period is unknown, for not all of the institutions' records have survived. Moreover, it is unlikely that those that are extant provide a completely accurate count. The best estimate for the years from opening through 1920 is 11,479; another 3,613 veterans gained admission sometime later, bringing the total number admitted to 15,092 (see Table 1). Of the former figure, Virginia inmates comprised the largest share (21.9 percent), followed by inmates in Texas (17.6 percent), North Carolina (11.4 percent), Louisiana (9.3 percent), Arkansas (7.8 percent), Georgia (6.9 percent), Mississippi (6.7 percent), Tennessee (6.2 percent), Alabama (6.1 percent), South Carolina (3.5 percent), and Florida (2.6 percent). Thus, the Virginia, Texas, Georgia, North Carolina, and Arkansas homes, combined, accounted for nearly two-thirds (65.6 percent) of the entire home population. From 1890 through 1928, more ex-Confederates resided in those five states than in any other state in the New South (see Tables 2, 3, and 4).

The fact that the sample is relatively sizable enhances the probability of matching the characteristics of the entire population. Each state sample has been properly represented: that is, of the 2,296 veterans, 503 (21.9 percent) resided in the Lee Camp Home of Virginia; 404 (17.6 percent) in the Texas home; 262 (11.4 percent) in the North Carolina institution; 212 (9.3 percent) in Louisiana's Camp Nicholls; 179 (7.8 percent) in the Arkansas home; 158 (6.9 percent) in the Georgia home; 154 (6.7 percent) at Beauvoir in Mississippi; 143 (6.2 percent) in the Tennessee home; and 140 (6.1 percent) at Alabama's Falkner Home. Only the Florida and South Carolina homes are misrepresented. Since most of the Florida institution's records are no longer extant, information on only 27 veterans has been located. So, I decided arbitrarily to analyze the records of an additional 33 veterans from the South Carolina home, bringing the total number for that sample to 114 (4.9 percent). Most statisticians require a sampling of at least 1,000 files. Although my entire sample of 2,296 clearly exceeds that demand, its reliability awaits further testing.

Whenever possible, parallel studies have been used as an indirect means of correlating data, testing the sample's reliability, and substantiating conclusions. For example, Table 5 illustrates the birthplaces of veterans admitted to four of the eleven homes. The table shows that about one-third (36.5 percent) of Confederate soldiers' home residents were natives of their respective states, whereas two-fifths (40.4 percent) had been born elsewhere in the South.

Immigrants and the northern-born comprised about one-fifth (22.9 percent) of the homes' population. The table also shows that Louisiana had the highest percentage of immigrants, Texas had the largest proportion of northerners, and Georgia was the most homogeneous or "southern" of the states, followed closely by Tennessee. These findings closely match those described in a parallel study by Bell Wiley, who examined the composition of Confederate military units based upon muster rolls. Wiley demonstrates that Louisiana contributed far more foreigners to Confederate service than any other state. Also, as clearly reflected in the table, Texas was a state composed largely of southern-born immigrants.[1]

Ultimately, the data's veracity—and in turn, the veterans' collective history—may never be conclusively determined. In the first place, as historical sources, applications and similar "single-round" survey questionnaires are not absolutely reliable. Data derived from both form-types are necessarily dependent upon the respondent's ability to give unequivocal answers to direct questions. A veteran's age, educational level, and emotional and physical health undoubtedly affected his responses. Secondly, a precoded form invariably produces data truncation; that is, only a preset range of questions was asked and no more, thereby resulting in a total lack of information on other, uninterrogated topics. In addition, official publications of the homes (for no apparent reason other than simple clerical oversight) were not immune to misreporting and underreporting.

In an effort to overcome such limitations, I have, whenever possible, extracted "external" data from other sources. For example, the ages (see Table 6) reported by veterans on their applications sometimes have been compared to the ones they disclosed to census takers in consecutive decades. Instances of dubious superintendent record-keeping have been cross-checked with physician and trustee accounts. In order to render the applicants' responses more useful, I have also found it necessary to manipulate information. Instead of giving their ages, veterans in many cases indicated their year of birth, which then had to be subtracted from their date of application, in order to extrapolate age at admission.

For the score or so of applicants who wrote "none" in reference to their marital status (see Table 13) and listed no dependents, I assumed they meant that they were indeed single men who perhaps had never married. The Georgia roster, for example, rarely indicates marital status. Yet it does list names of persons to be notified in the event of death. So, I assumed that when a "Mrs." bearing the identical surname as the veteran appeared, it meant that the veteran must have been married. If children were listed, but no "Mrs.," then he was a widower. And if names of other relatives (nieces, nephews, siblings, etc.) were provided, then the veteran probably was single. These

assumptions enabled me to answer more questions than the veterans themselves had been originally asked, thereby enlarging the scope of my analysis.

In determining whether a veteran suffered from a "war wound" (see Table
7), I considered only those physical ailments that conceivably could have been
caused by a "visible" war injury—such as the loss of a limb, a broken back, or a
fractured skull. At the same time I arbitrarily disregarded common disorders
of the aged—heart disease, sight and hearing loss, rheumatoid arthritis,
diarrhoeal ailments, general debility, etc.[2] Table 7 illustrates the percentage
distribution by state of Confederate soldiers' home residents afflicted with a
"war wound." Although not reflected in the table, a pattern of early admissions
for veterans who claimed a service-related disability revealed itself as I
analyzed the data. Of all the inmates wounded during the war, 312 were
admitted to a veterans' home during the first full decade of operation.

Occupational analysis (see Table 8) required considerably more manipulation in order to conform to modern conceptualizations and measurements of
socioeconomic standing. In fact, I discovered an earlier, but nonetheless adequate, study to be more useful for my New South subjects than more recent
approaches. I adopted William Hunt's simple four-category hierarchy and
nomenclature, not only because he analyzed census data for a similar time
period but also because he incorporated prestige as a subjective indicator of
occupational status.[3] With the notable exception of "farmer," all of the veterans' postwar occupations reported on applications or in official rosters fell
discretely under one of Hunt's four categories: proprietors/professional people, clerical workers, skilled workers, and the working or laboring class. Hunt
arbitrarily grouped property-owning farmers under the first category and
propertyless, or tenant, farmers—he referred specifically to them as "agricultural laborers"—under the fourth category. It stands to reason that a large
number of indigent, relief-dependent ex-Confederates were in fact farm
laborers rather than owners and thus fall in Hunt's fourth category. After all,
veterans had to meet strict needs-based requirements governing inmate admissions in each state. Those whose property values exceeded the allowable
limits prescribed by state laws were ruled ineligible for home admission. Yet, I
was unwilling to assume that just because a veteran listed "farmer" as his chief
postwar economic activity, he therefore owned no real estate whatsoever. He
probably did not, but I automatically assigned him to a fifth category, so as to
avoid any misunderstanding.

Although occupation is arguably the best measure of socioeconomic status,
it is possible to describe an individual's position within society by analyzing
multiple-item indicators.[4] The correlates of residence, literacy, disability, and
age undoubtedly affected a veteran's postwar economic activity and life
chances. Marital status and family size also enabled the aging veteran to avoid

or defer seeking relief. Wives and/or children of veterans potentially satisfied an economic need, providing financial assistance and guarantees of protection or support in old age. My research on the veterans' religious affiliation—another possible proxy for determining socioeconomic status—is inconclusive. Based upon my samples of Texas and North Carolina veterans only, almost three-fourths (70.9 percent) belonged to a mainline denomination such as Methodist, Baptist, Presbyterian, or Episcopalian, with a majority being Methodists and Baptists.

Data on military rank (see Table 10) also partially establishes an individual's antebellum socioeconomic status. I chose the highest rank held by the veteran in order to allow for field promotions and company elections, which sometimes involved prestige factors. Since applications to the Tennessee Confederate Soldiers' Home failed to provide a rank for each veteran, I consulted the ex-Confederates' compiled service records as indexed in *Tennesseans in the Civil War*. The inability to determine the rank held by all 143 Tennessee veterans may have skewed this tabulation. Even so, it appears that Confederate soldiers commanded other men on the basis of both their family's prewar wealth and the earlier esteem in which they had been held by others.[5]

Tracing family wealth values (see Tables 9, 11, and 12) as indicated in consecutive census schedules not only confirms this observation but also provides useful information about a veteran's postwar economic, residential, and occupational mobility patterns. I examined the wealth held by the 143 veterans in the Tennessee sample as reported in the 1860 and 1870 census schedules. Once again, the data required some manipulation. Because only 38 of the 143 men were heads of household in 1860, I chose family wealth aggregates rather than individual wealth as the basic unit of analysis. For each unmarried veteran who reported zero wealth, I included his parents' combined personal and real estate values, if any. If a veteran owned property—yet resided with his parents—I counted the family's composite wealth. In a few cases where a veteran boarded with a family whose members were apparently unrelated to him, I considered only my subject's wealth, not that belonging to his landlord or employer. I utilized the identical tracing procedures for the 1870 census data.

Lastly, I measured tenure (see Tables 14 and 15) by counting the time from when a veteran was first admitted to when he emigrated from the home for the first time. The out-migration figures for veterans in the Georgia, Louisiana, and Tennessee homes were based on deaths only. For veterans in the other five homes, I considered any form of out-migration, voluntary (furloughs, transfers, absences) as well as involuntary (deaths and dismissals). Among the Texas sample's 404 veterans, 259 (64.1 percent) died at the home; of the 164 South Carolinians, 79 left voluntarily.

Unless otherwise noted, all of the statistical tabulations involving inmate data in this study have been derived from the aforementioned sources. Each table gives the frequency distributions of one or two categorized variables. "N" always refers to the total number of files considered in a particular analysis. This number almost never equals the entire sample. Some of the tables also contain percentage values for a given category. Because of rounding, percentages rarely total 100. The information derived from the analyses, as well as my presentation of summary descriptions, should be considered exploratory, preliminary, and suggestive. Admittedly, more work remains to be done. My chief objective has been to provide a straightforward and readily interpretable description of a body of data (and its internal structure) that has been heretofore wholly unaggregated and unexamined.

Table 1. Number of Soldiers' Home Inmates, by State and Year of Admission

State (by Rank)	Admitted before 1920	Admitted after 1920	Total
1. Virginia	2,519	536	3,055
2. Texas	2,019	941	2,960
3. North Carolina	1,310	149	1,459
4. Louisiana	1,063	354	1,417
5. Arkansas	900	300	1,200
6. Georgia	792	277	1,069
7. Mississippi	767	360	1,127
8. Tennessee	708	266	974
9. Alabama	700	150	850
10. South Carolina	401	205	606
11. Florida	300	75	375
N	11,479	3,613	15,092

Table 2. Number and Percentage of Confederate Veterans, by State, in 1890

State (by Rank)	Number	Percentage of All Confederate Veterans
1. Texas	66,456	15.50
2. Virginia	48,448	11.28
3. Georgia	46,733	10.92
4. North Carolina	38,416	8.96
5. Alabama	33,871	7.88
6. Tennessee	31,727	7.42
7. Arkansas	26,582	6.18
8. Mississippi	26,582	6.18
9. South Carolina	23,581	5.46
10. Missouri	17,579	4.08
11. Louisiana	15,864	3.69
12. Kentucky	12,005	2.57
13. Florida	8,146	1.89
14. Maryland	8,000	1.86
All others	24,757	5.77
N	428,747	

Source: Bureau of the Census, "Soldiers and Widows," p. 593.

Table 3. Number and Percentage of Confederate Veterans, by State, in 1922

State (by Rank)	Number	Percentage of All Confederate Veterans
1. Texas	15,225	20.12
2. Georgia	9,105	12.03
3. Arkansas	9,100	12.02
4. North Carolina	6,370	8.42
5. Virginia	5,196	6.86
6. Alabama	4,376	5.78
7. Mississippi	3,796	5.01
8. South Carolina	3,788	5.00
9. Tennessee	2,540	3.35
10. Louisiana	2,341	3.09
11. Missouri	2,136	2.82
12. Florida	1,504	1.98
13. Oklahoma	1,484	1.96
14. Kentucky	1,190	1.57
All others	7,500[a]	9.91
N	75,651	

Source: "Surviving Confederate Veterans," *Con Vet* 30 (1922): 363.
a. estimated.

Table 4. Number and Percentage of Confederate Veterans, by State, in 1928

State (by Rank)	Number	Percentage of All Confederate Veterans
1. Texas	3,286	12.68
2. Georgia	3,070	11.84
3. Arkansas	2,875	11.09
4. Virginia	2,645	10.20
5. North Carolina	2,609	10.06
6. Mississippi	2,318	8.94
7. South Carolina	2,267	8.74
8. Alabama	2,094	8.08
9. Tennessee	1,552	5.99
10. Oklahoma	1,049	4.04
11. Louisiana	956	3.68
12. Florida	745	2.87
13. Kentucky	443	1.70
N	25,909	

Source: "Confederate Veterans and Widows," *Con Vet* 36 (1928): 408–9.

Table 5. Birthplace of Confederate Soldiers' Home Inmates, by State and Region (in Percentages)

Birthplace	Ga.	La.	Tenn.	Tex.	Total
Foreign-born	2.3	25.9	10.5	7.8	11.4
State native	76.2	39.6	71.8	6.8	36.5
C. S. A. native[a]	20.2	24.9	10.8	67.2	40.4
Union native[b]	1.3	9.6	6.9	18.2	11.5
N	158	212	143	404	917

a. Born in any of the eleven states that comprised the Confederate States of America.
b. Born in any state other than those comprising the Confederacy.

Table 6. Age and Age Range at Admission (from Opening Date to 1900), by State

	La.	Tenn.	Tex.	Va.
Mean age	59.8	62.8	63.2	60.5
Age range	41–80	49–87	45–91	38–88
N (566)	114	71	143	238

Table 7. Percentage of Confederate Soldiers' Home Residents with "War Wounds," by State

	Ga.	La.	N.C.	Tenn.	Tex.	Va.	Total
	32.9	23.5	35.5	33.6	21.5	19.1	24.9
N	158	212	262	143	404	503	1,682

Table 8. Occupation of Confederate Soldiers' Home Inmates, by State

Occupational Group	Number of Veterans							Percentage
	Ga.	La.	N.C.	S.C.	Tenn.	Tex.	Va.	
Professional	12	20	9	9	19	46	49	10.7
Clerical	3	30	1	4	11	7	31	5.7
Skilled	17	43	25	19	33	94	152	25.0
Laborer	—	90	8	16	39	30	78	17.1
Farmer	33	29	103	66	41	219	143	41.5
N	65	212	146	114	143	396	453	1,529

Table 9. 1860 Family Wealth for Tennessee Soldiers' Home Inmates

	Wealth Aggregate				
	$0	$1–1,000	$1,001–4,000	$4,001–10,000	$10,000+
Percentages of inmates	27.9	23.8	17.7	10.9	19.7
Mean wealth ($)	0	376	2,096	6,371	33,073
Percentage of total wealth	0	1.2	4.8	9.0	85.0

Note: Total wealth = $1,128,719; N = 143.

Table 10. Military Rank of Tennessee Soldiers' Home Inmates, by Antebellum Family Wealth (in Percentages)

	Wealth Aggregate			
Army Rank	$0	$1–1,000	$1,001–5,000	$5,000+
Private (N=84)	78.8	88.0	77.3	61.8
Corporal (N=3)	0.0	4.0	9.2	0.0
Sergeant (N=9)	15.2	4.0	4.5	5.9
Lieutenant (N=4)	3.0	0.0	0.0	8.8
Captain (N=5)	0.0	0.0	4.5	1.8
Major (N=1)	0.0	0.0	0.0	2.9
Other[a] (N=6)	3.0	4.0	4.5	8.8
Total mean wealth ($)	0	418	2,882	23,610

Note: N=114.
a. Unspecified ranks, such as surgeon, musician, or hospital steward.

Table 11. 1870 Family Wealth of Tennessee Soldiers' Home Inmates

	Wealth Aggregate				
	$0	$1–1,000	$1,001–4,000	$4,001–10,000	$10,000+
Percentage of inmates	40.0	28.7	16.9	8.8	5.1
Mean wealth ($)	0	335	1,875	6,042	28,814
Percentage of total wealth	0	3.9	13.1	21.9	61.0

Note: Total wealth= $830,403; N = 136.

Table 12. Tennessee Soldiers' Home Inmates, by Date Admitted and Antebellum Wealth (in Percentages)

	Wealth Aggregate				
Date Admitted	$0	$1–1,000	$1,001–4,000	$4,001–10,000	$10,000+
1890–1900	39.4	36.4	9.1	6.0	9.1
1901–22	18.2	14.3	25.9	15.6	26.0

Note: Mean wealth for inmates admitted 1890–1900 = $3,766 and for those admitted 1901–22= $10,120; N =143.

Table 13. Marital Status of Confederate Soldiers' Home Inmates, by State (from Opening to 1922, in Percentages)

	Ga.	La.	N.C.	S.C.	Tenn.	Tex.	Va.	Mean
Single	27.2	47.9	11.2	42.1	22.1	20.8	51.7	31.8
Married	14.6	12.1	15.0	21.0	23.2	17.1	26.2	18.5
Widowed	58.2	40.0	73.7	36.8	54.7	62.1	22.1	49.7
N (1,621)	158	140	259	114	95	404	451	

Table 14. Tenure of Confederate Soldiers' Home Residents, by State and Admission Date (in Mean Years)

Admission Date	Ark.	Ga.	La.	N.C.	Tenn.	Tex.	Va.	Average
Before 1900	a	a	2.14	a	9.28	5.07	4.46	5.23
1901–11	a	5.64	5.21	a	6.08	5.96	2.37	5.05
1912–21	3.15	3.33	3.67	3.60	9.00	5.81	1.65	4.31
N (1,660)	59	158	212	181	143	404	503	

a. Insufficient data available.

Table 15. Percentage of Confederate Soldiers' Home Residents with Tenure of One Year or Less, by State and Admission Date

Admission Date	Ark.	Ga.	La.	N.C.	Tenn.	Tex.	Va.	Average
Before 1900	a	a	63.1	a	28.2	18.4	25.6	33.8
1901–11	a	29.5	40.0	a	52.3	20.1	35.2	35.4
1912–21	40.6	38.0	20.8	32.6	30.0	18.5	55.7	33.7
N (1,660)	59	158	212	181	143	404	503	

a. Insufficient data available.

Table 16. Mean Age of Soldiers' Home Inmates, by State and Year of Admission

Year Admitted	Ga.	La.	N.C.	Tenn.	Tex.	Va.
1901–11	66.0	62.1	a	67.9	70.5	66.0
1912–22	74.0	74.5	78.9	75.1	74.4	77.5
N (1,082)	158	98	228	72	261	265

a. Insufficient data available

Table 17. In- and Out-Migration by Lee Camp Soldiers' Home Inmates, 1907–11 and 1913–17

Year	Inmates Admitted	Inmates Out-Migrating	Net Gain (Loss)[a]	Total Enrolled
1907	88	90	(2)	275
1908	80	84	(4)	
1909	75	69	6	
1910	84	73	11	
1911	71	67	4	290
1913	87	99	(12)	281
1914	85	68	17	
1915	77	86	(9)	
1916	82	78	4	
1917	56	64	(8)	273
N, 1907–11	398	383	15	
Annual average, 1907–11	79.5	76.6		
N, 1913–17	387	395	(8)	
Annual average, 1913–17	77.4	79.0		

a. Includes deaths, dismissals, discharges, and transfers to asylums.

Figure 1. Birth Dates of Confederate Soldiers' Home Inmates in Texas and Virginia

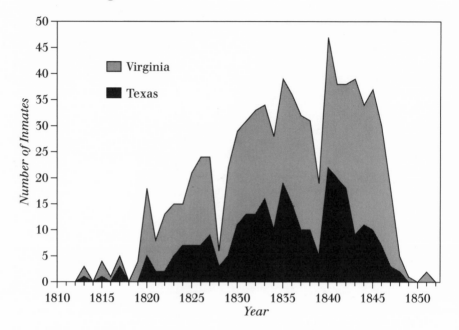

Figure 2. Estimated Average Enrollment in Confederate Soldiers' Homes, by State and Year

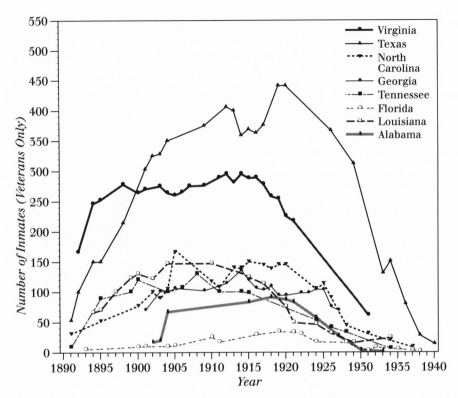

Figure 3. Number of Officers and Employees of Confederate Soldiers' Homes, by State and Year

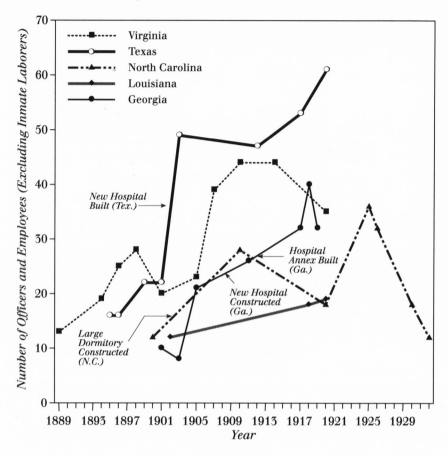

Figure 4. Estimated Public Appropriations for Confederate Soldiers' Homes, by State and Year Received

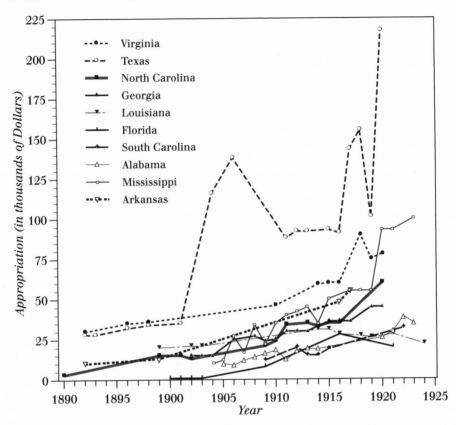

NOTES

Abbreviations

AA	Application for Admission
AAT	Association of the Army of Tennessee
AANV	Association of the Army of Northern Virginia
ArCH	Arkansas Confederate Home, Sweet Home
ArSA	Arkansas State Archives, Little Rock
Beauvoir	Beauvoir, the Jefferson Davis Memorial Shrine, Biloxi, Mississippi
CNSH	Camp Nicholls Soldiers' Home, New Orleans, Louisiana
Constitution	Atlanta *Constitution*
Con Vet	*Confederate Veteran*
GDAH	Georgia Department of Archives and History, Atlanta
GSH	Georgia Soldiers' Home, Atlanta
JDBMSH	Jefferson Davis Beauvoir Memorial Soldiers' Home, Biloxi, Mississippi
LCSH	Lee Camp Soldiers' Home, Richmond, Virginia
LHAC	Louisiana Historical Association Collection, Howard-Tilton Memorial Library, Tulane University, New Orleans, Louisiana
NCDAH	North Carolina Division of Archives and History, Raleigh
NCSH	North Carolina Soldiers' Home, Raleigh
SCCI	South Carolina Confederate Infirmary, Columbia
SCDAH	South Carolina Department of Archives and History, Columbia
TSH	Tennessee Soldiers' Home, Hermitage
TSLA	Tennessee State Library and Archives, Nashville
TxHM	Texas Home for Men, Austin
TxSA	Texas State Archives, Austin
USM	William D. McCain Library, University of Southern Mississippi, Hattiesburg
VHS	Virginia Historical Society, Richmond
VSL	Virginia State Library, Richmond

Preface

1. Edwards, *Road to Tara*, p. 287; *Constitution*, Dec. 13, 15–16, 1939; Hoar, *Last Boys in Gray*, pp. 187–90.

2. *Constitution*, May 23, 1890 (emphasis added).

Chapter 1

1. O'Connor, "A Late Encounter with the Enemy."

2. Cetina, "History of Veterans' Homes," pp. 10, 30, 48, 84, 122, 212. Ironically, as

president of the Confederacy, Davis in February 1864 vetoed on constitutional grounds an act establishing a national Confederate "Veteran Soldiers' Home." See *Journal of the Congress of the Confederate States of America*, 6:808–10.

3. Cetina, "History of Veterans' Homes." For a comparison, see also Goode, *United States Soldiers' Home*, and Bradley, *Veteran Care*, the latter of which concerns the southern branch of the National Homes for Disabled Volunteer Soldiers.

4. At its zenith the Wisconsin home consisted of 86 buildings and 167 employees to meet the needs of 423 veterans and widows. See Rood and Earle, *Wisconsin Veterans' Home*, pp. 33–34, 142.

5. For Virginia's home, see Williams, "'Home . . . for the Old Boys'"; for North Carolina's, Poole, "Final Encampment"; and for Oklahoma's, Lashley, "Oklahoma's Confederate Veterans Home."

6. Wilson, *Baptized in Blood*, p. 11.

7. Foster, *Ghosts of the Confederacy*, pp. 6–7.

8. Louisiana's (and the South's) first state-supported Confederate soldiers' home was chartered in March 1866. At that time a Democratic legislature—composed largely of former Confederate soldiers, merchants, and planters—was "easily persuaded" to appropriate $20,000 toward providing "shelter, food and clothing" for all indigent, wounded, and maimed soldiers who had served in Louisiana commands. Nowhere in the enabling act did the term "ex-Confederate" appear, though the measure was obviously intended to benefit the state's Civil War veterans, who were not otherwise eligible for federal pensions. After Governor J. Madison Wells signed into law Act No. 103, which chartered the home, he appointed eight members of the legislature (five of whom were ex-Confederate officers) to serve as a board of directors; the board made it clear from the outset that the planned institution was not a charity, but a "happy home" prepared by a proud and grateful people. Within a few months the board leased for purposes of the home the widow Doussan's Lake Shore Hotel, described as a "large and commodious" building, "healthily and pleasantly situated," overlooking Lake Pontchartrain, at Mandeville in St. Tammany Parish. Then a 2½ hour boat ride from New Orleans, the temporary home was fitted up with "every comfort," including "bathing houses and places of recreation." Soon work or "industrial departments" suited to the needs and abilities of the inmates were also added. Of the ninety-six inmates who eventually resided at the home, almost all were native Louisianians, and over half suffered from chronic disabilities. The home managed to receive an additional $10,000 in 1867, before a Republican-dominated government rescinded Act No. 103 in the following year. With no operating capital, the institution had to be abandoned. Some fifteen years of "pillage and humiliation of reconstruction and carpetbag rule" followed before Louisianians attempted to establish another Confederate home. New Orleans *Daily-Picayune*, Mar. 10, 11, 14, Apr. 6, May 4, 10, 26, 1866; Charlaron, "'Camp Nicholls,'" pp. 69–70. The phrase "easily persuaded" is from Coulter, *The South during Reconstruction*, pp. 352–53. Taylor, *Louisiana Reconstructed*, pp. 73, 82, 103, 174, discusses the Wells administration and the composition of the 1866 and 1868 legislatures. White, *Confederate Veteran*, p. 110, rehashes Charlaron's account. For the enabling legislation, see Loui-

siana *Acts* (1866), pp. 194, 196, 198. For a description of the home and its inmates, see *Goodspeed's Louisiana*, 1:266–68.

9. Although no complete published histories of either the AANV or AAT exist, the papers of these associations form the nucleus of the LHAC. For an introduction, see Hattaway, "United Confederate Veterans in Louisiana," pp. 5–7. Histories of the White League, on the other hand, are plentiful. For a sampling, see Landry, *Liberty Place*; Kendall, *History of New Orleans*, 1:359–75; Taylor, *Louisiana Reconstructed*, pp. 352–53; and Richardson, "Recollections." Richardson, who belonged to the Washington Artillery and the AAT, mentions other Confederate veterans who participated in the revolt. Landry, *Liberty Place*, pp. 234–40, provides a handy reference for cross-checking the names of other ex-Confederates against *Roll of the Association of the Army of Tennessee, Louisiana Division*. In "Southern Fraternal Organizations," p. 603, Sutherland points out that practically all fraternal societies of the period renounced political partisanship. In contrast, Dearing, *Veterans in Politics*, argues that Union veterans formed ostensibly charitable, but essentially political, organizations. McConnell, *Glorious Contentment*, adopts both interpretations. Although there is no evidence supporting the contention that either the AAT or the AANV volunteered as a unit for service in the White League, it is probable that both functioned as political pressure groups.

10. For references to the burial rituals of these and other associations, see Wilson, *Baptized in Blood*, pp. 28–29; White, *Confederate Veteran*, pp. 12, 20–22, 98–99, 103–4; and Foster, *Ghosts of the Confederacy*, p. 61. The quoted phrases come from the *Roll of the Association of the Army of Tennessee, Louisiana Division*, pp. 1–2.

11. Foster, *Ghosts of the Confederacy*, p. 242, determined the socioeconomic composition of the AAT. I have used his methodology to analyze the AANV. A list of 215 AANV members is available in *Roster, Louisiana Division, Army of Northern Virginia*. A search for each veteran's occupation in *Soard's New Orleans City Directory* revealed that more than two-thirds (71.4 percent) of the AANV members fall in Foster's top category (proprietary or professional). Among this group, 25 members practiced law, 34 owned mercantile establishments, 15 held city government positions, 17 were clergymen, and 22 practiced medicine, while 21 could not be found; fully one-half had been Confederate officers. This figure supports White, *Confederate Veteran*, p. 23, which asserts that former officers—especially "Generals and Colonels"—controlled Confederate veterans' organizations. When finally chartered in 1879, the AAT chose as its first president P. G. T. Beauregard, a former commander. *Roll of the Association of the Army of Tennessee, Louisiana Division*, pp. 1–2.

12. For a discussion of a number of yellow fever epidemics, including the terrible 1878 outbreak that ravaged New Orleans, see Duffy, *Medicine in Louisiana*, and Taylor, *Louisiana Reconstructed*, pp. 443–44. For Confederate veterans affected by the 1878 epidemic, consult the numerous letters contained in AAT Papers, Relief Committee Reports, LHAC. For example, see Philip Duffy to AAT, Aug. 11, 1878; John Curran to Relief Committee, Sept. 18, 1878; and Augustus Reichard to P. G. T. Beauregard, Sept. 20, 1878. The word "worthy" appears in William Kinney to AANV, Apr. 17, 1895, AANV Papers, Veterans Benefits, LHAC, and is used in reference to

relieving the "distress" of nonmembers. Confederate Veterans' Employment Bureau, *List of Applicants for Employment*, a palm-sized pamphlet printed by Gilmore's Sugar Planters publishing firm, contains the names of more than 200 individuals. For related correspondence, see J. Y. Gilmore to AANV, Oct. 12, 1895, AANV Papers, Veterans Benefits, LHAC; Gilmore et al. to The People of Louisiana, Nov. 16, 1895, and H. Dudley Coleman to AAT, May 11, 1897, both in AAT Papers, Veterans Benefits, LHAC. White, *Confederate Veteran*, p. 100, tells of a Nashville Confederate organization that sponsored an identical enterprise initiated in that city about the same time.

13. Under Act No. 69, Louisiana allocated $20,000 to purchase prostheses for "citizens" who had "lost limbs in Confederate service." By 1888 the law had been amended to award one-time, pro rata cash payments to veterans who had also lost their sight, hearing, voice, or mobility, provided that either the AAT or AANV verified the disability. Louisiana *Acts* (1880), pp. 65–66; (1882), p. 94; (1884), p. 56; (1886), pp. 212–13; (1888), pp. 23–24, 53–54; New Orleans *Times-Picayune*, Jan. 28, 1880. Georgia and North Carolina legislators enacted similar laws. See Georgia *Acts* (1878–79), pp. 41–42; (1880–81), p. 50; (1882–83), p. 44; (1884–85), p. 32; and White, *Confederate Veteran*, pp. 107–8. By 1886, under Act No. 69, 226 veterans and widows had been granted a total of 123,103 acres of public "swamp" land. Louisiana *Acts* (1884), pp. 123–24; (1886), pp. 213–15; (1896), pp. 90–91.

14. The Lee Camp charter is found in Virginia *Acts* (1884), pp. 521–22. The earliest record of the group administering relief is on Aug. 1, 1883, less than four months after its founding. See R. E. Lee Camp Records, Minutes, p. 39, VHS. For further references to the organization's establishment, see White, *Confederate Veteran*, pp. 22, 111; *Southern Historical Society Papers* 20 (1892): 316, 322; Foster, *Ghosts of the Confederacy*, pp. 93–94; and Williams, " 'Home . . . for the Old Boys,' " p. 40. A firsthand account of the origins of R. E. Lee Camp No. 1 is preserved in its Minutes, pp. 3–7, VHS, as well as in scattered issues of the Richmond *Times-Dispatch*, Apr. 6–19, 1883.

15. For Pollard's remarks, see "Tribute to the Late Gen. W. B. Taliaferro," *Con Vet* 8 (1900): 232–33. Pollard briefly served as commandant of LCSH (R. E. Lee Camp Records, Minutes, p. 12, VHS). Foster, *Ghosts of the Confederacy*, pp. 93, 242, analyzes the socioeconomic composition of the Lee Camp. I verified the occupations of members and officers in *Chataigne's Directory of Richmond*. Cooke, Lee, Wise, Ginter, and Pace served on the first executive board for the home. See LCSH, Board of Visitors, Minutes, VSL. In *Glorious Contentment*, McConnell demonstrates that the "typical" GAR camp derived its membership largely from white-collar, semiprofessional urban dwellers, much as the Lee Camp did.

16. Foster, *Ghosts of the Confederacy*, p. 242, also analyzes the socioeconomic composition of this veterans' society. Among the group's fourteen charter members, eight were merchants, two were lawyers, and two were physicians. Nashville Directory (1888); Wooldridge, *History of Nashville*, p. 564; Crew, *History of Nashville*, p. 566; *Minutes of the Second Convention of Confederate Soldiers*, pp. 4–5. For the society's strict eligibility requirements for membership, see *Con Vet* 2 (1894): 38.

17. For McMurray's background, consult Speer, *Prominent Tennesseans*, pp. 372–74. See also McMurray's *History of the Twentieth Tennessee Regiment*. Guild's history is

Fourth Tennessee Cavalry Regiment. Concerning Baskette, see Waller, *Nashville in the 1890s*, p. 239, and Nashville *Banner*, Sept. 7, 1889, for Baskette's censure of Anderson's work.

18. For Anderson's remarks, see his *Address.*

19. Baskette, a Confederate sergeant major, was a veteran of the campaigns of Shiloh, Vicksburg, Murfreesboro, Chickamauga, Dalton, and Atlanta. For Rector's comments, see Arkansas *Gazette*, May 9, 1889. For another panegyric to Johnny Reb, based on firsthand experience, see: "The Confederate Soldier," *Con Vet* 11 (1903): 322.

20. Wheeler to Jefferson M. Falkner, Dec. 29, 1902, quoted in Montgomery *Advertiser*, Jan. 4, 1903.

21. By the Johnny Reb "myth" is meant the complex mix of fact and distortion that comprised a particular attitude toward the Confederate common soldier. To many, Johnny Reb symbolized valor, obedience to duty, and self-sacrifice—true southern values. For a discussion of the myth's origins, its salient axioms, and its many expressions, see Stephen G. Davis, "Johnny Reb in Perspective." See also Foster, *Ghosts of the Confederacy* , pp. 122–26; White, *Confederate Veteran*, p. 37; Wilson, *Baptized in Blood*, pp. 37–54, 127, 189; and Vandiver, "The Confederate Myth."

Chapter 2

1. Rosenburg, *For the Sake of My Country*, p. 84. For a summary of Dawson's military career, see his Confederate Compiled Service Record, Record Group 109, National Archives, as well as his application for a Tennessee Confederate Pension, TSLA.

2. This assertion is based upon Livermore, *Numbers and Losses*, which estimated the number of three-year Confederate enlistees who survived the war to have been 928,822, and Bureau of the Census, "Soldiers and Widows," p. 593, which in 1890 reported 428,747 Confederate veterans, 46.2 percent of Livermore's 1865 total. Compare this percentage with Hesseltine, *Confederate Leaders*, p. 20, perhaps the earliest comprehensive attempt to treat the postwar careers of Confederate veterans. Among Hesseltine's 585 "leaders," only 281 (48 percent) survived until 1890. In "Southern Womanhood," pp. 97–98, Ruoff estimates that 31 percent of all Confederate veterans alive in 1890 had died by 1900. By 1928, the total number of survivors had dwindled to fewer than 26,000. *Con Vet* 36 (1928): 408–9.

3. In 1870 Dawson, a boarder and a farm laborer, possessed no material assets. A decade later he resided with a different family and listed "painter" as his occupation. His November 1895 TSH AA, TSLA, filled out and submitted by a former commander, bore Dawson's mark. Census (1870), Tenn., Smith, Dist. No. 14, p. 17; (1880), Dist. No. 1, p. 9.

4. For a discussion of the statistical methodology employed in compiling these and other analyses that appear throughout the work, see the Appendix.

5. For the relationship between self-reliance and "manliness," as well as the abhorrence of personal dependence, see Soltow, *Men and Wealth*, pp. 69–70; Klebaner, "Poverty and Its Relief"; and Wyllie, *Self-Made Man.* For veterans reluctant to accept

social welfare, see John O. Dean to W. Lowndes Calhoun, Jan. 14, 1901, GSH, Board of Trustees, Letters Received, GDAH; W. B. Taliaferro to Fitzhugh Lee, Aug. 19, 1887, and J. B. Clark to Lee, May 23, 1885, both in LCSH, Board of Visitors, Correspondence, VSL. See also Montgomery *Advertiser*, Apr. 27, 1902.

6. Livermore, *Numbers and Losses*, p. 63, provided the 1:5 estimate for all Confederate soldiers. For an explanation of the terminology and the analytical methodology used in the tabulation of veterans' disabilities by type and state, see the Appendix.

7. For Glynn's comments, see his letter to Fred A. Ober, June 16, 1886, AANV Papers, Membership, LHAC. For other disabled ex-Confederates requiring assistance in New Orleans, see P. M. McGrath to Joseph A. Charlaron, Sept. 12, 1882, Frank Herron to William Lambert, Jan. 15, 1883, Thomas Devine to Walter H. Rogers, Jan. 25, 1886, J. G. Blanchard to R. H. Brunet, May 9, 1887, and John M. Roberts to Nicholas Curry, Nov. 13, 1888, all in AAT Papers, Veterans Benefits, LHAC.

8. Roebuck, *My Own Personal Experience*, pp. 5–7; Montgomery *Advertiser*, June 22, July 1, 1902; Nathan J. Lewis to Managers of Confederate Soldiers Home, Feb. 3, 1885, Samuel V. Corbett to William H. Terry, Apr. 26, 1886, and S. J. Spindle to Secretary, R. E. Lee Camp, Aug. 30, 1885, all in LCSH, Board of Visitors, Correspondence, VSL. See also McNairy's TSH AA, TSLA, as well as the TSH AAs of Jesse C. McDaniel and H. B. Menees, who also suffered from physical ailments dating back to the war. For other veterans who moved westward after the war, only to encounter hardship and disappointment sometime later, see J. Medlock to James Hogg, Mar. 7, 1893, Hogg Papers, Governors Records, TxSA; A. L. Slack to James W. Pegram, June 1, 1891, and N. E. Edmundo to Charles U. Williams, June 17, 1883, both in LCSH, Board of Visitors, Correspondence, VSL; the AAs of Charles T. Clifford and Henry C. Nelson, TSH, TSLA; and Hiram Sample to Fred A. Ober, Nov. 12, 1911, AANV Papers, Veterans Benefits, LHAC.

9. See the TSH AAs of Hale, Toon, Fry, and Karr, TSLA. See also Census (1860), Tenn., Hawkins, Rogersville, 19; Maury, Mt. Pleasant, 31; McMinn, Sweetwater, 1; Williamson, Franklin, 30; (1870), Davidson, 10th Ward, Nashville, 509; Monroe, 1st Dist., Sweetwater, 13; Williamson, Franklin, 128.

10. For New Orleans veterans rendered ill and impoverished by the yellow fever epidemic, see the nearly one hundred documents contained in AAT Papers, Relief Committee Reports, LHAC, for the years 1878 through 1883, as well as those contained in the AANV Papers, Relief Committee Reports, LHAC, for the same period. For Saucier, see the letter from John Curran, Sept. 18, 1878, AANV Papers, Relief Committee Reports, LHAC. Boden's TSH AA, mentions the loss of his wife and children, TSLA. For Caylat's plight, see his letters to J. R. Richardson, Oct. 7, 1881, AANV Papers, Veterans Benefits, LHAC, and to Louis A. Adam, Aug. 10, 1886, AANV Papers, Membership, LHAC.

11. Regarding Holt, see J. A. Johnson to William H. Terry, Aug. 17, 1892, and J. S. Beasley to Terry, Aug. 17, 1892, both in Holt's LCSH AA, VSL. For Reese, see his letters to William H. Harrison, Nov. 20, 1911, to Horatio W. Bell, Jan. 4, 1912, and to the Georgia Board of Trustees, Nov. 29, 1911, all in GSH, Board of Trustees, Minutes, GDAH.

12. Montgomery *Advertiser*, June 22, July 18, 1902. Booth was not alone: in 1902 an

estimated one hundred Confederate veterans resided in Alabama's poorhouses. Montgomery *Advertiser*, June 5, 1902.

13. John M. DeSaussure to Thomas B. O'Brien, June 28, 1893, AANV Papers, Veterans Benefits, LHAC; William E. Todd to AAT, Aug. 11, 1889, F. A. Biers to Nicholas Curry, Aug. 28, 1889, Todd to Phillip Power, Aug. 29, 1908, all in AAT Papers, Veterans Benefits, LHAC. For Belcher, see his TSH AA, TSLA.

14. See Vaughn's TSH AA, TSLA. Regarding Clements, see his letter to James McGraw, June 17, 1895, R. E. Lee Camp Records, Correspondence, VHS. For Moore, see his letters of Aug. 26, 1880, June 6, 1881, and Oct. 7, 1887, all in AANV Papers, Veterans Benefits, LHAC. For Moore's military service record in the Fifth Louisiana Infantry, see Booth, *Louisiana Confederate Soldiers*, 2:1028. For other veterans who lost their jobs for one reason or another, see H. V. Ottmann to AAT, Apr. 10, 1883, N. T. U. Robinson to James Lingan, May 23, 1878, and A. S. Herbert to T. R. Juden, Aug. 11, 1900, all in AAT Papers, Veterans Benefits, LHAC. See also Daniel C. Hill's LCSH AA, VSL.

15. The unbroken chain analogy has been derived from Auriel Arnard to Walter H. Rogers, Nov. 14, 1887, CNSH, Board of Directors, Correspondence, LHAC. The assertion that half of all Confederates had been farmers is based upon Wiley, *Life of Johnny Reb*, p. 330. Evidence that these same men had more than likely held little or no property on the eve of the war has been provided in numerous works. See, among others, Escott, *Many Excellent People*; Campbell and Lowe, *Wealth and Power*; Hahn, *Roots of Southern Populism*; Ash, *Middle Tennessee*; and Shifflett, *Patronage and Poverty*.

16. Soltow, *Men and Wealth*, p. 65. Of course, total estate figures varied. For example, in East Tennessee the average per capita wealth in 1860 was $2,812, while in West Tennessee mean antebellum wealth was $17,090. Ash, *Middle Tennessee*, p. 11.

17. This unequal distribution of wealth is similar to the one Ash discovered for families residing in antebellum Middle Tennessee, where nearly two-thirds of the present sample lived. Ash, *Middle Tennessee*, pp. 42–44, found that 49 percent of the people in that region owned 90 percent of the wealth in 1860.

18. Bailey, *Tennessee's Confederate Generation*, p. 160.

19. Of Bailey's 188 men from "elite" families, 66.5 percent held the rank of private, while 19.1 percent were officers.

20. Montgomery *Advertiser*, Feb. 9, 1904.

21. For an introduction to the vast literature chronicling the postwar struggles of southern farmers, see Wright, *Cotton South*; Magdol and Wakelyn, *Southern Common People*, pt. 2; and Reid, "White Land, Black Labor."

22. For the impact of low socioeconomic status on physical capacity and body weight, especially among the aged, see Goodman, "Problems of Malnutrition"; Dovenmuele, Busse, and Newman, "Physical Problems of Older People"; 208–17; Richard J. Anderson, "Medical Diagnoses"; Rao, "Problems of Nutrition"; and Riley, *Aging*.

23. For these veterans, see their TSH AAs, TSLA. For additional information on Young, see his autobiographical sketch provided in Elliott and Moxley, *Tennessee Civil War Questionnaires*, 5:2260–61. For Denton's and Nance's prewar economic status, see

Census (1860), Tenn., Maury, Spring Hill, 151; Bedford, Shelbyville, 37. See also Wade's obituary, *Con Vet* 20 (1912): 241.

24. Of the forty-one farmers in the sample (Appendix, Table 8), 25 (61 percent) applied for admission between 1889 and December 1900. TSH, Register of Inmates, TSLA, lists Bonner, a former private in the Eighth Tennessee Infantry, as the first inmate admitted. Bonner's socioeconomic status may be traced in Census (1860), Tenn., Bedford, Shelbyville, 199; (1870), 380; and his TSH AA, dated Dec. 19, 1889, TSLA. Bonner obtained a discharge from the home in August 1894. A bachelor and a physician, Maney served briefly as a hospital steward during the war. See his TSH AA, TSLA, and Census (1860), Tenn., Williamson, Franklin, 32.

25. Roe had been wounded in the left knee at Shiloh, in the wrist at Selma, in the right hip at Brice's Crossroads, and in the groin on retreat from Corinth. When applying for admission, he estimated his total estate amounted to $25.00, which was precisely the same amount he had reported on the eve of the war. Census (1860), Tenn., Tipton, Covington, 10.

26. Fully 40 percent of the married and widowed Tennessee veterans in the sample had no children. The large number of single veterans far exceeded national population averages. For example, between 1890 and 1930 the percentage of all males (age fifty-five and over) who had never married ranged from a low of only 5.6 percent in 1890 to a high of 10.1 percent in 1930. The percentage of widowed Tennessee veterans was nearly two times the national average of 23.3 percent in 1890 and 27.1 percent in 1910 for all men sixty-five years and older. Thompson and Whelpton, *Population Trends*, p. 204. Being single or being a widower, both of which could threaten economic independence, appear to have acted as trigger mechanisms for home admission. See Ward, "The Never-Married in Later Life," and Turner, "Personality Traits." For the possibility that veterans may have suffered from acute delayed stress after the Civil War, see Dean, "'We Will All Be Lost.'" For a statistical analysis of inmate tenure and mortality rates in the various homes, see the Appendix

27. See the veterans' TSH AAs, TSLA. See also Nevins's Tennessee Confederate Pension Application, TSLA, and Vinson's sketch in Elliot and Moxley, *Tennessee Civil War Questionnaires*, 5:2110–12. Before the war each of the families in question owned more than $10,000 worth of assets, including slaves. Census (1860), Tenn., Rutherford, Smyrna, 53; Haywood, Brownsville, 47; Sumner, Gallatin, 22; (1870), Rutherford, Murfreesboro, 264; Haywood, Brownsville, 387; Sumner, Gallatin, 749. See also John H. Cocke to John P. Hickman, May 7, 1895, accompanying Whitmore's TSH AA, and R. P. McClain to Hickman, June 16, 1909, attached to Scobey's TSH AA, both in TSLA. See also Census (1860), Tenn., Wilson, Green Hill, 46; Fayette, Somerville, 70; (1870), Wilson, Green Hill, 354; Fayette, Somerville, 293.

28. From an undated newspaper clipping, Beauvoir.

Chapter 3

1. For contemporary descriptions of the meeting, see the New York *Sun*, New York *Tribune*, and New York *Times*, Apr. 10, 1884.

2. For background information on Gordon, see Eckert, *John Brown Gordon*. Regarding Gordon's affiliation with the Virginia home, see Gordon to Charles U. Williams, Apr. 7, 1884, and William H. Clarke to Williams, Dec. 20, 1884, LCSH, Board of Visitors, Correspondence, VSL.

3. Concerning Blue-Gray reunions, see Buck, *Road to Reunion*, pp. 135–39, 246, 256–60, and Foster, *Ghosts of the Confederacy*, pp. 67–68. For the particular reunion that may have contributed to the founding of the Virginia home, see Benson, *"Yank" and "Reb."* See also "The Confederate Soldiers Home of Richmond, Va.," *Con Vet* 34 (1926): 411–12.

4. Regarding Tanner, see Dearing, *Veterans in Politics*, pp. 327, 362, 379, 392–96, 432, and Smith, *A Famous Battery*, pp. 179–216. For portions of Tanner's speech, see the New York *Sun* and New York *Tribune*, Apr. 10, 1884. See also Williams, "'Home . . . for the Old Boys,'" p. 41; Corporal James Tanner to Capt. Arthur A. Spitzer, Aug. 3, 1884, LCSH, Board of Visitors, Correspondence, VSL; and R. E. Lee Camp Records, Minutes, p. 133, VHS.

5. New York *Sun* and New York *Tribune*, Apr. 10, 1884. On the speaker's platform also sat Generals Floyd King of Louisiana and George Sheridan, who spoke that night. For a sketch of the reunion medal, see James Tanner to W. C. Carrington, Apr. 28, 1884, R. E. Lee Camp Records, Correspondence, VHS.

6. The New York Soldiers' Home had sponsored a benefit in the Academy of Music seven years earlier. Cetina, "History of Veterans' Homes," p. 218. For the Virginia home fund-raising galas, see James Tanner to W. C. Carrington, Apr. 28, 1884, R. E. Lee Camp Records, Correspondence, VHS; William H. Clarke to Charles U. Williams, Dec. 20, 1884, LCSH, Board of Visitors, Correspondence, VSL; and Smith, *A Famous Battery*, p. 194.

7. For a sampling of contributions received, see Thomas Pearson [Newark, N.J.] to R. E. Lee Camp, Oct. 23, 1883, M. A. Dillon [Washington, D.C.] to Sir, Dec. 29, 1883, Charles Robinson [Davenport, Iowa] to Post of Confederate Soldiers, July 22, 1883, H. C. Kessler [Butte, Mont.] to W. C. Carrington, Mar. 30, 1884, Charles Spenser [Richmond] to Arthur A. Spitzer, May 15, 1885, J. Kling [Sing Sing, N.Y.] to R. E. Lee Camp, May 11, 1887, Washington [D.C.] Aid Association to Captain Charles U. Williams, Dec. 13, 1884, and C. A. DeFrance [St. Louis] to Williams, Dec. 12, 1884, all in LCSH, Board of Visitors, Correspondence, VSL; and C. A. Spencer [Grand Junction, Colo.] to R. E. Lee Camp, Feb. 24, 1885, R. E. Lee Camp Records, Correspondence, VHS. See also Williams, "'Home . . . for the Old Boys,'" p. 41; Foster, *Ghosts of the Confederacy*, pp. 61, 94; and *Con Vet* 34 (1926): 411–12. For nearly three consecutive weeks in May 1884, a hundred ex-Confederate wives, widows, and daughters held a bazaar in the Richmond armory. The ladies eagerly collected more than $30,000 in receipts for the home. For references to the work of the "Fair" committee that organized this bazaar, see R. E. Lee Camp Records, Minutes, pp. 92, 96, 124, 131, VHS. See also *Southern Historical Society Papers* 12 (1884): 238–39, and 20 (1892): 316; and *Constitution*, Apr. 9, 1889. Not all gifts were accepted, however. For example, see the entry in R. E. Lee Camp Records, Minutes, VHS, for May 7, 1885, in which "Professor King," a balloonist, proposed to make an "ascension" for the benefit of the home. The next words read, "Motion tabled."

8. Fitzhugh Lee to Arthur A. Spitzer, Aug. 13, 1884, and Charles U. Williams to A. S. Venable, Feb. 22, 1885, both in LCSH, Board of Visitors, Correspondence, VSL; *Southern Historical Society Papers* 20 (1900): 316; LCSH, Board of Visitors, Minutes, 1:62, VSL.

9. At one point in his keynote address, General Gordon had referred to the home as an "enduring monumen[t] to real peace and real union." New York *Sun*, May 3, 1884. Archer Anderson, *Address*, pp. 3–12. Five years later Anderson, a member of the Lee Memorial Association, delivered the commemorative address at the unveiling of Robert E. Lee's statue on Richmond's Monument Avenue, before an estimated 150,000 people. Foster, *Ghosts of the Confederacy*, p. 101. The Lee Camp Home operated on voluntary contributions for two years, until the state assumed control.

10. Georgetown *Weekly Times*, July 13, Nov. 30, 1881; Nov. 14, 1883; Confederate Soldiers' Home, Subscribers to the Confederate Soldiers' Home and Widows' and Orphans' Asylum," Kentucky State Archives, Frankfort; *Southern Historical Society Papers* 11 (1883): 432.

11. *Con Vet* 10 (1902): 254, 385, 558–61; 16 (1908): 466; 18 (1910): 261.

12. "Confederate Monuments," *Con Vet* 1 (1893): 7; Col. J. A. Charlaron, "Louisiana Soldiers' Home," CNSH, Board of Directors *Report* (1902), pp. 71–72, LHAC. AAT Papers, Minutes, 2:65–68, 136–37, LHAC. The idea for a home may have originated with Union veterans who had recently visited New Orleans during a Blue-Gray Memorial Day celebration. Foster, *Ghosts of the Confederacy*, pp. 67–68, describes the reunion and, pp. 109–10, provides a sketch of Charlaron, who is also featured in Hattaway, "Clio's Southern Soldiers," pp. 216–17.

13. Col. J. A. Charlaron, "Louisiana Soldiers' Home," CNSH, Board of Directors *Report* (1902), pp. 71–72, LHAC; AAT Papers, Minutes, 2:71, LHAC. For Leake's arguments, see CNSH, Clippings and Pamphlets, LHAC. One of Leake's colleagues, the bill's co-sponsor, Senator Robert S. Perry of New Iberia, called Leake "devoted and gallant." See Perry's letter to Charlaron, July 22, 1882, AAT Papers, Correspondence, LHAC. Leake probably would have favored a law based upon the Georgia act that empowered each county to provide $100 per year for every resident who had lost a limb in the "defense of the South" and who possessed less than $1,000 of taxable property. Ten years later state lawmakers dropped the latter requirement. Georgia *Laws* (1875), pp. 107–8; (1885), p. 112.

14. There already exists an enormous literature that discusses changing American attitudes toward social welfare. Katz, *In the Shadow of the Poorhouse*, is particularly informative. For southern attitudes, Wisner, *Social Welfare in the South*, and Bellows, "Tempering the Wind," are useful. In the 1860s and 1870s, some northern reformers objected to the establishment of a national asylum and state-supported veterans' homes in their region for, ostensibly, the same reasons as Leake and other southern conservatives. See Cetina, "History of Veterans Homes." See also McConnell, *Glorious Contentment*, pp. 153–65 for indications that some Union veterans shared Leake's opposition to soldiers' homes and pensions on the grounds that they would threaten a veteran's autonomy and manliness. Proponents dealt successfully with these worries by arguing that relief fulfilled the terms of the nation's "sacred contract" with her veterans.

15. Col. J. A. Charlaron, "Louisiana Soldiers' Home," CNSH, Board of Directors

Report (1902), pp. 70, 75, LHAC. For negative attitudes toward pensions, see Wilson, *Baptized in Blood*, pp. 82–83; *Con Vet* 6 (1898): 473–74; 7 (1899): 25; 16 (1908): 81; and *Constitution*, Apr. 10, 1889. The phrases attributed to Gilmore and Coleman can be found on the first page of Confederate Veterans' Employment Bureau, *List of Applicants for Employment*. For a copy of the AAT's July 1882 resolution censuring Leake, see Thomas Papers, William R. Perkins Library, Duke University, Durham, N.C. For Leake's response to the New Orleans veterans' societies—in which he did not hold membership—see his letter to Charlaron, July 13, 1882, Charlaron Papers, LHAC. Foster, *Ghosts of the Confederacy*, pp. 24–35, argues that ex-Confederates remained highly concerned about honor and masculinity, vital components of a traditional value system discussed in Wyatt-Brown, *Southern Honor*.

16. Senator Perry of New Iberia called "maimed and infirm" veterans "living monuments." See his letter to Charlaron cited in note 13 above. For Augustin's remarks, see his report to the AAT, Sept. 11, 1883, AAT Papers, Minutes, 2:123, 138–39, LHAC. Governor Foster's message appears in Louisiana *House Journal* (1900), p. 11. The final quoted phrases are those of Fred A. Ober, AANV vice-president, in his letter to Peter J. Trezevant, Louisiana House clerk, May 29, 1886, AANV Papers, Correspondence, LHAC.

17. Louisiana *Acts* (1882), p. 73. The House approved the measure (62-3) and the Senate voted in favor (27-5). Louisiana *House Journal* (1882), p. 409; Louisiana *Senate Journal* (1882), p. 293. The overwhelming support of the bill came at a time when Bourbon Democrats actively promoted a program of fiscal retrenchment. See Hair, *Bourbonism and Agrarian Protest.* Levy's statement is found in his letter to AANV, Oct. 14, 1911, AANV Papers, Veterans Benefits, LHAC. In the end, Louisiana's constitution had to be formally amended in order to accommodate the soldiers' home. Louisiana Constitution (1898), Art. XVIII, Sec. 1.

18. *Confederate Gray Book*; Austin *Daily Statesman*, Dec. 10, 1884; Austin *Confederate Drummer*, Sept. 1886; *Southern Bivouac* 3 (1885): 220. See also the accounts by charter members Fred Carleton in Houston *Chronicle*, Feb. 20, 1944, and Henry E. Shelley in a letter to Col. Henry C. Lindsey, Nov. 23, 1898, Lindsey Papers, Barker Texas History Center, University of Texas, Austin.

19. For the camp's fund-raising efforts, see the broadside describing the "Grand Gift Concert and Drawing" (Austin Public Library, Austin, Tex.) that took place in Austin, featuring locally prominent musicians and singers and a raffle of more than 2,000 donated prizes. Previously postponed because of low ticket sales blamed on "drought and other disasters," the long-awaited gala of December 1886 generated about $11,000. Austin *Confederate Drummer*, Sept. 1886; Austin *Daily Statesman*, Dec. 27, 1886; Frank Brown, "Annals of Travis County," 30:103, TxSA; and Lasswell, *Rags and Hope*, pp. 7–8. For the home's purchase, opening, and formal dedication, see Henry E. Shelley, "The Confederate Home for Texas," *Con Vet* 6 (1896): 156–57; Austin *Record*, Mar. 12, 1887; Austin *Daily Statesman*, Nov. 1, 1888; and John B. Armstrong and wife to Hood Camp, Feb. 19, 1886, Texas Statutory Documents, Deeds, Abstracts and Cessions of Jurisdiction, State Eleemosynary Institutions, TxSA.

20. Texas Constitution (1876), Art III, Sec. 51.

21. For Confederate veterans dominating Texas politics, see White, *Confederate Veteran*, pp. 83–86. For Harrison's enabling bill, see Raines, *Year Book for Texas, 1901*, p. 54. Texas *House Journal* (1881), pp. 151–52, contains the final vote for the artificial limbs bill and Carleton's stated objection. Concerning the land certificate bill, see Gammel, *Laws*, 9:122, and Miller, "Texas Land Grants."

22. Raines, *Year Book for Texas, 1901*, pp. 54–55; Gammel, *Laws*, 9:138. For Ross, who later served as president of Texas A&M University, see Benner, *Sul Ross*, pp. 185–86. Benner argues that Ross, symbol of the Lost Cause, pushed for economic modernization of Texas and sectional cooperation.

23. The portion of Ross's biennial message to the legislature that concerned the home is found in Texas *House Journal* (1891), pp. 49–50. For Texas ex-Confederate involvement in the election of 1890, see Raines, *Year Book for Texas, 1901*, p. 56; "The Confederate Home in Austin before the Turn of the Century," Texas Confederate Museum, Austin; and Frank Brown, "Annals of Travis County," 30:103–10, TxSA. For Hogg's statements, see Raines, *Year Book for Texas, 1901*, p. 56, and Texas *House Journal* (1891), pp. 110–11.

24. The circuitous path the bill took, after Terrell read it for the first time on January 23, may be followed in Texas *House Journal* (1891), pp. 134–36, 319, 334, 336–39; Texas *Senate Journal* (1891), pp. 211, 217, 232, 238–39; *House Journal* (1891), pp. 398, 416; *Senate Journal* (1891), pp. 255–56, 264; and *House Journal*, (1891), pp. 419, 438. See Gammel, *Laws*, 10:14–17, for the final product, its approval date, and the voting margins. See also Raines, *Year Book for Texas, 1901*, p. 56.

25. Article III, Sec. 51, of the Texas Constitution was amended another eight times over the course of the next seventy-three years. For example, in 1910 the maximum appropriation for the Confederate home was increased from $100,000 to $150,000 annually. The other seven changes related to Confederate pensions, which were first granted in 1898 under the same constitutional provision that had legalized the home. Texas *House Journal* (1895), pp. 324, 358, 423–24, 562, 584–85, 602, 606, 616, 623; Gammel, *Laws*, 10:42–44.

26. Col. J. A. Charlaron, "Louisiana Soldiers' Home," CNSH, Board of Directors *Report* (1902), p. 73, LHAC.

27. Ibid.; *Goodspeed's Louisiana*, 1:147–48; Casey, *Encyclopedia*, pp. 141–42, 262; *Southern Bivouac* 2 (1884): 508–11. A broadside dated Aug. 9, 1883, addressed to the state's police juries can be found in CNSH, Board of Directors, Correspondence, LHAC. The lottery—a contrivance Nicholls considered anathema "to true southern values," according to Wilson, *Baptized in Blood*, p. 89—and the sham battle are described in John Augustin's letter to the AAT, Aug. 14, 1883, AAT Papers, Executive Committee Reports, LHAC; New Orleans *Times-Democrat*, Sept. 16–17, 1883; AAT Papers, Minutes, 2:118, 123, 128, LHAC; Col. J. A. Charlaron, "Louisiana Soldiers' Home," CNSH, Board of Directors *Report* (1902), pp. 74–75, LHAC; and White, *Confederate Veteran*, 94. New Orleans was not alone among southern cities in having a GAR post; Union veterans tended to establish posts wherever they settled after the war, so that New South cities such as Nashville, Richmond, Atlanta, and Chattanooga, as well as New Orleans, were home to GAR organizations and activities.

28. Casey, *Encyclopedia*, p. 142; *Goodspeed's Louisiana*, 1:148; Col. J. A. Charlaron, "Louisiana Soldiers' Home," CNSH, Board of Directors *Report* (1902), pp. 74–75, LHAC; White, *Confederate Veteran*, p. 110; *Southern Historical Society Papers* 28 (1900): 229, 231–36.

29. Civil War Papers, Wharton J. Green Scrapbook, p. 369, NCDAH; "A Confederate Movement," Charlotte *Home-Democrat*, May 23, 1884. For information on Carr, see Webb, *Jule Carr*. See also the article in *Con Vet* 6 (1898): 234, which addresses Carr's specific involvement with the North Carolina home. Section 3 of the charter for the Confederate Veterans Association of North Carolina—as documented in North Carolina *Laws*, (1889), p. 683—permitted the group to found "a home or homes for indigent, infirm and invalid Confederate soldiers and sailors, or their widows and orphans." Carr was among the incorporators. Regarding what was probably the very first effort at forming a statewide association of Confederate veterans, in October 1881, see the description of the establishment of the North Carolina Society of Ex-Confederate Soldiers and Sailors in Green's Scrapbook, p. 368, and the handwritten constitution of the society in Polk Papers, NCDAH.

30. For a sketch of the work of the Ladies Memorial Association, which included several Confederate veterans as officers and advisers, see the clipping from Raleigh *Daily Call*, May 10, 1889, the undated article, "The Narrative of a Half Century of Faithful Work," written by Fred A. Olds for the Raleigh *News and Observer*, and the society's Minutes, all in Wake County Ladies Memorial Association Papers, NCDAH. Imitating the Lee Camp, the group sponsored a four-day Confederate military bazaar, which netted about $2,000 for the home project. See Jones, "Ladies Memorial Association," Wake County Ladies Memorial Association Papers, NCDAH; "Home for Old Confeds in Carolina a Great Success," *Constitution*, Jan. 6, 1901; and Poole, "Final Encampment," p. 12. A clipping pasted inside the cover of the scattered and incomplete NCSH, Board of Incorporators, Minutes, NCDAH, and the *Roster of Inmates of the Soldiers' Home, Raleigh*, treat the rental home, which has since been moved to 415 East Street. See also Olds, "History of the Soldiers' Home at Raleigh," which discusses the historic significance of Pettigrew Hospital, the home site. The names of the eighty-eight members of the Confederate Veterans Association of North Carolina who incorporated the Soldiers' Home Association of North Carolina, as well as the purpose of the organization, are provided in North Carolina *Laws* (1891), pp. 793–96. The list included many of the same individuals associated with the North Carolina Confederate Home Association in 1884. For the legislature's handling and approval of the act founding the Soldiers' Home Association, see North Carolina *Senate Journal* (1891), pp. 179, 227, 241, 265, 268, 271, 380, and North Carolina *House Journal* (1891), pp. 272, 292, 327, 371. For Carr's recollection, see his handwritten letter to the Raleigh *News and Observer*, c. Sept. 1902, Carr Papers, Southern Historical Collection, Wilson Library, University of North Carolina, Chapel Hill.

31. NCSH, Board of Incorporators, Minutes, NCDAH; Poole, "Final Encampment," p. 12; Connor, *Manual of North Carolina*, p. 166; Daniel G. Fowle to Samuel A. Ashe, Mar. 25, 1891, Fowle Papers, NCDAH; William C. Stronach to Alfred M. Scales, July 17, 1891, Scales Papers, NCDAH. Beasley served as president of the North Carolina

Confederate Home Association until his resignation in April 1886, after "earnest efforts" at fund-raising proved unsuccessful. Other directors elected were Senator Matt Ransom, Judge Thomas Fuller, and railroad executive Alexander B. Andrews.

32. For information on Rothrock, see Evans, *Confederate Military History*, 8:690–91.

33. Benjamin F. Cheatham Bivouac Minutes, 1:33, TSLA. For a published report of the meeting, see Nashville *Banner*, Nov. 3, 1888. Mark Cockrill and Mrs. John P. Hickman also produced their own versions of the meeting. See Cockrill's story in the Nashville *Banner*, May 13, 1892, and Hickman's paper presented to the historical committee, UDC, as reprinted in Nashville *Banner*, Mar. 7, 1908. The Nashville City Directory (1888) listed the men's occupations and Rothrock's multiple posts.

34. The first public announcement of the bill appeared in the Nashville *Banner*, Jan. 30, 1889. See also Nashville *Daily American*, Feb. 9, 1889. The quoted phrases have been extracted from the measure's final version, as found in Tennessee *Acts* (1889), pp. 342–44.

35. The first pension measure, signed by Governor William B. Bate, provided $10.00 per month until death to any Tennessee ex-Confederate who had lost his vision "while engaged in battle." Tennessee *Acts* (1888), pp. 323–24. The second program increased the monthly allotment to $25.00 and extended entitlement to limbless veterans. Tennessee *Acts* (1887), pp. 105–6. The computations for the political affiliations in the General Assembly may be found in White and Ash, *Messages of the Governors of Tennessee*, 8:283. See McBride, *Biographical Directory*, for each member's Confederate background.

36. Memphis *Daily Appeal*, as quoted in the Nashville *Banner*, Jan. 7, 1889. For other editorials concerning the project, see the debate and final vote coverage in the Nashville *Daily American*, Mar. 16, 1889; Nashville *Banner*, Mar. 29, 1889; Chattanooga *Daily Times*, Mar. 16, 1889; Knoxville *Journal*, Mar. 30, 1889; and Memphis *Daily Appeal*, Mar. 25, 1889. White and Ash, *Messages of the Governors of Tennessee*, 7:221, 344, reproduces Taylor's eulogy.

37. The legislative wrangling and maneuvering over the bill, from first reading to final vote, may be followed in Tennessee *Senate Journal* (1889), pp. 196, 215, 413–15, 513, and Tennessee *House Journal* (1889), pp. 557, 588, 671, 684–87, 729, 731, 754, 757. See also the newspaper accounts cited in note 36 above. For an earlier, aborted attempt by a group of Tennessee lawmakers to convert the Hermitage into a home for Mexican-American War veterans, see Tennessee *Senate Journal* (1885), p. 439; Nashville *Daily American*, Mar. 18, 1885; and Rutland, "Captain William B. Walton," pp. 177–78.

38. Dorris, *Preservation of the Hermitage*, p. 22.

39. The first quoted material is from a letter, signed by "Jackson," in Nashville *Banner*, Jan. 7, 1889. Original members of the Ladies Hermitage Association are listed in *Constitution*, Apr. 26, 1889, and Wooldridge, *History of Nashville*, pp. 566–67. The account of the compromise meeting between the Ladies Hermitage Association and Cheatham Bivouac representatives is based on the article that appeared in Nashville *Banner*, Jan. 12, 1889. For a review of the controversy, see Nashville *Banner*, Mar. 7,

1908; Horn, *The Hermitage*, pp. 44–45; Nashville *Tennessean Magazine*, Jan. 3, 1954; and Dorris, *Preservation of the Hermitage*, pp. 44–46.

40. Benjamin F. Cheatham Bivouac Minutes, 2:60–63, TSLA. The House voted on the measure four separate times, the Senate only once. By "consistent supporter" is meant someone who cast his vote in favor of the Crews bill each time. For the final House vote (57-33), see Tennessee *House Journal* (1889), p. 731. For the Senate tally (21-8), see Tennessee *Senate Journal* (1889), p. 513. Background information for the 119 Tennessee lawmakers who deliberated the bill's fate is available in McBride, *Biographical Directory*.

41. Tennessee *Acts* (1889), p. 344. For Moody's speech, see Nashville *Daily American*, Mar. 16, 1889. Fort's comments are available in Knoxville *Journal*, Mar. 30, 1889. The argument by Morris, a former Nashville mayor, is in Nashville *Banner*, Mar. 29, 1889, and Nashville *Daily American*, Mar. 30, 1889. Pyott's explanation appears in Nashville *Banner*, Mar. 15, 1889, and Chattanooga *Daily Times*, Mar. 16, 1889. For David R. Nelson, the East Tennessee senator representing Blount, Monroe, and Roane counties, see Nashville *Banner*, Mar. 15, 1889.

42. Tennessee *Senate Journal* (1891), pp. 173–74.

43. For a sketch of Garrett, a Confederate partisan ranger who later taught history at Peabody College and edited the *American Historical Magazine*, see Evans, *Confederate Military History*, 8:492–95.

44. The account of the ceremony is based largely on a story in Nashville *Banner*, May 13, 1892.

45. For more information regarding the careers of these men, see Donovan and Gatewood, *Governors of Arkansas*, pp. 86–90; Herndon, *Centennial History of Arkansas*, 1:435, 3:853–54; and Hempstead, *Historical Review of Arkansas*, 1:312. For coverage of the initial and subsequent meetings, see *Con Vet* 31 (1923): 48; Arkansas *Gazette*, May 4, 1889, Aug. 7, 1892; and Gaither, *Arkansas Confederate Home*, p. 2.

46. Arkansas *Gazette*, May 9, 1889.

47. Arkansas *House Journal* (1891), p. 252. Gaither, *Arkansas Confederate Home*, pp. 2–3; *Con Vet* 31 (1923): 48; Lea, "Personal Recollections," p. 28; Herndon, *Centennial History of Arkansas*, p. 435.

48. Thomas, *Arkansas and Its People*, 1:235; Roberts and Moneyhon, *Portraits of Conflict*, p. 212; Arkansas *Gazette*, July 5, 7, 17, Aug. 4, Sept. 4, 1889, July 31, Aug. 6, 15, 24, 1890, Aug. 5, Sept. 27, 1891, Aug. 7, 12, 1892; Herndon, *Centennial History of Arkansas*, p. 436.

49. William Baya to Albert J. Russell, Aug. 16, 1892, Florida Soldiers' Home Papers, Jacksonville Public Library, Jacksonville, Fla.; Russell, *Life and Labors*, pp. 268–72, 279, 283; Florida *Laws* (1893), pp. 191–92; *Con Vet* 1 (1893): 63; T. Frederick Davis, *History of Jacksonville*, p. 198; Florida *Times-Union*, Apr. 7, 1892.

50. Maryland *Laws* (1888), p. 338; *Maryland Line Confederate Soldiers' Home*; Baltimore *American*, June 28, 1888. See also *Con Vet* 2 (1894): 9–10, 17–19, 41–43, 83–84, 364–66; 34 (1926): 90–91.

51. *Con Vet* 1 (1893): 25, 258, 302; 5 (1897): 179–80; 36 (1928): 299–301.

52. W. L. Peters to James W. White, May 3, 1888, R. E. Lee Camp Records, Correspondence, VHS; *Con Vet* 3 (1895): 57.

Chapter 4

1. *Constitution*, Oct. 1–2, 1901; *Con Vet* 10 (1902): 490.

2. For Stewart's decision to go north, as well as the quoted word regarding the advent of Grady's editorial, see Frank Brown, "Annals of Travis County," 30:107, TxSA, and Raines, *Year Book for Texas, 1901*, pp. 54–55. For Grady's reverence of the past, see Gaston, *New South Creed*, p. 165; and Foster, *Ghosts of the Confederacy*, p. 80. See also Nixon, *Grady*, p. 305.

3. *Constitution*, Apr. 6, 1889; Raines, *Year Book for Texas, 1901*, p. 55; New York *Journal*, quoted in *Constitution*, Apr. 10, 1889. For comments by the Texas press, see *Constitution*, Apr. 18, 1889, and Austin *Daily Statesman*, June 23, 1889. Soon, Stewart heeded their call and abandoned his work.

4. See "The First Resolution Ever Passed," *Constitution*, Apr. 13, 1889, regarding the claim for Roach. In his letter printed in *Constitution*, Apr. 18, 1889, Massengale endorsed Grady's effort. He also viewed the proposed home as a "monument" honoring "living heroes," which evidently triggered his recollection of his Warrenton speech. See also George T. Fry's April 1888 recommendation to the Fulton County Confederate Veterans Association that a grand fair be held in order to raise money for a home. *Constitution*, Apr. 11, 1889. As the old saying goes, success has a thousand parents.

5. The only known account of this fascinating meeting is an undated, loose clipping with the headline, "Indigent Veterans. A Movement Started to Give Them a Permanent Home. S. M. Inman Starts the Ball. An Earnest Meeting of the Ladies and Members of the Veterans' Association—Entertainment to be Given." Confederate Veterans File, Atlanta Historical Society, Atlanta, Ga. The clipping matches the type, column width, and four-point headline style used by the *Constitution*, but its exact date has not been determined. The August 1887 date is predicated in part upon the fact that references to the upcoming Piedmont Exposition, which took place in October 1887, were made during the meeting. The meeting is also alluded to in Rodgers, *Confederate Veterans Association of Fulton County*, pp. 121–22, 128. For Calhoun, consult Northen, *Men of Mark*, 3:165–66. Nixon, *Grady*, pp. 271–72, discusses the link between Hemphill, Grady, and Inman. For Colquitt's participation in the Maryland home's opening ceremonies, see Baltimore *American*, June 28, 1888.

6. In fact Grady himself had helped craft, if not popularize, the "sorry tale" of Johnny Reb—the gaunt, limping, battle-scarred, and impoverished Confederate soldier—the same image he criticized Major Stewart for exploiting. See, Nixon, *Grady*, pp. 343–44, and Osterweis, *Myth of the Lost Cause*, pp. 127–42, which discusses Grady's contributions as an imagemaker.

7. The word "immortal" used to describe Grady's editorial appears in W. H. Carr, "The Founding of the Home," in *Thin Gray Line*, p. 47. For the historic founding of the veterans' association and Davis's visit, see Rodgers, *Confederate Veterans Associa-*

tion of Fulton County, pp. 6–10, 12–13, 102, 108–18; *Constitution*, Oct. 22, 1888; Foster, *Ghosts of the Confederacy*, p. 95; and Woodward, *Origins of the New South*, p. 155.

8. Unless other sources are credited, the sources on which my account of the the Atlanta Ring is based are two articles by Harold E. Davis, "Henry W. Grady, Master of the Atlanta Ring," and "Henry W. Grady, the Atlanta *Constitution* and the Politics of Farming" as well as his book, *Henry Grady's New South*. The idea of controlling the black vote was the "central consideration" in Georgia postwar politics. Bartley, *Modern Georgia*, p. 98.

9. For Grady's advice to Northen, see Nixon, *Grady*, pp. 311–13, and Woodward, *Tom Watson*, p. 164. For more about the 1890 Georgia election, the farmer's threat in that state, and Grady's political agenda, see Arnett, *Populist Movement*, pp. 102–16; Shaw, *Wool-Hat Boys*, pp. 22–44; and Wynne, *Continuity of Cotton*, pp. 81–96, 146–75.

10. Holmes, in "Georgia Alliance Legislature," pp. 486–87, computed the number of Confederate veterans in the 1890 House. The same source that he used—thumbnail sketches of House members as provided by the *Constitution*, July 19, 1891—indicates that 52.6 percent were sons of veterans. See also McMath, *Populist Vanguard*, p. 162, which indicates that 44.2 percent of southern Alliance leaders were ex-Confederates.

11. See Grady's rousing editorial with boldface type in the *Constitution*, Apr. 7, 1889, especially page 17, which he devoted entirely to the home project. Regarding Gordon, Brown, and John Inman's endorsements, see ibid., Apr. 9, 1889.

12. *Constitution*, Apr. 7, 1889. Hillyer advised Grady: "Keep the Confederate veterans' names out of the dust." Ibid., Apr. 11, 1889. Graves, a prominent and respected Democrat, was a lifelong admirer of Grady. See Nixon, *Grady*, pp. 285, 291, 331.

13. For Grady's feud with Bullock and their eventual reconciliation, as well as his differences with Jones, see Nixon, *Grady*, pp. 72–73, 313, 319, and Woodward, *Tom Watson*, pp. 125–26, 133. For Black's and Walsh's comments, see *Constitution*, Apr. 7, 1889.

14. The *Constitution*, Apr. 28, 1889, reported that pledges totaled $42,598. Yet the total amount actually received fell several thousand dollars short of that figure. For a directory of contributors—which included Henry W. Grady, Jr., the editor's son—see GSH, List of Persons Subscribing Contributions Towards the Erection of the Home, GDAH. The proceedings of the subscribers' meeting are found in *Constitution*, Apr. 17, 1889.

15. *Constitution*, Apr. 11, 1889.

16. Ibid., Apr. 17, 1889. For information on Kimball, see Range, "Hannibal I. Kimball."

17. *Constitution*, Apr. 19, 1889; GSH, Board of Trustees, Minutes, 1:1–7, GDAH; Rodgers, *Confederate Veterans Association of Fulton County*, p. 178.

18. GSH, Board of Trustees, Minutes, 1:7–21, GDAH; *Constitution*, Apr. 17, 19, 1889; *Con Vet* 10 (1902): 490; Rothman, *Conscience and Convenience*, p. 10.

19. GSH, Board of Trustees, Minutes, 1:7–22, GDAH; Bruce and Morgan, Architects Business File, Atlanta Historical Society, Atlanta, Ga.; Nixon, *Grady*, pp. 330–31.

20. Rodgers, *Confederate Veterans Association of Fulton County*, p. 182; GSH, Board of Trustees, Minutes, 1:23, 28–30, GDAH; *Constitution*, Apr. 26, 1890.

21. Sealed in the cornerstone were some Confederate currency, minié balls, war diaries, letters from Jefferson and Varina Davis, an immortelle from the sarcophagus of Grady, and, curiously, a copy of Lee's plans on how to use blacks in the war. *Constitution*, Apr. 25–27, 1890; Rodgers, *Confederate Veterans Association of Fulton County*, pp. 182–83; GSH, Board of Trustees, Minutes, 1:33, GDAH.

22. GSH, Board of Trustees, Minutes, 1:41, 44, 53–56, GDAH; *Constitution*, Dec. 7, 1890; Georgia *House Journal* (1890), p. 244; Georgia *Laws* (1887), pp. 27–28; (1889), pp. 39–40. Regarding Cutts, who attended the home's dedication, see Holmes, "Georgia Alliance Legislature," p. 488, and *Constitution*, Apr. 26, 1890, July 19, 1891. A separate bill increasing pension allowances for widows also failed to pass in the Senate, which the Alliance controlled too. According to Holmes, "Georgia Alliance Legislature," p. 507, the farmers' legislature unanimously approved a bill providing widows of Confederate veterans $100 per year. Although Georgia *House Journal* (1890), p. 30, supports that assertion, the bill actually remained in the Senate finance committee at the time the session ended. Georgia *Senate Journal* (1890), p. 86; *Constitution*, Sept. 10, 1891. See also Young, "Confederate Pensions," pp. 47–52, which notes that payments to widows did not go into effect until 1892.

23. GSH, Board of Trustees, Minutes, 1:45, 57–62, GDAH; *Constitution*, Aug. 26, 1891. For more concerning Clark Howell, see Northen, *Men of Mark*, 4:233–37.

24. For coverage of the legislative debate concerning the Confederate home bill, the best source is *Constitution*, Aug. 26–27, 1891. Biographical profiles of the House members are available in ibid., July 19, 1891.

25. Ibid., July 19, Aug. 26–27, 1891.

26. Ibid., Aug. 28, 1891.

27. The bill's course, from its introduction by Cutts to the final vote, may be followed in Georgia *House Journal* (1891), pp. 474, 534, 590, 640–41, 647–50.

28. *Constitution*, Aug. 27, 1891.

29. Ibid., Aug. 28–Sept. 10, 1891; Arkansas *Gazette*, Aug. 29, Sept. 4, 1891.

30. An Allianceman who supported the home defended Livingston, claiming that he had introduced a resolution in favor of the home during their recently concluded convention. *Constitution*, Aug. 29, 1891.

31. Ibid., Aug. 27–28, 1891; Woodward, *Tom Watson*, pp. 177–78. Of the two black members (both Republicans) who sat in the 1891 Georgia House, J. M. Holzendorf, a thirty-five-year-old farmer-teacher from Camden, joined ninety-three other representatives in voting against the bill, while Lectured Crawford, a minister and former slave representing McIntosh County, abstained. *Constitution*, July 19, 1891; Georgia *House Journal*, (1891), p. 648; Holmes, "Georgia Alliance Legislature," p. 507. For the colorful Small, a reformed alcoholic who soon aligned with the Populists, see *Constitution*, Sept. 3–4, 1891, and Shaw, *Wool-Hat Boys*, pp. 31, 60, 66–67.

32. *Constitution*, Aug. 28–31, 1891; Holmes, "Georgia Alliance Legislature," p. 508. For Mattox, see *History of Clinch County*, p. 274.

33. *Constitution*, Aug. 29, 1891, Oct. 26, 1892.

34. GSH, Board of Trustees, Minutes, 1:63–73, GDAH; *Constitution*, Aug. 29–30, Sept. 1–3, 9–10, 12, 1891.

35. Holmes, "Georgia Alliance Legislature," p. 515. The figures used in describing the composition of the 1892 House have been arrived at by comparing the names of members listed in Georgia *House Journal* (1890), pp. 753–57, with those that appear on the roll in Georgia *House Journal* (1892), pp. 3–6.

36. *Constitution*, Oct. 27–29, Nov. 23, 1892; GSH, Board of Trustees, Minutes, 1:81–82, GDAH; Georgia *House Journal* (1892), p. 14.

37. *Constitution*, Nov. 24, Dec. 3, 1892. In honor of his defense of the home, Styles—a vocal opponent of Jim Crow legislation—received a gold-headed ebony cane presented by negrophobe Sam Small, on behalf of the Fulton County Confederate Veterans Association. An imaginative reporter wrote that Styles's acceptance speech was greeted with applause so thunderous that it "shook the roof til the pictures of Lee and Davis on the wall bowed" and the "old Confederate flag quivered." Ibid., Dec. 20, 1892; Shaw, *Wool-Hat Boys*, pp. 60, 138–39; Georgia *House Journal* (1892), p. 469.

38. *Constitution*, Dec. 3, 9, 1892; Georgia *House Journal* (1892), pp. 469–73.

39. *Constitution*, Dec. 9, 1892; Shaw, *Wool-Hat Boys*, pp. 66, 96–97.

40. *Constitution*, Dec. 13–15, 1892; Georgia *Senate Journal* (1892), pp. 340, 350, 363, 368–71, 383–84. "Shame! Shame!! Shame!!!," scolded the Brunswick (Georgia) *Times*. For reaction by other newspapers regarding the legislature's "mischief" and "cowardice," see *Constitution*, Dec. 20, 1892, and *Con Vet* 1 (1893): 9.

41. *Constitution*, Dec. 15, 17, 20, 1892, Jan. 13, Feb. 14, 1893, Dec. 20, 1894; GSH, Board of Trustees, Minutes, 1:83–89, GDAH. The board's minutes end with the January 1893 meeting and do not resume until two years later.

42. *Constitution*, Jan. 29–30, 1895, Oct. 28, 1897; GSH, Board of Trustees, Minutes, 1:90–99, GDAH.

43. The board's minutes end abruptly following its October 25, 1897, meeting to discuss the court's decree. No date for Romare's loan of more than $5,000 has been found, though it is believed to have been made before the forced sale in April 1898, when the home was $4,600 in arrears. GSH, Board of Trustees, Minutes, 1: 99–106, GDAH; *Constitution*, Apr. 3–6, 1898, Jan. 23, 1901.

44. *Constitution*, Apr. 3–4, 1898; *Con Vet* 6 (1898): 145.

45. Exactly why the board's deal with the UDC fell through is unclear. *Constitution*, Apr. 6–8, 1898; *Con Vet* 6 (1898): 145.

46. *Constitution*, June 5, July 20–24 , Oct. 26, 1898, June 4, 1901.

47. On connections between the Civil War and the Spanish-American War, see Foster, *Ghosts of the Confederacy*, pp. 145–49; Buck, *Road to Reunion*, pp. 306–7; and Linderman, *Embattled Courage*, pp. 296–97.

48. ArCH, Superintendent's *Report*, (1915–1916), p. 10, ArSA.

49. *Constitution*, Oct. 26, Nov. 8–11, 22, 1898, May 3, 1899. Georgia *House Journal* (1898), p. 391. Without the aid of the board's official minutes or any other firsthand account, I have been unable to fill the void between May 1899 and October 1900.

50. Georgia *House Journal* (1900), pp. 126, 533, 562–65; *Constitution*, Oct. 30, Dec. 4, 13, 1900, June 4, 1901. No other representative, according to Gary, was either a

veteran or a son of a veteran. In the following legislature, however, ex-Confederates reportedly occupied a total of fifteen seats in both houses. White, *Confederate Veteran*, p. 86.

51. Georgia *House Journal* (1900), pp. 562–65, 796; *Constitution*, Dec. 13, 16, 1900; Georgia *Senate Journal* (1900), pp. 435, 454, 487–89.

52. *Constitution*, Dec. 16, 1900; Georgia *Senate Journal* (1900), pp. 488–89. True to his word, Tatum was among the Senators voting for the bill.

53. *Constitution*, Nov. 16, Dec. 13, 20, 22, 1900, Jan. 12, 23–25, Apr. 12, 1901; Georgia *Laws* (1900), pp. 86–88.

54. *Constitution*, Jan. 19–20, 1901; Young, "Confederate Pensions," pp. 48–49. Moreover, legislation permitting the state's disabled and indigent ex-Confederates to sell life insurance and "intoxicants" and practice medicine without a license was on the books by 1900. Georgia *Laws* (1895), pp. 92–94; (1897), pp. 24–25; (1899), p. 99.

55. *Constitution*, June 3–4, 1901. See also Stephen D. Lee to W. Lowndes Calhoun, May 11, 1901, Calhoun Papers, William R. Perkins Library, Duke University, Durham, N.C.

56. *Constitution*, June 4, Oct. 1–2, 1901; Georgia *House Journal* (1901), pp. 159, 679–70; Georgia *Senate Journal* (1901), pp. 433, 532–33; Georgia *Laws* (1901), p. 14; *Con Vet* 10 (1902): 490–91.

57. Montgomery *Advertiser*, Nov. 14, 1901, Feb. 18, June 15, July 20, 1902, Sept. 4, 11, 25, Oct. 16, 31, 1903.

58. Pass Christian *Coast News*, Dec. 7, 1893, in M. James Stevens notebook, Beauvoir; *Con Vet* 11 (1903): 54, 104; 23 (1915): 300; 26 (1918): 499; 34 (1926): 117–18; Warranty Deed, Varina Davis to Mississippi Division of the United Sons of Confederate Veterans, Oct. 10, 1902, Beauvoir; Biloxi *Daily Herald*, Mar. 16, 1962; *Inaugural Addresses of the Governors of Mississippi*, pp. 31–32. The fate of the bill accepting Beauvoir as a gift from the SCV may be followed in Mississippi *House Journal*, (1904), pp. 175, 387, 498–99, 518, and Mississippi *Senate Journal* (1904), pp. 505, 566. Background information regarding the members of the legislature is available in Rowland, *Official and Statistical Register*.

59. For legislation extending various benefits to South Carolina's Confederate veterans, see South Carolina *Acts* (1866), p. 433; (1879), p. 186; (1881), pp. 563–64; (1886), pp. 708–9; (1887), pp. 826–29; (1901), p. 855; (1905), p. 954; and (1906), pp. 118–19. For the women's home, see *Southern Historical Society Papers* 5 (1878): 254. For the earlier home endeavors, see *Con Vet* 8 (1900): 359, and Charleston *News and Courier*, June 23, 1963.

60. Regarding the fate of the infirmary bill, specifically, see South Carolina *Acts* (1908), pp. 1074–75; South Carolina *Senate Journal* (1907), pp. 207, 304, 407–8, 431; (1908), p. 682; and South Carolina *House Journal* (1907), pp. 525, 529, 682; (1908); pp. 339, 430–31, 465–66; (1909), pp. 455, 720. For the incensed veteran's comments, see Columbia *State*, Feb. 19, 1908.

61. For coverage of the opening and dedicatory ceremonies, see Columbia *State*, May 11, 29, June 3–4, 1909. Sketches of Brooks, Smith, and Weston may be found in Hemphill, *Men of Mark*, 4:44–47, 347–48, and 386–87, respectively.

Chapter 5

1. For accounts of almshouse conditions, see Shifflett, *Patronage and Poverty*, p. 72, 138; Jackson, *New Orleans in the Gilded Age*, pp. 190–93; and Rothman, *Conscience and Convenience*, pp. 22–24. For avowals by those determined to prevent ex-Confederates from suffering the indignity of the asylum, see Frank Freeman to John P. Hickman, May 20, 1901, TSH AA, W. G. W. Clay, TSLA; A. T. Barnes to Hickman, Apr. 19, 1912, TSH AA, G. W. Bruer, TSLA; R. C. Taylor to [James W. Pegram], Mar. 13, 1890, LCSH AA, William Johnson, VSL; and Rebecca Cameron to Lisa T. Rodman, Oct. 30, 1900, and Rodman to Daughters of the Confederacy, Nov. 14, 1900, both in Hinsdale Papers, William R. Perkins Library, Duke University, Durham, N.C. See also Calvin C. Burnette to J. E. Graves, July 15, 1910, LCSH AA, Burnette, VSL. The establishment of soldiers' homes in the North was also prompted in part by the fact that many Union veterans resided in poorhouses. See McConnell, *Glorious Contentment*, and Cetina, "History of Veterans' Homes," pp. 114–121.

2. LCSH, Board of Visitors *Report* (1896), p. 5, VSL; *Southern Historical Society Papers* 20 (1892): 315–16; *Constitution*, Sept. 12, 1891; GSH, Board of Trustees, Minutes, 2:102, GDAH.

3. Montgomery *Advertiser*, Feb. 3, 1903; *Constitution*, Apr. 7, 1889.

4. *Con Vet* 1 (1893): 59; 12 (1904): 325; Nashville *Banner*, May 12, 1892, Mar. 7, 1908.

5. SCCI, Executive Committee, Minutes, May 11, 1923, p. 128, SCDAH; L. R. Wallace, H. H. Turner, J. T. Green to Supt., July 13, 1922, ArCH AA, George W. Glen, ArSA.

6. Board of Visitors to J. C. Batchelder, Apr. 16, 1912, LCSH, Board of Visitors, Correspondence, VSL; Raines, *Year Book for Texas, 1901*, p. 58; GSH, Board of Trustees, Minutes, 2:102, 182–83, 3:237 4:40, GDAH.

7. Jefferson Manly Falkner Soldiers' Home, Superintendent *Report* (1904), Alabama Department of Archives and History, Montgomery; Joseph H. Cocke to John P. Hickman, May 7, 1895, TSH AA, Edwin Whitmore, TSLA; Poole, "Final Encampment," pp. 12–13; W. N. Jones to Charles Dupry, Oct. 11, 1893, North Carolina Board of Public Charities, Report, NCDAH.

8. *Constitution*, Apr. 9, 1889.

9. Arkansas *Gazette*, Aug. 15, 1890.

10. New Orleans *Picayune*, Dec. 13, 1899; Russell, *Life and Labors*, p. 274; Lea, "Personal Recollections," p. 28; *Con Vet* 16 (1908): 151, 182.

11. GSH, Board of Trustees, Minutes, 2:61, 146, 293, GDAH. Beginning in 1906, administrators finally began hiring black servants to relieve inmates of the more undesirable and strenuous chores. GSH, Board of Trustees *Report* (1906), p. 9, GDAH. Tennessee trustees reserved the right to establish either a farm or factory, whichever would render the "charity" as "nearly self-sustaining as possible." Tennessee *Acts* (1889), pp. 342–44.

12. "Texas Confederate Soldiers' Home A Model," *Con Vet* 20 (1912): 61; TxHM, Board of Managers *Report* (1892), pp. 13–18, TxSA; Texas *House Journal* (1895), pp. 392–93; (1905), pp. 298–99; (1911), pp. 762–64; Austin *Daily Statesman*, Dec. 7, 1913.

13. Williams, "'Home . . . for the Old Boys,'" pp. 43–44; LCSH, Board of Visitors, Investigative Committee Report (1892), pp. 71–75, 80, 90–91, 124, VSL; LCSH, Board of Visitors, Minutes, 1:24, 45, VSL. See also inmate J. H. Allen to Board of Visitors, c. 1885, LCSH, Board of Visitors, Correspondence, VSL.

14. As a work incentive, the board threatened to "debar" violators from the privileges of the home for up to one year. CNSH, Board of Directors, Minutes, 2:22, 141, 474, 5:87–88, LHAC; CNSH, Superintendent Report (1891), LHAC; CNSH, Board of Directors, House Committee Report (1900), LHAC; CNSH, Rules and Regulations (1882), LHAC.

15. W. W. Heard to Michael B. Bergeron, Dec. 29, 1903, CNSH, Board of Visitors, Correspondence, LHAC; Heinrich Dübel to Board of Visitors, Apr. 4, 1887, Samuel V. Corbett to William H. Terry, Apr. 26, 1886, V. Wren to James F. Chalmers, May 8, 1892, Nathan J. Lewis to James W. Pegram, Mar. 15, 1885, A. B. Carter to Fitzhugh Lee, Feb. 11, 1885, G. W. Richardson to Pegram, Feb. 19, 1886, and J. B. Clark to Lee, May 23, 1885, all in LCSH, Board of Visitors, Correspondence, VSL; Daniel C. Hill to W. P. Smith, July 11, 1890, R. E. Lee Camp Records, Correspondence, VHS. See also TSH AAs, Robert F. Cattels and James Cowen, TSLA.

16. Vick was eventually permitted to enter the Arkansas home on October 1, 1920, only to be discharged for an unspecified reason twenty days later. Newton to Vick, Dec. 28, 1916, ArCH AA, Vick, ArSA.

17. Admission requirements comprised part of the enabling act for a number of soldiers' homes. See Georgia *Laws* (1900), pp. 86–88; Virginia *Acts* (1884), pp. 521–22; Texas *Laws* (1895), pp. 42–44; Tennessee *Acts* (1889), pp. 342–44; Louisiana *Acts* (1882), p. 73. For the South Carolinian's remarks, see W. W. Morris to G. Valentine, June 9, 1913, TSH AA, J. F. Houser, TSLA. See also E. Murray to Maj. Harry Hammond, Nov. 25, 1910, SCCI AA, J. D. Everett, SCDAH, and SCCI, Executive Committee, Minutes, Feb. 10, 1922, p. 86, SCDAH. For Ober's quip, see his letter to Peter J. Trezevant, May 11, 1886, AANV Papers, Correspondence, LHAC. Despite the stringent selection criteria, imposters occasionally gained admittance to the homes; however, they were usually dismissed. See GSH, Board of Trustees, Minutes, 3:72–73, 76, GDAH; NCSH, Board of Incorporators, Minutes, 103, NCDAH; New Orleans *Daily-Picayune*, Jan. 19, 1913; and *Con Vet* 17 (1909): 562. See also LCSH, Board of Visitors, Minutes, 1:205, VSL, in which an inmate confessed to having deserted but was allowed to remain in the home because he had been a "good soldier."

18. SCCI AA, A. O. Banks, SCDAH.

19. Austin *Daily Statesman*, Dec. 7, 1913; Texas *Laws* (1895), pp. 42–44; TxHM, Board of Managers *Report* (1892), p. 16, TxSA. E. P. Wright to John W. A. Sanford, Jan. 21, 1909, Sanford Papers, Alabama Department of Archives and History, Montgomery.

20. Rufus McDaniel to H. C. Wheeler, Mar. 26, 1923, ArCH AA, Wheeler, ArSA.

21. Louisiana *Acts* (1900), pp. 124–26; TxHM, Board of Managers *Report* (1892), p. 9, TxSA; Walter Guion to Henry H. Ward, Oct. 30, 1900, CNSH, Board of Directors, Correspondence, LHAC.

22. One Tennessee veteran admitted owning 160 acres, which he said he would

gladly deed to the home if granted entrance. The board, however, denied his plea. F. M. Vaughn to John P. Hickman, June 1, 1899, TSH AA, John S. Gregory, TSLA.

23. The phrase attributed to the Lee Camp was printed on its application for admission. For the other quoted statements, see TxHM, Superintendent *Report* (1892), (1898), (1904), (1909), TxSA.

24. SCCI, Executive Committee, Minutes, May 12, 1922, p. 93–94, SCDAH.

25. J. W. Wilks and W. H. Edwards to Board of Directors, May 3, 1909, SCCI AA, W. G. Parker, SCDAH.

26. For examples of veterans promising to cooperate with home authorities, see E. F. Grigg to R. H. Bosher, Oct. 15, 1902, and Clarence Thomas to James Pegram, Sept. 30, 1887, both in LCSH, Board of Visitors, Correspondence, VSL; and Washington Taylor to Norman V. Randolph, Apr. 10, 1893, LCSH AA, R. B. Banks, VSL. For moral endorsements see, for example, TSH AAs, George W. Brown, Joseph C. Alsup, Patrick Butler, Vincent Willoughby, A. W. Baxter, and Charles T. Clifford, TSLA. For a highly unfavorable report, see J. B. Pleasants to Charles H. Epps, July 22, 1886, LCSH AA, John E. Brooke, VSL. Regarding administrators' expectation of gentlemanly deportment among inmates, see GSH, Board of Trustees, Minutes, 3:264–65, 4:18–19, GDAH, and A. J. Montague to Norman V. Randolph, Apr. 12, 1899, LCSH, Board of Visitors, Correspondence, VSL. See Wilson, *Baptized in Blood*, p. 87, for a discussion of the claim that Johnny Reb was sober—almost a teetotaler—as a soldier.

27. The emphasis placed upon order came, of course, at a time when there was a tremendous preoccupation with personal self-control and stability within society. Wiebe, *Search for Order*. GSH, Board of Trustees, Minutes, 2:36; 3:246–47, GDAH; GSH, Board of Trustees *Report* (1906), p. 10, GDAH; Investigation of the Georgia Soldiers' Home, (1906), p. 191, GDAH; CNSH, Board of Directors, Minutes, 2:386, LHAC; CNSH, Board of Directors *Report* (1902), LHAC; CNSH, President Report (1911), LHAC; TxHM, Superintendent *Report* (1909), TxSA; TxHM, Board of Managers *Report* (1892), TxSA; (1902); (1904), Austin Public Library, Austin, Tex.

28. For a rare glimpse of the daily routine within a Confederate veterans' institution, see Austin *Confederate Home News*, Feb. 23, 1912. Regarding the use of bells in dictating inmate functions, as well as policies regulating personal hygiene, see TxHM, Board of Managers *Report* (1892), pp. 15–18, TxSA. For roll calls, inspections, curfews, passes, guards, and other surveillance devices, see *Confederate Soldiers' Home of Georgia* (1901); New Orleans *Daily-Picayune*, Jan. 19, 1913; Investigation of the Georgia Soldiers' Home (1906), pp. 19, 148, 164–65, 458, GDAH; JDBMSH, Board of Directors, Minute Book, 1:222, USM. For uniforms, see TxHM, Board of Managers *Report* (1892), p. 14; (1893), p. 6, TxSA; LCSH, Board of Visitors, Minutes, 1:22, 2:133, VSL; CNSH, Board of Directors, Minutes, 2:5–7, 28, 55, 304, LHAC; TSH, Board of Trustees, Minutes, 35, TSLA; GSH, Board of Trustees, Minutes, 2:35, 201, 219, 3:132, 4:22–24, GDAH; Poole, "Final Encampment," pp. 12–13; South Carolina *Laws* (1912), sec. 178; Arkansas *Gazette*, Aug. 7, 1892; V. B. Mass, "Dining Room Record," p. 39, Beauvoir; and JDBMSH, Board of Directors, *Ninth Biennial Report*, USM. In 1896, Texas superintendent William P. Hardeman recommended that a barbed-wire fence some six to ten feet tall be strung "entirely around the premises" so as to ensure

against the "constant aggression of hogs and dogs," as well as to deter theft. TxHM, Board of Managers, Superintendent *Report* (1896), TxSA. For other home enclosures, both suggested and actual, see *Con Vet* 1 (1893): 59; 31 (1923): 48; J. B. Hodgkin to Henry C. Stuart, Feb. 10, 1914, Executive Papers, Henry C. Stuart, VSL; Crew, *History of Nashville*, p. 566; SCCI, Confederate Home Commissioners *Report*, (1913); and Jefferson Manly Falkner Soldiers' Home, Superintendent *Report* (1904), Alabama Department of Archives and History, Montgomery.

29. Rules governing inmate behavior were reminiscent of the discipline prescribed in wartime hospitals and for every member of the southern armed forces as defined by the Articles of War enacted by the Confederate Congress. See Cunningham, *Doctors in Gray*, pp. 90–93, 211–12; *Regulations for the Army of the Confederate States*, pp. 407–13; Russell, *Life and Labors*, p. 272; TxHM, Board of Managers *Report* (1892), pp. 13–18, TxSA; New Orleans *Daily-Picayune*, Jan. 19, 1913; *Confederate Soldiers' Home of Georgia* (1901); GSH, Board of Trustees, Minutes, 2:49, GDAH; LCSH, Board of Visitors, Minutes, 1:158, 2:410, VSL; Texas *House Journal* (1895), pp. 392–93.

30. Gaither, *Arkansas Confederate Home*, p. 3; *Southern Historical Society Papers* 20 (1892): 324; GSH, Board of Trustees, Minutes, 2:30, 55, 3:92, 269–70, 272–73, 276, 4:2–5, 22–24, 66, GDAH; TxHM, Board of Managers *Report* (1892), 5, 10–11, TxSA; LCSH, Board of Visitors, Minutes, 1:62, VSL; Austin *Confederate Home News*, Feb. 17, 1912; CNSH, Board of Directors *Report* (1902), LHAC; *Southern Bivouac* 3 (January 1885): 511; SCCI, Confederate Home Commissioners, Minutes, June 12, 1923, SCDAH; N. W. Brooker to Coleman L. Blease, Jan. 27, 1911, Blease Papers, SCDAH; Montgomery *Advertiser*, Apr. 3, 1904.

31. The particular occupations cited at the beginning of the paragraph were those of the Georgia home's first five superintendents, from 1901 to 1906. See Investigation of the Georgia Soldiers' Home (1906), pp. 167, 229, 233, 244, 249, 290, GDAH, in which inmates were asked to critique their superiors' performances. Superintendents, as well as other home officers, were subject to annual elections, which explains, in part, their high turnover rate. For the application letters of several candidates, see GSH, Board of Trustees, Minutes, 2:152–4, 156, 3:240, GDAH, wherein Saussey's comments may be found. For Loggins's description, see Investigation of the Texas Home for Men, (1917), p. 3, TxSA.

32. CNSH, Board of Visitors, Minutes, 2:267, 392–93, LHAC; CNSH, Rules and Regulations (1884), pp. 4–8, LHAC; GSH, Board of Trustees, Minutes, 3:229, GDAH; GSH, Board of Trustees, Investigating Committee Report, June 24, 1904 [located in Minutes], GDAH; GSH, Board of Trustees *Report* (1906), pp. 6–7; (1914), pp. 6–7, GDAH; *Con Vet* 16 (1908): 181; TxHM, Board of Managers *Report* (1904), Austin Public Library, Austin, Tex.; Texas *House Journal* (1901), pp. 638–39; (1913), pp. 942–43; Mrs. F. C. Miller to Francis P. Fleming, Jan. 19, 1902, Florida Soldiers' Home Papers, Jacksonville Public Library, Jacksonville, Fla.

33. TxHM, Board of Managers *Report* (1892), pp. 8, 16, TxSA; CNSH, Board of Directors *Report* (1887), p. 4, LHAC; CNSH, Rules and Regulations (1888), LHAC; GSH, Board of Trustees, Minutes, 2:34, 4:116, GDAH; Investigation of the Georgia Soldiers' Home (1906), p. 398, GDAH; *Confederate Soldiers' Home of Georgia* (1917), pp. 8, 19.

34. A. J. Montague to Norman V. Randolph, Apr. 12, 1899, LCSH, Board of Visitors, Correspondence, VSL; LCSH, Board of Visitors, Minutes, 1:41, 45, VSL; LCSH, Board of Visitors, Investigating Committee Report (1892), VSL; Investigation of the Georgia Soldiers' Home (1906), pp. 325–30, 468–69, GDAH; TxHM, Board of Managers *Report* (1892), p. 17, TxSA; GSH, Board of Trustees, Minutes, 2:50; 4:263, GDAH; GSH, Board of Trustees *Report* (1906), p. 11, GDAH; Tennessee *House Journal* (1911), p. 947.

35. GSH, Board of Trustees, Minutes, 2:241, GDAH; GSH, Board of Trustees *Report* (1906), p. 11, GDAH; LCSH, Board of Visitors, Minutes, 1:128, VSL.

36. For a discussion of this notion, see Van de Wetering, "Popular Concept of 'Home,'" and Ownby, *Subduing Satan*, p. 4.

37. TxHM, Board of Managers *Report* (1892), p. 3, TxSA; GSH, Board of Trustees, Minutes, 2:273, 3:144, 246–47, GDAH; CNSH, Board of Directors, Minutes, 2:392–93, LHAC; W. W. Heard to Michael B. Bergeron, Dec. 29, 1903, and Feb. 10, 1904, CNSH, Board of Directors, Correspondence, LHAC; LCSH, Board of Visitors, Executive Committee Orders, No. 27, May 28, 1908, VSL.

38. CNSH, Board of Directors *Report* (1886), p. 5; (1902), p. 14, LHAC; CNSH, Board of Directors, Minutes, 2:25–26, LHAC; GSH, Board of Trustees, Minutes, 1:290, 2:83, 218, 290, 3:7, GDAH; GSH, Board of Trustees *Report* (1901), GDAH; *Confederate Soldiers' Home of Georgia* (1917), p. 12; Investigation of the Georgia Soldiers' Home (1906), p. 177, GDAH; TxHM, Board of Managers *Report* (1892), 16, TxSA; Lawdon R. Mason to Charles P. Bigger, Feb. 28, 1899, J. J. Quantz to Lee Camp, c. Aug. 1888, both in LCSH, Board of Visitors, Correspondence, VSL; Tennessee *Acts* (1909), p. 41; Nashville *Banner*, Mar. 7, 1908; Saussey Diary, GDAH; Raleigh *News and Observer*, Dec. 5, 1920; R. E. Lee Camp Records, Lee Camp Soldiers' Home Library Register, VHS; TSH, Board of Trustees, Minutes (1909), pp. 38, 51, TSLA; Poole, "Final Encampment," p. 17; Virginia *Senate Journal* (1899), p. 5; LCSH, Board of Visitors *Report* (1904), p. 6, VSL; Martha Haywood to James Joyner, c. 1915, Joyner Papers, NCDAH; *Con Vet* 9 (1901): 549–50.

39. The phrase and thesis "more than a roof" is borrowed from McClure, *More Than a Roof*. See also *Constitution*, Sept. 12, 1891; GSH, Board of Trustees, Minutes, 2:36, 102, 133, 139, 3:52, GDAH; "Texas Confederate Soldiers' Home A Model," *Con Vet* 20 (1912): 61; TxHM, Board of Managers *Report* (1892), p. 14, TxSA; Raines, *Year Book for Texas, 1901*, p. 56; Fred A. Ober to Peter J. Trezevant, May 29, 1886, AANV Papers, Correspondence, LHAC; AAT Papers, Minutes, 2:123, 138–39, LHAC; CNSH, Board of Directors, Minutes, 4:53–56, LHAC.

40. Edwardsville, Ala., *Standard News*, Apr. 18, 1902; Julian S. Levy to AANV, Oct. 14, 1911, AANV Papers, Veterans Benefits, LHAC; New Orleans *Daily-Picayune*, Jan. 19, 1913; Texas *House Journal* (1911), 50; GSH, Board of Trustees, Minutes, 2:123, 3:200, 263, 4:43–44, 279, GDAH; LCSH, Board of Visitors *Report* (1918), p. 5, VSL; *Con Vet* 8 (1900): 264; 24 (1916): 439; 34 (1926): 472; CNSH, Board of Directors, Minutes, 2:104–6, LHAC; *Constitution*, Apr. 9, 1889, Sept. 12, 1891; Raines, *Year Book for Texas, 1901*, 56; New Orleans *Daily-Picayune*, Jan. 19, 1913; Texas *House Journal* (1911), p. 50. See also *Southern Bivouac* 2 (July 1884): 508–11; Russell, *Life and Labors*, p. 272; and *Inaugural Addresses of the Governors of Mississippi*, pp. 98–100.

41. For the clearest presentation of the concept of "total institution," see Goffman, *Asylums*. Also useful are Foucault, *Discipline and Punish*, and Katz, *In the Shadow of the Poorhouse*. For an assessment of the "social control" theory and its critics, see Trattner, "Social Welfare or Social Control?."

42. CNSH, Board of Directors *Report* (1886), p. 4, LHAC.

Chapter 6

1. Cole, "Life in Camp Lee Soldiers' Home."

2. Biloxi *Daily Herald*, June 14, Oct. 6, 1919; John H. Owens to Lida Owens, c. Apr. 22, 1912, M. James Stevens notebook, Beauvoir; *Con Vet* 21 (1913): 478; 33 (1925): 349; Montgomery *Advertiser*, Aug. 6, 1902; Austin *Confederate Home News*, Feb. 17, 1912; JDBMSH, Register of Inmates, p. 59, Mississippi Department of Archives and History, Jackson.

3. SCCI, Confederate Home Commissioners, Minutes, undated clipping, SCDAH; "Last of the Southern Confederacy and Our Most Romantic Heritage," Raleigh *News and Observer*, Dec. 5, 1920; "The Last Roll," New Orleans *Daily-Picayune*, Jan. 19, 1913; "The Confederate Homes of Texas," *Con Vet* 24 (1916): 489; "U.D.C. Notes," *Con Vet* 34 (1926): 472; Columbia *State Record*, Dec. 29, 1924; Jefferson Manly Falkner Soldiers' Home, Superintendent *Report* (1904), Alabama Department of Archives and History, Montgomery; Montgomery *Advertiser*, June 21, 1904. For others' impressions of the homes from the outside, see *Con Vet* 24 (1916): 570; 31 (1923): 37; Gaither, *Arkansas Confederate Home*, p. 5; Biloxi *Daily Herald*, May 30, 1919; and *Southern Bivouac* 2 (July 1884): 508–11.

4. "The Last Roll," New Orleans *Daily-Picayune*, Jan. 19, 1913.

5. The poem appeared in Thompson's Austin *Confederate Home Vidette*, May 15, 1912, which superseded the *Home News*.

6. B. G. McDowell to John P. Hickman, June 28, 1900, TSH AA, William G. Roberts, TSLA; C. W. Frazer to Hickman, July 19, 1895, TSH AA, John Huffernan, TSLA. See also Charles Moore, Jr., to AANV, Aug. 26, 1880, AANV Papers, Veterans Benefits, LHAC; John A. Clements to "Tip" Harrison, June 1, 1901; John O. Dean to W. Lowndes Calhoun, Jan. 14, 1901, GSH, Board of Trustees, Correspondence, GDAH; W. B. Taliaferro to Fitzhugh Lee, Aug. 19, 1887, LCSH, Board of Visitors, Correspondence, VSL; and Francis H. Williams to James S. Hogg, Nov. 24, 1890, Governors Records, James S. Hogg, TxSA. Branum noted that "a few inmates are inclined to be supersensitive, and attribute their presence in the home to some weakness which might have been averted." New Orleans *Daily-Picayune*, Jan. 19, 1913. See also E. L. McLendon [County Clerk, Cleveland County, Arkansas] to Rufus McDaniel, Sept. 10, 1923, ArCH AA, J. Stroud Gill, ArSA.

7. Cole, "Life in Camp Lee Soldiers' Home."

8. Wall to James W. Pegram, Nov. 4, 1895, LCSH, Board of Visitors, Correspondence, VSL; B. F. Watson to Rufus G. McDaniel, Mar. 23, 1922, ArCH AA, Watson, ArSA.

9. See the letters to Charles Euker, Nov. 30, 1905, and J. E. Graves, Mar. 7, 1910, LCSH AAs, H. O. Bass and Thomas S. Bullock, respectively, VSL. For Hodgkin's

complaints (and suggestions), see his letter to Henry C. Stuart, Jan. 22, 1914, Executive Records, Henry C. Stuart, VSL.

10. W. W. Coldwell to E. J. Boshee, June 11, 1902, LCSH AA, Asa Wall, VSL.

11. For inmate complaints, see letter from "6 inmates" to James Hogg, Mar. 1, 1891, Governors Records, James S. Hogg, TxSA; Texas *House Journal* (1897), pp. 101, 692–93; (1905), pp. 298–99, 1078, 1216–17; (1919), pp. 299, 544, 582, 668, 673; Texas *Laws* (1905), p. 409; Austin *Confederate Home Vidette*, Jan. 1, 1913; Disabled Veterans to AANV, Jan. 8, 1885, AANV Papers, Correspondence, LHAC; Charles A. Roberts to Fred Ober, Nov. 22, 1906, Auriel Aurand to Board of Directors, Sept. 30, 1903, "16 Veterans" to Board of Directors, May 13, 1919, Board of Directors to T. O. Moore, Sept. 8, 1909, all in CNSH, Board of Directors, Correspondence, LHAC; CNSH, Board of Directors, Investigating Committee Report (Oct. 6, 1889), LHAC; John Watson to Board of Directors, May 3, 1919, CNSH, Board of Directors, Minutes, LHAC; GSH, Board of Trustees, Minutes, 2:99, 107, 141, 150–51, 157, 219, 3:132–35, GDAH; William DeJournett to Charles D. Phillips, June 25, 1907; M. A. Fowler et al. to "Guardians of Home," Dec. 12, 1903, GSH, Board of Trustees, Correspondence, GDAH; GSH, Board of Trustees, *Report* (1906), p. 11, GDAH; LCSH, Board of Visitors, Minutes, 1:171, VSL; letter from Green B. Samuels, July 17, 1899; J. H. Allen to Fitzhugh Lee, Oct. 13, 1885, LCSH, Board of Visitors, Correspondence, VSL; South Carolina *House Journal* (1920), pp. 10–11; J. C. Bridges et al. to Board of Directors, Feb. 20, 1902, Florida Old Confederate Soldiers and Sailors Home, Board of Directors, Letters Received, Jacksonville Public Library, Jacksonville, Fla.; "Cousin Yam" to "Cousins Nellie & Bessie," May 25, 1921, Beauvoir.

12. C. M. Hooper to Board of Directors, June 23–25, 1901, Florida Old Confederate Soldiers and Sailors Home, Board of Directors, Letters Received, Jacksonville Public Library, Jacksonville, Jacksonville, Fla. See also Hooper to F. P. Fleming, July 5, 13, 15, 1901, and M. E. Gainey to Fleming, Dec. 14, 1902, both in ibid.

13. Ruffin to F. P. Fleming, July 9, 1902, Florida Old Confederate Soldiers and Sailors Home, Board of Directors, Letters Received, Jacksonville Public Library, Jacksonville, Jacksonville, Fla. See also John McCormack to D. E. Maxwell, June 23, 1901, ibid.

14. Discipline among male inmates was a universal cause of concern in nineteenth-century almshouses. See, for example, Weiler, "The Aged, the Family, and the Problems of a Maturing Industrial Society," p. 158. For particular complaints regarding inmate behavior, see GSH, Board of Trustees, Minutes, 2:78, 99, 110, 112–13, 130, 150–56, 218, 297–98, 3:88, GDAH; Investigation of the Georgia Soldiers' Home (1906), pp. 447, GDAH; J. B. Hodgkin to Henry C. Stuart, Jan. 22, 1914, Executive Records, Henry C. Stuart, VSL; North Carolina Department of Human Services, Inspection of NCSH, Oct. 2, 1920, NCDAH.

15. South Carolina *Reports and Resolutions* (1916), 3:621.

16. CNSH, Board of Directors, Minutes, 2:187, 242, LHAC; CNSH, Board of Directors, Secretary Report (May 5, 1906), LHAC; CNSH, Board of Directors, President Report (May 5, 1906), LHAC; CNSH, Board of Directors, Investigating Committee Report (Feb. 6, 1909); (Jan. 15, 1918), LHAC; New Orleans *Daily-Picayune*, Jan.

19, 1913; GSH, Board of Trustees, Minutes, 2:160, 185, 191, 218–19, 242, 269, 293, 3:6, 12, 142–44, 237, 254, GDAH; Investigation of the Georgia Soldiers' Home (1906), pp. 251–53, 255, 265, GDAH; Saussey Diary, GDAH; J. E. Graves to Charles J. Anderson, Feb. 22, 1917, LCSH, Board of Visitors, Correspondence, VSL; LCSH, Board of Visitors, Minutes, 1:105–6, VSL; TSH, Board of Trustees, Minutes, p. 46, TSLA; TxHM, Board of Managers *Report* (1894), p. 3, TxSA; Investigation of the Texas Home for Men (1917), p. 188, TxSA; Mass Diary, 4:256, USM.

17. GSH, Board of Trustees, Minutes, 3:83–85, 4:113, GDAH; LCSH, Board of Visitors, Minutes, 3:325, VSL; Investigation of the Texas Home for Men (1917), pp. 12, 28–29, 160, 162, 165, TxSA.

18. *Southern Bivouac* 2 (July 1884): 510; Investigation of the Georgia Soldiers' Home (1906), p. 448, GDAH; GSH, Board of Trustees, Minutes, 2:96, 141, 224–25, 3:95, 102, 145–46, GDAH.

19. McCampbell, *Ex-Confederate Soldiers' Home, Richmond.*

20. Felix G. Swaim to "Whom it may Concern," Aug. 14, 1909, ArCH AA, Griffing, ArSA; JDBMSH, Register of Inmates, p. 15, Mississippi Department of Archives and History, Jackson.

21. See Chambers, Longhurst, and Pacey, *Seasonal Dimensions to Rural Poverty*; Sakamoto-Momiyama, *Seasonality in Human Mortality*; and Henry, *Population*, pp. 37–38. For reports of suicides, see Austin *Confederate Home Vidette*, June 1, 1912; *Constitution*, Apr. 5, 1903; and LCSH, Board of Visitors, Minutes, 2:25, VSL.

22. Rufus McDaniel to Mrs. Pearl Sims, Mar. 20, 1926, Jan. 24, 1927, ArCH AA, Wesley Givens, ArSA; Charles Allen to J. E. Graves, Feb. 7, 1912, and Mrs. Clark to Charles Bigger, Oct. 1, 1893, LCSH AAs, Allen and Clark, respectively, VSL.

23. McDaniel to Mrs. Lilly Pinson, Feb. 25, 1924, McDaniel to E. L. McLendon, Sept. 11, 1923, both in ArCH AA, J. Stroud Gill, ArSA.

24. Roebuck, *My Own Personal Experience*, pp. 5–7.

25. He was unsuccessful in his appeal. Boisseau to J. E. Graves, Feb. 8, 1913, LCSH AA, David G. Boisseau, VSL.

26. John W. Meeks to Rufus G. McDaniel, June 13, Aug. 8, 1922, McDaniel to Meeks, Aug. 7, 1922, both in ArCH AA, Robert Burrow, ArSA.

27. For an introduction to the "relocation mortality effect" syndrome, see Lawton and Yaffe, "Mortality, Morbidity and Voluntary Change of Residence"; Markus et al., "Impact of Relocation"; and Lieberman, "Relationships of Mortality Rates to Entrance to a Home."

28. GSH, Register of Inmates, 1:48, GDAH; Warren G. French to [Mrs. Jesse Rankin], Mar. 4, 1948, JDBMSH, Board of Directors, Correspondence, USM; *Con Vet* 26 (1918): 499; SCCI AA, James M. Hughes, SCDAH.

29. See the Appendix for the method used in calculating inmates' tenure.

30. GSH, Register of Inmates, 1:52, 67, 503, GDAH; *Thin Gray Line*, p. 74; NCSH, Inmate Register, NCDAH; SCCI AA, Joe Boatright, SCDAH; JDBMSH, Register of Inmates; TxHM, Roster of Inmates, TxSA.

31. For specific acts of inmate roughhousing, especially during the twentieth century, see Austin *Confederate Home Vidette*, Jan. 1, 1913; "Texas Confederate

Soldiers' Home a Model," *Con Vet* 20 (1912): 61; GSH, Board of Trustees, Minutes, 3:187, 193, 287–88, 4:106, 139, GDAH; Investigation of the Georgia Soldiers' Home (1906), pp. 168, 450–52, GDAH; TSH, Board of Trustees, Minutes, p. 51, TSLA; CNSH, Board of Directors, Investigating Committee Report (1899–1924), LHAC; E. P. Wright to John W. A. Sanford, Jan. 21, 1909, Sanford Papers, Alabama Department of Archives and History, Montgomery.

32. SCCI, Confederate Home Commissioners, *Report* (1914), SCDAH; Biloxi *Daily Herald*, Nov. 8, 9, 1916. See also Kapnick, Goodman, and Cornwell, "Political Behavior in the Aged"; President Henry E. Shelley's remark that a "large majority" of the Texas inmates participated in political campaigns, in TxHM, Board of Managers *Report* (1894), p. 4, TxSA; and the Texas-inmate newspaper that served as a Democratic organ, Austin *Confederate Home Vidette*, May 15, 1912.

33. GSH, Board of Trustees, Minutes, 2:76, 89, 91, 98, 101, 3:32–33, 38, 158, 165–67, 171, 177, 194, GDAH; GSH, Board of Trustees *Report* (1911), GDAH; Investigation of the Georgia Soldiers' Home (1906), pp. 389, 450–52, GDAH; CNSH, Board of Directors, Minutes, 5:6, 7, 30, LHAC; CNSH, Board of Directors, President Report (Nov. 30, 1900), LHAC; Melzar Titus to F. W. Gras, Feb. 5, 1916, CNSH, Board of Directors, Correspondence, LHAC; NCSH, Superintendent's Inmate Behavior Log, p. 107, NCDAH; Raleigh *News and Observer*, Apr. 24–25, 1935; LCSH, Board of Visitors, Minutes, 2:410, VSL; W. L Morris to Fitzhugh Lee, Feb. 3, 1885, J. H. Allen to Lee, Oct. 13, 1885, both in LCSH, Board of Visitors, Correspondence, VSL; Investigation of the Texas Home for Men (1917), pp. 69–71, TxSA; Austin *Confederate Home Vidette*, May 1, 1913.

34. Goffman, *Asylums*, pp. 60–63; Investigation of the Texas Home for Men (1917), p. 5, TxSA; Mary E. Smith to Board of Visitors, n.d., LCSH, Board of Visitors, Correspondence, VSL.

35. For an introduction to the role of reminiscing, see Feldman, Mulcahey, and Brudno, "A Different Approach to the Treatment of the Older Male Veteran Patient"; Friedman, "Spatial Proximity and Social Interaction"; Friedman, "Age, Length of Institutionalization, and Social Status"; Lewis, "Reminiscing and Self-Concept"; Havighurst and Glasser, "An Exploratory Study of Reminiscence"; Tobin, "Preservation of the Self"; and Richter, "Attaining Ego Integrity through Life Review."

36. "The Last Roll," New Orleans *Daily-Picayune*, Jan. 19, 1913; *Con Vet* 10 (1902): 296; 20 (1912): 61; Williams, " 'Home . . . for the Old Boys,' " p. 45. See also Columbia *Record*, Feb. 14, 1932, for an article entitled "Remnant of Gray Hosts Clings to Spirit of Sixties; Vets at Columbia Home Spin Stories of Battle and Hardship." The story included two photographs and interviews with six veterans, ranging in ages from eight-seven to ninety-one.

37. Julian Levy to AANV, Oct. 14, 1911, AANV Papers, Veterans Benefits, LHAC.

38. *Southern Historical Society Papers* 26 (1898): 303; SCCI, Confederate Home Commissioners, Minutes, Sept. 9, 1924, SCDAH; Montgomery *Advertiser*, Oct. 5, Nov. 18, 1902; interviews with Mrs. Daniels (Aug. 16, 1984), with Lillie Patterson (June 11, 1984), and with Bob Griffin (n.d.), Fritz Hamer Research Notes, Confederate Memorial Park, Marbury, Alabama; Mass Diary, 1:87, USM; JDBMSH, Board of Directors, Minute Book, 1:61, USM; Lumpkin, *Making of a Southerner*, p. 125.

39. Newspaper clipping, Feb. 28, 1929, and undated clipping, both in JDBMSH, Board of Directors, Minute Book 1, USM. See also, Biloxi *Daily Herald*, June 17, 1922, for what happened to one Mississippi inmate who got separated from the others while attending the 1922 UCV reunion at Richmond, missed the train home, and was forced to remain in the Virginia home for a few days before the superintendent was able to go fetch him. In addition, see the record of J. D. Binion, whose two-and-a-half-year tenure as a Georgia inmate tragically ended in June 1917, when he fell off a train en route to Atlanta from a veterans' reunion. GSH, Inmate Register, 2:89, GDAH.

40. Biloxi *Daily Herald*, Aug. 6, 1923.

Chapter 7

1. Biloxi *Daily Herald*, Dec. 6, 1916.

2. McCampbell, *Ex-Confederate Soldiers' Home, Richmond*; TxHM, Board of Managers *Report* (1902), pp. 3–4, Austin Public Library, Austin, Tex.; (1918), p. 12, TxSA; Investigation of the Texas Home for Men (1917), p. 238, TxSA; GSH, Board of Trustees, Minutes, 2:223, 3:121, GDAH; Investigation of the Georgia Soldiers' Home (1906), pp. 398, 428–31, GDAH; New Orleans *Daily-Picayune*, Jan. 19, 1913; GSH, Board of Trustees, Minutes, 2:87–88, 100, 290, 3:56, 64, 180–81, 189–90, 4:18–19, 141, GDAH; John Watson to Board of Directors, May 3, 1919, CNSH, Board of Directors, Minutes, LHAC; Texas *House Journal* (1913), pp. 942–43; Ben S. Williams to S. E. Welch, Dec. 3, 1920, SCCI, Confederate Home Commissioners, Minutes, SCDAH; J. W. Bryant to Clarence P. Newton, Oct. 18, 1915, ArCH AA, Bryant, ArSA; South Carolina *Reports and Resolutions* (1913), 3:687–88.

3. For the complete testimony of Mills, see Investigation of the Georgia Soldiers' Home (1906), pp. 187–205, GDAH. See also Mills to W. Lowndes Calhoun, Apr. 1, 1900, GSH, Board of Trustees, Letters Received, GDAH, and J. W. Bryant to Clarence P. Newton, Oct. 18, 1915, ArCH AA, Edward Tillotson, ArSA. For instances of inmate drunkenness and management disgust, see GSH, Board of Trustees *Report* (1906), pp. 6–7, 9–10, GDAH; GSH, Board of Trustees, Minutes, 2:48–50, 133, 3:185, 244, 266–67, GDAH; LCSH, Board of Visitors, Report by Commandant William H. Terry (c. May 1887), Correspondence, VSL; CNSH, Board of Directors, Minutes, 2:190, 197, LHAC; TxHM, Board of Managers *Report* (1892), p. 6, TxSA.

4. GSH, Board of Trustees, Minutes, 2:123–24, 147, 165, 299, GDAH; LCSH, Board of Visitors, Minutes, 3:36, VSL; TxHM, Board of Managers *Report* (1900), p. 9, TxSA; James S. Fouché to Dr. W. T. C. Bates, Oct. 9, 1924, SCCI, Confederate Home Commissioners, Minutes, SCDAH; SCCI, Executive Committee, Minutes, Oct. 1923, pp. 144–45, SCDAH; SCCI, Confederate Home Commissioners *Report* (1913), SCDAH. Morphine addiction in the United States after the Civil War was known as the "army disease," as numerous physicians prescribed opium or morphine to diseased or disabled veterans in order to relieve their physical pain and perhaps their mental anguish as well. See Courtwright, "Opiate Addiction."

5. TxHM, Board of Managers *Report* (1901), p. 7, Austin Public Library, Austin, Tex.; Carr to Martha Haywood, Dec. 22, 1920, Nov. 6, 1922, Haywood Papers, NCDAH;

GSH, Board of Trustees, Minutes, 2:273, GDAH. See also Mrs. James Pleasants to Norman V. Randolph, Jan. 9, 1893, LCSH, Board of Visitors, Correspondence, VSL, regarding a dismissed insubordinate inmate who earnestly desired "the helpful restraints" of the home.

6. Of the 46 inmates questioned by the Georgia investigating committee in December 1905, 23 had no complaints; 18 indicated that drunkenness and cursing by fellow inmates worried them the most; 8 criticized the home's clothing and food quality; 2 specifically expressed displeasure for passes, curfews, and the management; while only 3 made a positive statement of their treatment in the home. GSH, Board of Trustees, Minutes, 3:3, GDAH.

7. "The Confederate Soldiers' Home of Georgia," *Atlanta Journal Magazine*, Apr. 28, 1912; GSH, Board of Trustees, Minutes, 2:180, 3:103, 113, GDAH; CNSH, Board of Directors, Minutes, 2:44, 4:15, LHAC; CNSH, Board of Directors, President Report (June 2, 1906), LHAC; LCSH, Board of Visitors, Minutes, 1:141, 158, 2:352, VSL; Austin *Confederate Home News*, Feb. 17, 1912; "Sermon from a Veteran to Comrades," *Con Vet* 9 (1901): 549–50; SCCI, Executive Committee, Minutes, May 12, 1922, pp. 93–94, SCDAH.

8. McCampbell, *Ex-Confederate Soldiers' Home, Richmond.*

9. Texas *Senate Journal* (1913), p. 93; TSH, Board of Trustees, Minutes, 58–59, TSLA; SCCI, Executive Committee, Minutes, Apr. 13, 1922, p. 90, SCDAH; James W. Pegram to Comrades, Oct. 27, 1893, W. Gordon McCabe to James Pegram, Oct. 30, 1893, and Charles W. Bingley to Norman V. Randolph, Apr. 14, 1891, all in LCSH, Board of Visitors, Correspondence, VSL.

10. CNSH, Board of Directors, Minutes, 2:30, LHAC; Fred Ober to Alex N. Power, Sept. 7, 1907, CNSH, Board of Directors, Correspondence, LHAC.

11. South Carolina *Reports and Resolutions* (1918), 2:62–64; SCCI, Confederate Home Commissioners, Minutes, June 6, 1922, June 12, 1923, SCDAH. See CNSH, Board of Directors, Minutes 2:397, LHAC, which undoubtedly offered a better alternative than Director B. T. Walshe's recommendation that "any inmate who caused any disturbance . . . would be sent to prison." See also Tennessee *House Journal* (1911), pp. 947–48.

12. South Carolina *Reports and Resolutions* (1913), 3:687–88; JDBMSH, Board of Directors, *Fifth Biennial Report* (1912–13), pp. 4–5, USM. For Thompson's observations, see Investigation of the Georgia Soldiers' Home (1906), pp. 329–32, 327, GDAH. For Ober's remarks, see CNSH, Board of Directors, President Report (May 5, 1906), LHAC.

13. See L. R. Wallace, H. H. Turner, J. T. Green to Supt. [McDaniel], July 13, 1922, and McDaniel's reply of July 17, 1922, both in ArCH AA, George W. Glen, ArSA.

14. See LCSH AA, Marshall S. Brown, VSL, which also has the veteran's record as an inmate; LCSH, Board of Visitors, Minutes, 1:45, 50, 79–80, VSL; GSH, Board of Trustees, Minutes, 2:159, 185, 191, 3:70–72, 140–41, 146, 167, GDAH; TSH, Board of Trustees, Minutes, pp. 20–21, TSLA; CNSH, Board of Directors, Minutes, 2:275, LHAC; CNSH, Board of Directors, President Report (June 3, 1904), LHAC; CNSH, Board of Directors, Investigating Committee Report (Nov. 17, 1897), LHAC; and

SCCI, Executive Committee, Minutes, May 12, 1922, p. 93, and July 11, 1924, pp. 189–90, SCDAH.

15. Cardwell to W. G. Peterson, Dec. 16, 1910, SCCI AA, John F. Johnson, SCDAH; SCCI, Confederate Home Commissioners, Minutes, Sept., 18, 1923, SCDAH.

16. J. M. Hughey to Cardwell, Jan. 10, 1910, SCCI AA, Hughey, SCDAH.

17. William Barr to John C. Loggins, Oct. 16, 1918, TxHM, Board of Managers, Correspondence, TxSA; GSH, Board of Trustees, Mintues, 2:42, 3:88, 101, 176, GDAH; Edward Travers to T. C. Will, Dec. 27, 1908, and John Edens to H. H. Ward, Sept. 3, 1907, both in CNSH, Board of Directors, Correspondence, LHAC; James E. Childress to A. L. Phillips, June 25, 1902, LCSH AA, Childress, VSL; R. P. Williford to William J. McMurray, Mar. 22, 1893, TSH AA, Williford, TSLA; Tennessee *Acts* (1899), p. 1257.

18. G. W. Thompson to Felix G. Swaim, Oct. 5, 1909, ArCH AA, Thompson, ArSA.

19. Soon afterward, Thompson left. But twelve years later he was readmitted—along with his wife—and he died at the home in January 1928. Felix G. Swaim to Adjutant General's Office, Apr. 19, May 6, 14, 1911, ArCH AA, G. W. Thompson, ArSA.

20. Bonham to W. D. Starling, Oct. 2, 1909, SCCI AA, Riley Rowland, SCDAH; Malachi Whittle to B. T. Walshe, June 25, 1899, CNSH, Board of Directors, Correspondence, LHAC; GSH, Board of Trustees, Minutes, 3:8–11, 39, GDAH. See also a pair of Delbridge's clemency petitions, one handwritten and dated Jan. 15, 1907, the other typed and dated July 7, 1907, GSH, Board of Trustees, Letters Received, GDAH.

21. Rufus K. Houston to Board of Directors, May 1918, CNSH, Board of Directors, Correspondence, LHAC; LCSH, Board of Visitors, Minutes, 3:178–79, 186–87, VSL.

22. Austin *Confederate Home Vidette*, May 15, 1912; CNSH, Board of Directors, Minutes, 2:148, LHAC; CNSH, Board of Directors, President Report (Jan. 25, 1909), LHAC.

23. About a year and a half following his readmission, Horton was granted a discharge at his own request. He died of bronchitis six months later. SCCI, Executive Committee, Minutes, Mar. 31, 1920; J. L. Wardlaw to Gov. R. A. Cooper, Aug. 27, 1920, and S. E. Welch to Wardlaw, Oct. 25, 1920, both in SCCI, Confederate Home Commissioners, Minutes; SCCI, Inmate Records, 1:160, SCDAH.

24. SCCI, Confederate Home Commissioners *Report* (1913), SCDAH; SCCI, Executive Committee, Minutes, July 11, 1922, June 1923, pp. 98, 96, 130, SCDAH.

25. For Severn's ordeal, see his letter to the Board of Directors, Aug. 31, 1900, John J. Aubertin to Alden McLellan, Sept. 1, 1900, Severn to E. E. Smart, Oct. 2, 1900, and McLellan to Leon Jastremski, Oct. 15, 1900, all in CNSH, Board of Directors, Correspondence, LHAC.

26. For a published account of the sensational Ripley case, see Board of Directors to AANV and AAT, Sept. 9, 1893, CNSH, Board of Directors, Correspondence, LHAC. See also CNSH, Board of Directors, Minutes, 2:99–100, LHAC; Louisiana *House Journal* (1894), pp. 824–25; and New Orleans *Daily-Picayune*, June 11, 1894.

27. For criticisms by inmates, see Investigation of the Georgia Soldiers' Home (1906), pp. 100, 117–128, 136–41, 228–29, 232, 280, 287–90, 292, 365, 367–68, 374,

GDAH. The committee's findings begin on p. 466. For the committee's origins, see Georgia *Laws* (1906), pp. 1164–65. Regarding legislative investigations of other homes, see the petition by E. G. Wall et al., July 4, 1892, LCSH, Board of Visitors, Correspondence, VSL; LCSH, Board of Visitors, Minutes, 1:359–66, 2:22–25, VSL; CNSH, Board of Directors, Minutes, 5:76–78, LHAC.

28. See Investigation of the Texas Home for Men (1917), pp. 34–36, 39–40, 45, 85–87, 91, 114–15, 177, TxSA.

29. South Carolina *Reports and Resolutions* (1913), 3:687–88; South Carolina *House Journal*, (1920), pp. 10–11; David Cardwell to Martin Ansel, May 6, 1910, and Ansel to Cardwell, May 7, 1910, both in Ansel Papers, SCDAH. Regarding the generally nonchalant attitude toward inmate allegations, see Texas *House Journal* (1901), pp. 638–39; New Orleans *Daily-Picayune*, Jan. 19, 1913. For overwhelmingly favorable endorsements of home administrations, see GSH, Board of Trustees, Minutes, 2:149, 4:27, 29–30, 43, GDAH; Texas *House Journal* (1895), p. 457; (1907), p. 694; Georgia *House Journal* (1913), pp. 1140–42, 1255–57; LCSH, Board of Visitors, Minutes, 1:149–51, VSL. For the defensive posture adopted by home officials, see Investigation of the Georgia Soldiers' Home (1906), p. 177, GDAH; CNSH, Board of Directors, Minutes, 5:75–77, LHAC; CNSH, Board of Directors, Investigating Committee Report (Sept. 7, 1918), LHAC; Board of Visitors to J. C. Batchelder, Apr. 16, 1912, LCSH, Board of Visitors, Minutes, VSL; Rev. G. Croft Williams to Capt. J. L. Wardlaw, Sept. 3, 1920, and Wardlaw to Williams, Sept. 7, 1920, both in SCCI, Confederate Home Commissioners, Minutes, SCDAH.

30. For allegations of retribution against inmates, see Tennessee *Senate Journal* (1897), pp. 805–7; H. H. Mashburn to Julian S. Carr, Nov. 3, 1922, Haywood Papers, NCDAH; the 176-page stenographic report filed in reaction to the petition by E. G. Wall et al., July 4, 1892 (esp. pp. 36, 39–40, 95), VSL; John N. Opie to Norman V. Randolph, Feb. 7, 1900, LCSH, Board of Visitors, Correspondence, VSL; Investigation of the Georgia Soldiers' Home (1906), pp. 22–24, 40–51, 221, GDAH; CNSH, Board of Directors, Minutes, 5:84, 91–92, 95–96, LHAC.

31. Norman V. Randolph to John N. Opie, Feb. 7, 1900, LCSH, Board of Visitors, Correspondence, VSL.

32. GSH, Board of Trustees, Minutes, 2:87–88, 100, 290, 3:56, 64, 180–81, 189–90, 4:18–19, 141, GDAH; John Watson to Board of Directors, May 3, 1919, CNSH, Board of Directors, Minutes, LHAC; Texas *House Journal* (1913), pp. 942–43; Ben S. Williams to S. E. Welch, Dec. 3, 1920, SCCI, Confederate Home Commissioners, Minutes, SCDAH.

33. For the etymology of "inmate," see *Oxford English Dictionary*, 5:307. For formal petitions presented by inmates and management alike, see the handwritten "Exhibit A" by M. L. Faries et al., c. Apr. 1905, GSH, Board of Trustees, Minutes, 2:200–201, GDAH; CNSH, Board of Directors, Minutes, 3:265, 270, 279, 280–300, LHAC; TSH, Board of Trustees, Minutes, 45, TSLA; Unsigned to The Executive Committee, Dec. 27, 1905, Jefferson Manly Falkner Soldiers' Home records, Alabama Department of Archives and History, Montgomery.

Chapter 8

1. Foster, *Ghosts of the Confederacy*, pp. 3–5, 7, 178–79, 197.

2. Every home had a hospital, a noteworthy addition that eventually transformed each institution. See Olds, "History of the Soldiers' Home at Raleigh," pp. 1, 8; GSH, Board of Trustees, Minutes, 2: 80–82, GDAH; GSH, Board of Trustees *Report* (1914), p. 3, GDAH; LCSH, Board of Visitors *Report* (1897), p. 4, VSL; Tennessee Board of Charities *Report* (1915), p. 31; J. L. Wardlaw to H. E. Thompson, Jan. 5, 1917, SCCI, Confederate Home Commissioners, Minutes, SCDAH; South Carolina *Reports and Resolutions* (1911), 5:114–15; (1917), 2:63–64.

3. CNSH, Board of Directors *Report* (1886), p. 9; (1894), pp. 7–9; (1896), pp. 7–8; (1898), pp. 12–14, LHAC; CNSH, Board of Directors, Minutes, 2:171, LHAC. The term "trivial" is used by Surgeon F. T. Fry in LCSH, Board of Visitors *Report* (1899), p. 7, VSL.

4. CNSH, Board of Directors *Report* (1906), pp. 19–20; (1908), pp. 17–18; (1914), pp. 17–18, LHAC; M. James Stevens notebook, Beauvoir. The Arkansas home hospital, originally built in 1894, was first expanded in 1907, then enlarged and refurbished in 1917, and added to a third time in 1923. *Con Vet* 16 (1908): 182; Gaither, *Arkansas Confederate Home*, p. 4. By 1915 there were three hospitals on the grounds of the Kentucky Confederate Soldiers' Home. *Con Vet* 23 (1915): 462–63.

5. For an unfavorable critique of hospital care, see GSH, Board of Trustees, Minutes, 2:143, GDAH. For Moore's optimistic data, see TxHM, Board of Managers *Report* (1912), p. 9, Austin Public Library, Austin, Tex. Life expectancy in 1900 for American men aged sixty-five was 11.9 years; from age seventy-five it was 7.1 years. Faber, *Life Tables*.

6. Clarence P. Newton to George Brackman, Oct. 12, 1918, ArCH AA, Brackman, ArSA.

7. LCSH, Board of Visitors *Report* (1905), p. 7; (1910), p. 7; (1915), pp. 8–9; (1918), pp. 8–9, VSL; JDBMSH, Board of Directors, *Fifth Biennial Report* (1912–13), pp. 5–6, USM.

8. CNSH, Board of Directors *Report* (1896), p. 7; (1902), p. 13, LHAC; GSH, Board of Trustees *Report* (1906), p. 7, GDAH.

9. TxHM, Board of Managers *Report* (1892), pp. 4, 8; (1894), p. 5, TxSA; Stith, "Plat of the Confederate Home at Austin, Texas," Texas Confederate Museum, Austin; Raines, *Year Book for Texas, 1901*, p. 58; CNSH, Board of Directors, Minutes, 2:4 69, LHAC; CNSH, Board of Directors *Report* (1906), pp. 4, 26–39; (1908), pp. 24–25, LHAC; GSH, Board of Trustees, Minutes, 2:87, GDAH; Poole, "Final Encampment," pp. 12–13.

10. South Carolina *Reports and Resolutions* (1918), 2:62–64.

11. "Gold Key Souvenir of Beauvoir" (c. 1929), JDBMSH, Correspondence, USM; Biloxi *Daily Herald*, Mar. 27, 1919; *Con Vet* 36 (1928): 186–87.

12. The Lee Camp Home's monthly per capita expenses from 1884 to 1898 averaged $8.09. During that same period, the home received $428,056, 63.8 percent of which represented state appropriations, the remainder being city and private contributions.

LCSH, Board of Visitors, Minutes, 1:45, 77, 102–03, 167, 182–83, VSL; LCSH, Board of Visitors *Report* (1895), pp. 5–6; (1896), p. 4; (1898), pp. 5–6, VSL. The Arkansas home got off to a shaky start. After less than one full year, it fell into arrears by some $2,500, a debt that the legislature had to make good in 1893. Arkansas *Gazette*, Aug. 7, 1892; Thomas, *Arkansas and Its People*, 1:235.

13. Herndon, *Centennial History of Arkansas*, 1:436. For a glimpse of the terrible time the Arkansas home administrators had with their finances, see ArCH, Superintendent's *Report* (1915–16), pp. 5–10. The difficulty in balancing budgets is further illustrated in CNSH, Board of Directors *Report* (1914), pp. 12–13, LHAC. The report shows that during the biennial period 1912–14, the institution's expenses surpassed receipts by more than $2,000.

14. See, for example, the records of the Arkansas home for the period 1923–24. The provisions, fuel, and payroll costs accounted for more than two-thirds of the total operating expenses of $163,013.62. The cost for care and treatment of the inmates was roughly $15,000, or 9 percent of the total disbursements. At approximately the same time the medical staff consisted of a resident physician, an assistant physician, a pharmacist, a hospital matron, a nurse, and various "helpers." ArCH, Board of Managers *Report* (1924), p. 12.

15. For just a few construction and repairs costs, see Georgia *Laws* (1906), pp. 19–20; (1911), pp. 37–38; and Texas *Laws* (1917), pp. 86–88. Between 1905 and 1918 the Lee Camp Home's monthly per capita expenses for food and tobacco alone averaged $13.47. LCSH, Board of Visitors *Report* (1905), pp. 5–6; (1910), p. 5; (1915), p. 5; (1918), p. 7, VSL. Concerning the spiraling inflation Texas officials grappled with, see TxHM, Board of Managers *Report* (1904), p. 6; (1916), pp. 6–7, Austin Public Library, Austin, Tex.; (1918), p. 6, TxSA.

16. By way of comparison, the Louisiana state constitution of 1898 fixed Camp Nicholls's annual per capita appropriations at $130. Beauvoir's allotment from 1909 to 1919 was set at 60 cents per capita per day, while the state of Texas originally placed a cap on soldiers' home funds at $100,000 per year. CNSH, Board of Directors *Report* (1906), p. 7, LHAC; Raines, *Year Book for Texas, 1901*, 57; Biloxi *Daily Herald*, Apr. 26, 1916.

17. This figure has been computed by multiplying the per capita allowance times the standard one hundred inmates times fifteen. As Figure 2 in the Appendix indicates, enrollment in the Tennessee institution did not reach one hundred until 1899, after which inmate population continued to climb until it reached its apex of 130 in 1908. From that point on inmate population gradually, then rapidly, declined. Tennessee *Senate Journal* (1891), p. 174; (1897), pp. 118, 922; Tennessee *House Journal Appendix* (1895), pp. 3–4; Tennessee *House Journal* (1899), p. 303; Tennessee *House and Senate Journal Appendix* (1905), p. 1; Tennessee *Acts* (1909), p. 41; (1911), pp. 17–18; (1915), p. 98.

18. According to White, *Confederate Veteran*, pp. 113–14, the total cost for all fifteen Confederate homes in 1914 alone amounted to $518,000; truly a bargain, compared to Confederate pension payments by southern states, which totaled $7.4 million during the same year. For debt amortization and miscellaneous disbursements

in the Tennessee and other homes, see Tennessee *Senate Journal* (1909), p. 41; Tennessee *Acts* (1911), pp. 17–18; Connor, *Manual of North Carolina*, p. 167; Louisiana *Acts* (1902), pp. 382–83; and Texas *Laws* (1917), pp. 86–88. For Superintendent Tartt's request, see JDBMSH, Board of Directors, *Eighth Biennial Report* (1918–19), Beauvoir.

19. GSH, Board of Trustees *Report* (1910), p. 7, GDAH; TxHM, Superintendent *Report* (1904), p. 8, TxSA; CNSH, Board of Directors *Report* (1902), p. 5, LHAC; LCSH, Board of Visitors *Report* (1901), p. 5, VSL; *Con Vet* 18 (1910): 280.

20. Charter members of the Nashville auxiliary included men—Governor Peter Turney, John Overton, *American* editor Duncan Cooper, attorney John Childress—as well as the wives of veteran activists George Guild, John Hickman, and Gideon Baskette. Poppenheim, *United Daughters of the Confederacy*, 1:234; Nashville *Daily American*, Apr. 10, 1890. For a rendering of some of the group's many gifts, see TSH, Board of Trustees, Minutes, p. 56, TSLA; and *Con Vet* 23 (1915): 441–42; 16 (1908): 180. See also, Climer, "Protectors of the Past"; and Cody, *Tennessee Division United Daughters of the Confederacy*, pp. 39–46.

21. The phrase "secondary bureaucracy" has been borrowed from Hall, *The Organization of American Culture*, pp. 262–63, though it is used differently here. For the emotional visit to the Tennessee home, see *Con Vet* 14 (1906): 271. Regarding visits to other homes, see CNSH, Board of Directors, Minutes, 2:75, 385, LHAC; CNSH, Board of Directors, House Committee Report (Dec. 2, 1905), LHAC; CNSH, Board of Directors, President Report (June 6, 1900); (Sept. 30, 1900); (May 7, 1904); (June 3, 1904), LHAC; Raleigh *News and Observer*, Dec. 5, 1920; Poole, "Final Encampment," p. 16; White, *Confederate Veteran*, p. 113; *Con Vet* 2 (1894): 367; 5 (1897): 114–15, 546; 18 (1910): 280; Montgomery *Advertiser*, May 26, 1903; and Mountain Creek, Ala., *News*, Apr. 21, 28, 1904.

22. *Con Vet* 5 (1897): 179; 9 (1901): 226–27; Ben S. Williams to Mrs. Cornelia G. Walker, Nov. 29, 1929, SCCI, Confederate Home Commissioners, Minutes, SCDAH; Biloxi *Daily Herald*, Nov. 23, 1914, Feb. 4, 8, May 8, July 4, Oct. 6, 10, 25, 1916. For the "proper" role of women in the veterans' institutions, see GSH, Board of Trustees, Minutes, 3:11, 13, GDAH. For other clashes between women and management, see TSH, Board of Trustees, Minutes, 45, TSLA; GSH, Board of Trustees, Minutes, 3:234, 243, GDAH; Saussey Diary, GDAH; Georgia *House Journal* (1925), pp. 1280–84; letters from Mrs. Norman V. Randolph, May 3, 1899, and Mrs. Kate P. Minor, c. 1899, both in LCSH, Board of Visitors, Correspondence, VSL; and letters from Mrs. Edward Gottschalk, Aug. 1, 1912, and George H. Lord, Aug. 21, 1912, both in CNSH, Board of Directors, Correspondence, LHAC.

23. Huey, *Alabama Division, United Daughters of the Confederacy*, pp. 81–86.

24. In the end, only the Florida home excluded women inmates. SCCI, Inmate Records, SCDAH. For the shift in women's roles at Camp Nicholls, see CNSH, Board of Directors *Report* (1904), p. 6; (1918), p. 15; (1922), p. 4, LHAC; CNSH, Board of Directors, Minutes, 4:145, 147, LHAC; New Orleans *Times-Picayune*, Jan. 5, 1921; and CNSH, Board of Directors, House Committee Report (Mar. 31, 1921), LHAC, in which the committee chairman commenced, "Ladies and Gentlemen . . ." For a similar

change in the North Carolina institution, see William C. Stronach to Rebecca Cameron, Oct. 23, 1900, Hinsdale Papers, William R. Perkins Library, Duke University, Durham, N.C.; North Carolina *Laws* (1891), p. 795; NCSH, Warrants and Weekly Payroll (1910), NCDAH; and North Carolina Department of Human Services, Inspection of NCSH, 1920 and 1924, NCDAH. See also South Carolina *Acts* (1921), pp. 119–20; Biloxi *Daily Herald*, Mar. 16, 1962; and *Con Vet* 35 (1927): 197.

25. In 1949, after the last Confederate veteran had died, the home was opened to veterans of all wars. Lashley, "Oklahoma's Confederate Veterans Home," pp. 34–45; Lashley, "Confederate Veterans in Oklahoma."

26. Richardson, Wallace, and Anderson, *Lone Star State*, p. 316.

27. See Williams, " 'Home . . . for the Old Boys,' " p. 41, which argues that, as the age of residents increased, problems of misbehavior at the Lee Camp Home were fewer and the rules were altered to accommodate older men. Notwithstanding this argument, the official records of the institution reveal otherwise. From 1897 to 1899, for example, as many as sixteen Lee Camp Home inmates were dismissed for cause; between 1915 and 1917, fourteen were expelled, only a slight decrease. LCSH, Board of Visitors *Report* (1898–1900, 1916–18), VSL. See also CNSH, Board of Directors, Investigating Committee Report (1900, 1915, 1919), LHAC. Between July 1, 1899, and Nov. 16, 1900, Camp Nicholls officials cited 101 inmates for rules violations ranging from intoxication to disturbing the peace, assault and battery, threats, and insubordination. Between Jan. 4, 1913, and Dec. 5, 1914, thirty inmates were brought up on charges: fourteen for drunkenness and bootlegging, eight for disturbing the peace and fighting, and four for threatening and abusing home officers. In 1918, eight inmates were found guilty of creating disturbances, including climbing the front fence. So, while the number of infractions clearly appears to have decreased over time, the presumption that aged inmates tended to be more passive in latter years is questionable indeed.

28. See GSH, Board of Trustees, Minutes, 4:279, GDAH, and NCSH, Superintendent's Inmate Behavior Log (1923–24), pp. 107–8, NCDAH, for recorded breaches in discipline. For the words "creditable appearance," see CNSH, Board of Directors, House Committee Report (June 6, 1919), LHAC. For examples of a superintendent's continued concern for veterans' hygiene, see Mass Diary, 1:26–27, 39, 41, USM.

29. For Rixey's proposals, see *Cong. Rec.*, 55th Cong., 3rd sess., vol. 32, pt. 1, p. 268; 57th Cong., 1st sess., vol. 35, pt. 1, pp. 627, 632, 637; and 58th Cong., 2nd sess., vol. 38, pt. 2, p. 1873. For reaction to the Virginian's bills, see *Cong. Rec.*, 57th Cong., 1st sess., vol. 35, pt. 1, pp. 628–34, and pt. 8, Appendix, pp. 91–92. For the statement attributed to Gardner, see Montgomery *Advertiser*, Apr. 27, 1902.

30. See Senate Committee on Military Affairs, *Homes for Confederate Veterans Hearing*, and House Committee on Invalid Persons, *Claims of Confederate Soldiers Hearing*. See also *Con Vet* 23 (1915): 102–3; 24 (1916): 8, 56, 90.

31. *Cong. Rec.*, 64th Cong., 1st Sess., pp. 24, 83. For Wilson's remarks, see *Con Vet* 25 (1917): 296–97, and Link, *Papers of Woodrow Wilson*, 42:451–53. Regarding how the First World War reminded southerners of their "sacred duty" to Johnny Reb, see *Con Vet* 25 (1917): 143, 232–33, 364, 506–12; 28 (1918): 240, 428–29, 539; 27 (1919): 35, 45, 409–10, 478.

32. *Con Vet* 18 (1910): 33, 280; 34 (1926): 118; Gaither, *Arkansas Confederate Home*, 18. For a mournful account of a visit to the Confederate home at Pikesville, Maryland, see *Con Vet* 29 (1921): 176–78.

33. *Con Vet* 18 (1910): 6.

34. Texas Board of Control *Report* (1920), TxSA; Texas *Laws* (1919), pp. 323–27. The Texas home retained "Confederate" in its official title until its closing, though the last Confederate veteran in residence had died in 1954. Newspaper accounts are useful in reconstructing the institution's latter years, when it served as a state hospital. See especially Austin *American Statesman*, May 25, 1941, June 5, 1957, May 21, 1963, Aug. 11, 1966, Nov. 4, Dec. 20, 1970.

35. Lancaster, *Florida Division, United Daughters of the Confederacy*, pp. 11–13; Florida *Laws* (1921), pp. 262–64.

36. LCSH, Board of Visitors *Report* (1921), pp. 3–4, VSL; Williams, " 'Home . . . for the Old Boys,' " p. 46.

37. W. J. Edwards, the last veteran admitted to the Tennessee home (in 1937), died three years after his enrollment. TSH, Record of Inmates (1918), p. 129, TSLA. Tennessee Department of Institutions, *Biennial Report* (1934); Poole, "Final Encampment," 14–17; Casey, *Encyclopedia*, p. 142; CNSH, Board of Directors *Report* (1938), LHAC; Florida Treasurer's *Report* (1940), p. 105; Florida *Laws* (1921), pp. 262–64; Lancaster, *Florida Division, United Daughters of the Confederacy*, p. 19; *Con Vet* 34 (1926): 90; 39 (1931): 431.

38. For example, the first of eighty-two widows and wives was admitted to the South Carolina Confederate Infirmary on April 4, 1925. The first of seventy-five daughters was admitted in September 1935. The first sister of a veteran (age seventy years or older) was admitted in July 1930, by virtue of a legislative act passed the previous year; and beginning in 1943, the state allowed nieces to be admitted if they had been born prior to 1873.

39. *Confederate Veteran—Official Bulletin, South Carolina Division, UCV* (July 1935), p. 3; South Carolina *Statutes at Large* (1957), p. 446; Columbia *State*, June 30, 1957, June 18, 1963; Columbia *Record*, Feb. 11, June 12, 1957; Charleston *News and Courier*, June 23, 1963.

40. Kane, *Dear Dorothy Dix*, pp. 270–71.

41. J. L. Peete to Mrs. Josie C. Rankin, June 9, 1948, Warren G. French to [Rankin], Mar. 4, 1948, and Mrs. Emile Joffrion to [Rankin], Jan. 20, 1948, all in JDBMSH, Board of Directors, Correspondence, USM. See also Thomas F. Richardson (of New Haven, Conn.) to Old Soldiers Home, Sept. 29, 1947, and Rankin to C. C. Shores (of Oklahoma City), Sept. 3, 1947, both in ibid.

42. Mississippi *Laws* (1940), pp. 569–73; (1955), pp. 287–88; New Orleans *Times-Picayune*, Jan. 11, 1954; *Dixie Times-Picayune States Roto Magazine*, June 5, 1955; Bassett, "History of Beauvoir—Jefferson Davis Shrine," pp. 47–66; McCain, *Minutes, Board of Directors*, pp. 108–9; Biloxi *Daily Herald*, Mar. 16, 1962.

43. Gaither, *Arkansas Confederate Home*, p. 6; *Con Vet* 18 (1910): 11, 224; 21 (1913): 348; 29 (1921): 177; M. L. Smith to [Pension Commissioners for York County], Apr. 4, 1911, SCCI AA, Thomas Thomasson, SCDAH.

Epilogue

1. *Con Vet* 34 (1926): 73; 37 (1929): 164, 191, 311, 432; 38 (1930): 200; Los Angeles *Times*, Apr. 16, 1929.

Appendix

1. Wiley, *Life of Johnny Reb*, pp. 322–24.
2. Hammond, "Common Disorders of the Aged"; Chen, "Control and Diarrhoeal Disease, Morbidity and Mortality"; Richard J. Anderson, "Medical Diagnoses."
3. Hunt, "Workers at Gainful Occupations," pp. 393–425.
4. See Powers, *Measures of Socioeconomic Status*.
5. *Tennesseans in the Civil War*. For a related study linking socioeconomic status and rank, see Krick, *Lee's Colonels*.

BIBLIOGRAPHY

Primary Materials

OFFICIAL HOME RECORDS

Alabama Department of Archives and History, Montgomery
   Jefferson Manly Falkner Soldiers' Home, Mountain Creek
      Cemetery Rosters
      Insurance Papers
      Superintendent *Reports*
Arkansas State Archives, Little Rock
   Arkansas Confederate Soldiers' Home, Sweet Home
      Applications for Admission
      Board of Managers *Reports*
      Superintendent's *Reports*
Austin Public Library, Austin, Texas
   Texas Confederate Home for Men, Austin
      Board of Managers *Reports*
Georgia Department of Archives and History, Atlanta
   Georgia Soldiers' Home, Atlanta
      Applications for Admission
      Board of Trustees
         Letters Received
         Minutes
         Reports, 1901–14
      Hospital Record Book
      Invoices for Supplies and Services
      List of Persons Subscribing Contributions Towards the Erection of the Home
      Payrolls for Staff Salaries
      Payrolls of Payments to Inmates
      Record Book of Miscellaneous Home Functions
      Record of Admissions, Discharges and Deaths
      Record of Donations, Entertainments and Religious Services
      Register of Inmates
      George N. Saussey Diary
      Visitors' Register
Jacksonville Public Library, Jacksonville, Florida
   Florida Old Confederate Soldiers and Sailors Home, Jacksonville
      Applications for Admission
      Board of Directors, Letters Received

Kentucky State Archives, Frankfort
  Confederate Soldiers' Home, Georgetown
    Subscribers to the Confederate Soldiers' Home and Widows' and Orphans'
      Asylum
  Kentucky Confederate Soldiers' Home, Pewee Valley
    Board of Trustees, Minutes
    Clothing Issue Book
    Commandant Reports
    Hospital Register
    Inmates Register
    Miscellaneous Reports
    Officer and Employee Payroll
    Physician and Undertaker Records
    Purchase Ledgers
    Rules and Regulations
Louisiana Historical Association Collection, Howard-Tilton Memorial Library,
  Tulane University, New Orleans
  Camp Nicholls Soldiers' Home, New Orleans
    Board of Directors
      Correspondence
      House Committee Reports
      Investigating Committee Reports
      Membership Lists
      Minutes
      President Reports
      Reports, 1886–1938
      Secretary Reports
    Clippings and Pamphlets
    Financial Records
    Rules and Regulations
    Superintendent Reports
    Surgeon Reports
William D. McCain Library, University of Southern Mississippi, Hattiesburg
  Jefferson Davis Beauvoir Memorial Soldiers' Home, Biloxi, Mississippi
    Board of Directors
      Correspondence
      Minute Book, 1920–36
      Reports
Mississippi Department of Archives and History, Jackson
  Jefferson Davis Beauvoir Memorial Soldiers' Home, Biloxi
    Register of Inmates
North Carolina Division of Archives and History, Raleigh
  North Carolina Soldiers' Home, Raleigh
    Board of Incorporators, Minutes

Building and Maintenance Expenses
Drug and Whiskey Account
Hospital Record of Patients
Hospital Register
Inmate Expenses
Inmate Record
Inmate Register
Inmate Roll Book
Ledger Accounts Paid
Record of Clothing Issued
Superintendent's Inmate Behavior Log
Visitors' Register
Warrants and Weekly Payroll
South Carolina Department of Archives and History, Columbia
South Carolina Confederate Infirmary, Columbia
Applications for Admission
Confederate Home Commissioners
Minutes
Reports
Executive Committee, Minutes
Inmate Records
Tennessee State Library and Archives, Nashville
Tennessee Soldiers' Home, Hermitage
Applications for Admission
Board of Trustees
Minutes
Report, 1894
Financial Reports
Record of Inmates, 1918
Register of Inmates
Texas State Archives, Austin
Texas Confederate Home for Men, Austin
Applications for Admission
Blueprints and Drawings
Board of Managers
Correspondence
Reports, 1891–1920
Patients' Ledger, Hospital Record
Roster of Inmates
Superintendent *Reports*, 1892–1909
Virginia State Library, Richmond
Lee Camp Soldiers' Home, Richmond
Applications for Admission
Board of Visitors

Executive Committee Orders
Correspondence
Investigative Committee Reports
Minutes
Reports, 1886–1931
Register of Inmates

MANUSCRIPTS

Alabama Department of Archives and History, Montgomery
  John W. A. Sanford Papers
Atlanta Historical Society, Atlanta, Georgia
  Bruce and Morgan, Architects Business File
  Confederate Veterans File
Barker Texas History Center, University of Texas, Austin
  Henry C. Lindsey Papers
Beauvoir, the Jefferson Davis Memorial Shrine, Biloxi, Mississippi
  V. B. Mass, "Dining Room Record of the Jefferson Davis Soldiers' Home, Beauvoir, Miss, 1917–18, Book No. 1"
  M. James Stevens Notebook
Confederate Memorial Park, Marbury, Alabama
  Fritz Hamer Research Notes
Georgia Department of Archives and History, Atlanta
  Joint Committee of House and Senate Investigation of the Confederate Soldiers' Home of Georgia, Stenographer's Transcription, 1906
Jacksonville Public Library, Jacksonville, Florida
  Florida Soldiers' Home Papers
Louisiana Historical Association Collection, Howard-Tilton Memorial Library, Tulane University, New Orleans
  Association of the Army of Northern Virginia Papers
    Correspondence
    Membership
    Relief Committee Reports
    Veterans Benefits
  Association of the Army of Tennessee Papers
    Correspondence
    Executive Committee Reports
    Membership
    Minutes
    Relief Committee Reports
    Veterans Benefits
  Joseph A. Charlaron Papers
William D. McCain Library, University of Southern Mississippi, Hattiesburg
  V. B. Mass Diary, 1919–20
National Archives, Washington, D.C.

Confederate Compiled Service Records
North Carolina Division of Archives and History, Raleigh
  Civil War Papers
    Wharton J. Green Scrapbook
  Daniel G. Fowle Papers
  Martha Haywood Papers
  James Y. Joyner Papers
  North Carolina Board of Public Charities, Report
  North Carolina Department of Human Services, Engineering Files for State
    Board of Health Inspection of State Institutions, Inspection Records, North
    Carolina Soldiers' Home, Raleigh, 1920–1934
  North Carolina Pension Applications
  Fred A. Olds Papers
  Leonidas L. Polk Papers
  Alfred M. Scales Papers
  Wake County Ladies Memorial Association Papers
    Clippings
    Correspondence
    Mrs. Garland Jones, "Ladies Memorial Association of Raleigh, North Car-
      olina," c. 1902
    Minutes
    Treasurer's Books
William R. Perkins Library, Duke University, Durham, North Carolina
  William Lowndes Calhoun Papers
  John W. Hinsdale Papers
  Charles E. Jones Papers
  William H. Thomas Papers
South Carolina Department of Archives and History, Columbia
  Martin F. Ansel Papers
  Coleman L. Blease Papers
Southern Historical Collection, Wilson Library, University of North Carolina,
  Chapel Hill
  Julian S. Carr Papers
  Raleigh E. Colston Papers
Tennessee State Library and Archives, Nashville
  Benjamin F. Cheatham Bivouac Minutes
  Tennessee Confederate Pension Applications
Texas Confederate Museum, Austin
  "The Confederate Home in Austin before the Turn of the Century," 1954
  D. C. Stith, "Plat of the Confederate Home at Austin, Texas, Containing 25
    Acres"
Texas State Archives, Austin
  Frank Brown, "Annals of Travis County and the City of Austin (From the Ear-
    liest Times to the Close of 1875)," unpublished scrapbook

Governors Records
  M. A. Ferguson
  James S. Hogg
  Dan Moody
Texas Legislative Committee to Investigate State Departments and Institutions,
  Confederate Home for Men, Stenographer's Transcription, 1917
Texas Statutory Documents. Deeds, Abstracts and Cessions of Jurisdiction, State
  Eleemosynary Institutions
Virginia Historical Society, Richmond
  Grand Camp Confederate Veterans, Department of Virginia, R. E. Lee Camp No.
  1, Richmond, Va., Records
  Correspondence
  Lee Camp Soldiers' Home Library Register
  Minutes
  Roster
Virginia State Library, Richmond
  Executive Papers
    Westmoreland Davis
    Fitzhugh Lee
    Henry C. Stuart
    Claude A. Swanson

MEMBERSHIP ROLLS, ROSTERS, AND BIOGRAPHICAL COMPILATIONS

Booth, Andrew B., comp. *Records of Louisiana Confederate Soldiers and Louisiana Confederate Commands*. 3 vols. 1920; reprint, Spartanburg, S.C., 1984.
Confederate Gray Book, John Bell Hood Camp, No. 103, U.C.V. Austin, [c. 1904].
Confederate Veterans' Employment Bureau. *List of Applicants for Employment*. New Orleans, [c. 1895].
Donovan, Timothy P., and Willard B. Gatewood, eds. *The Governors of Arkansas: Essays in Political Biography*. Fayetteville, Ark., 1981.
Elliott, Colleen M., and Louise A. Moxley, eds. *The Tennessee Civil War Questionnaires*. 5 vols. Easley, S.C., 1985.
Evans, Clement A., ed. *Confederate Military History: A Library of Confederate States History*. 12 vols. Atlanta, 1899.
Frank Cheatham Bivouac, U.C.V., Nashville. Confederate Gray Book. Nashville, 1911.
Garrett, William. *Reminiscences of Public Men in Alabama*. 1875; reprint, Spartanburg, S.C., 1975.
Goodwin, Adolph O., comp. *Who's Who in Raleigh*. Raleigh, 1916.
Hemphill, J. C. *Men of Mark in South Carolina*. 4 vols. Washington, D.C., 1907.
Inaugural Addresses of the Governors of Mississippi, 1890–1980. Oxford, Miss., 1980.
Krick, Robert K. *Lee's Colonels: A Biographical Register of the Field Officers of the Army of Northern Virginia*. Dayton, Ohio, 1979.
McBride, Robert M., ed. *Biographical Directory of the Tennessee General Assembly*. 5 vols. Nashville, 1975–.

Mathes, James H. *The Old Guard in Gray: Researches in the Annals of the Confederate Historical Association.* Memphis, 1897.

Men of Affairs in Progressive New Orleans. New Orleans, 1908.

Northen, William J., ed. *Men of Mark in Georgia.* 7 vols. 1907; reprint, Spartanburg, S.C., 1974.

Roll of the Association of the Army of Tennessee, Louisiana Division, Camp No. 2, U.C.V. New Orleans, 1902.

Roster, Louisiana Division, Army of Northern Virginia, New Orleans, La., Camp. No. 1, U.C.V. New Orleans, 1893.

Roster of Inmates of the Soldiers' Home, Raleigh, North Carolina. Raleigh, 1904.

Speer, William S., comp. *Sketches of Prominent Tennesseans.* Nashville, 1888.

Tennesseans in the Civil War: A Military History of Confederate and Union Units, with Available Rosters of Personnel. 2 parts. Nashville, 1964.

Who's Who in Tennessee. Memphis, 1911.

NEWSPAPERS, PERIODICALS, AND CITY DIRECTORIES

Arkansas *Gazette* (Little Rock), 1889–92.

Atlanta *Constitution*, 1889–1959.

Atlanta *Journal*, 1965.

Atlanta *Journal Magazine*, 1912.

Austin *American Statesman*, 1941–70.

Austin *Confederate Drummer*, 1886.

Austin *Confederate Home News*, 1912.

Austin *Confederate Home Vidette*, 1912–13.

Austin *Daily Statesman*, 1884–1913.

Austin *Record*, 1887.

Baltimore *American*, 1888.

Biloxi *Daily Herald*, 1914–62.

Carolina *Free Press* (Columbia), 1931.

Charleston *News and Courier*, 1963.

Charlotte *Home-Democrat*, 1884.

Chataigne's Directory of Richmond, Va., 1883–84.

Chattanooga *Daily Times*, 1889.

Clanton, Ala., *Banner*, 1902.

Columbia *Record*, 1957.

Columbia *State* , 1908–63.

Confederate Veteran, 1892–1987.

Confederate Veteran—Official Bulletin, South Carolina Division, UCV (Columbia), 1935.

Dixie, Times-Picayune States Roto Magazine (New Orleans), 1955.

Edwardsville, Ala., *Standard News*, 1902.

Florida Times-Union (Jacksonville), 1892–1939.

Georgetown, Ky., *Weekly Times*, 1881–83.

Houston *Chronicle*, 1944.

Knoxville *Journal*, 1889.

Memphis *Daily Appeal*, 1889.

Montgomery *Advertiser*, 1901–4.

Mountain Creek, Ala., *News*, 1904.

Nashville *Banner*, 1887–1908.

Nashville City Directories, 1883–1901.

Nashville *Daily American*, 1885–89.

New Orleans *Daily-Picayune*, 1866–1913.

New Orleans *Picayune*, 1894–1954.

New Orleans *Times-Democrat*, 1883.

New Orleans *Times-Picayune*, 1880–1921.

New York *Journal*, 1889.

New York *Sun*, 1884.

New York *Times*, 1884.

New York *Tribune*, 1884.

Orphans Friend and Masonic Journal (Raleigh), 1926.

Pass Christian, Miss., *Coast News*, 1893.

Polk's Atlanta City Directory for 1889.

Raleigh *Daily Call*, 1889.

Raleigh *News and Observer*, c. 1902–35.

Richmond *Times-Dispatch*, 1883–1989.

Soard's New Orleans City Directory for 1883.

Southern Bivouac, 1884–85.

Southern Historical Society Papers, 1883–92.

PUBLISHED REPORTS, ADDRESSES, CONTEMPORARY HISTORIES, AND YEARBOOKS

Anderson, Archer. *Address on the Opening of the Lee Camp Soldiers' Home.* Richmond, 1885.

Association of Confederate Soldiers, Tennessee Division. *Minutes.* Nashville, 1898.

Benson, C. H. *"Yank" and "Reb": A History of a Fraternal Visit Paid by Lincoln Post, No. 11, G.A.R. of Newark, New Jersey.* Newark, 1884.

Charlaron, Joseph A. "'Camp Nicholls,' The Soldiers' Home of Louisiana." Official Souvenir and Hand Book. New Orleans, 1903.

Cody, Annie E., comp. *History of the Tennessee Division United Daughters of the Confederacy.* Nashville, [c. 1947].

Cole, Howson, ed. "Life in Camp Lee Soldiers' Home." *Virginia Magazine of History and Biography* 70 (1962): 468–70.

Confederate Veterans Annual Yearbook. Atlanta, 1923.

Crew, H. H. *History of Nashville, Tennessee.* Nashville, 1889.

Davis, T. Frederick. *History of Jacksonville, Florida and Vicinity, 1513–1924.* 1925; reprint, Gainesville, Fla., 1964.

Dorris, Mary C. *Preservation of the Hermitage, 1889–1915: Annals, History, and Stories.* Nashville, 1915.

Gaither, Zella H. *Arkansas Confederate Home*. Little Rock, 1922.

Gobrecht, J. C. *History of the National Homes for Disabled Volunteer Soldiers*. Dayton, Ohio, 1875.

Goodspeed's Biographical and Historical Memoirs of Louisiana. 3 vols. Chicago, 1892.

Guild, George B. *A Brief Narrative of the Fourth Tennessee Cavalry Regiment, Wheeler's Corps, Army of Tennessee*. Nashville, 1913.

Hempstead, Fay. *Historical Review of Arkansas*. 3 vols. Chicago, 1911.

Herndon, Dallas T. *Centennial History of Arkansas*. 3 vols. Little Rock, 1922.

History of Clinch County [Georgia]. Macon, Ga., 1916.

Huey, Mattie M. *History of the Alabama Division, United Daughters of the Confederacy*. Opelika, Ala., [c. 1937].

Hunt, William C. "Workers at Gainful Occupations at the Federal Censuses of 1870, 1880 and 1890." *Bulletin of the Department of Labor*, no. 11. Washington, D.C., 1897.

Kendall, John S. *History of New Orleans*. 3 vols. New Orleans, 1922.

Lasswell, Mary, comp. and ed. *Rags and Hope: The Recollections of Val C. Giles, Four Years with Hood's Brigade, Fourth Texas Infantry, 1861–1865*. New York, 1961.

Lea, Mrs. R. J. "My Personal Recollections of the Arkansas Confederate Home." *Southern Magazine* 2 (1935–36).

Link, Arthur S., ed. *The Papers of Woodrow Wilson*. 67 vols. Princeton, 1966–.

Livermore, Thomas L. *Numbers and Losses in the Civil War: 1861–1865*. 1900; reprint, Bloomington, Ind., 1957.

Lumpkin, Katherine DuPre. *The Making of a Southerner*. New York, 1947.

McCain, William D., comp. *Minutes, Board of Directors, Mississippi Division, United Sons of Confederate Veterans, June 4, 1954–June 3, 1958*. Hattiesburg, Miss., 1958.

McCampbell, S. J. N. *The Ex-Confederate Soldiers' Home, Richmond, Va., in Verse, by an Inmate*. Richmond, 1886.

McMurray, William J. *History of the Twentieth Tennessee Regiment Volunteer Infantry, C.S.A.* Nashville, 1975 [1904].

Maryland Line Confederate Soldiers' Home. Baltimore, 1889.

Minutes of the Second Convention of Confederate Soldiers, Tennessee Division. Nashville, 1889.

Olds, Fred A. "History of the Soldiers' Home at Raleigh." *Orphans Friend and Masonic Journal*, Dec. 1926.

Poppenheim, Mary B. *The History of the United Daughters of the Confederacy*. 2 vols. Raleigh, 1956.

Richardson, Frank L. "My Recollections of the Battle of the 14th of September, 1874." *Louisiana Historical Quarterly* 3 (1920): 498–501.

Rodgers, Robert L., comp. *History of the Confederate Veterans Association of Fulton County, Georgia*. Atlanta, 1890.

Roebuck, J. E. *My Own Personal Experience and Observation as a Soldier in the Confederate Army*. N.p., 1911.

Rood, Hosea W., and E. B. Earle, comps. *History of the Wisconsin Veterans' Home, 1886–1926.* Milwaukee, 1926.

Rosenburg, R. B., ed. *"For the Sake of My Country": The Diary of Colonel William W. Ward, 9th Tennessee Cavalry, Morgan's Brigade, C.S.A.* Murfreesboro, Tenn., 1992.

Russell, Mrs. A. J. *Life and Labors of Albert J. Russell.* Jacksonville, Fla., 1897.

Smith, James E. *A Famous Battery and Its Campaigns, 1861-'64.* Washington, D.C., 1892.

Thin Gray Line, 1861–1922. Atlanta, 1922.

Thomas, David Y., ed. *Arkansas and Its People.* 4 vols. New York, 1930.

Waddill, Edward M. *The Song of the Soldiers Home of Raleigh.* Raleigh, 1895.

White, Robert H., and Stephen V. Ash, eds., *Messages of the Governors of Tennessee.* 10 vols. Nashville, 1952–90.

Wooldridge, J., ed. *History of Nashville, Tennessee.* Nashville, 1890.

STATE RECORDS AND GOVERNMENT PUBLICATIONS

Arkansas *House Journal.*

"Camp Nicholls—The Soldiers' Home of Louisiana." Louisiana Secretary of State Report. Baton Rouge, 1894.

Confederate Soldiers' Home of Georgia: Act of the General Assembly and Rules and Regulations Governing the Home. Atlanta, 1917.

Confederate Soldiers' Home of Georgia: Act of the General Assembly, Board of Trustees, Rules and Regulations. Atlanta, 1901.

Connor, R. D. W., ed. *A Manual of North Carolina.* Raleigh, 1913.

Florida *Laws.*

Florida Treasurer's *Report.*

Gammel, H. P. N., comp. *Laws of Texas, 1822–1897.* 10 vols. Austin, 1898.

Georgia *House Journal.*

Georgia *Laws.*

Georgia *Senate Journal.*

Journal of the Congress of the Confederate States of America. 7 vols. Washington, D.C., 1905.

Louisiana *Acts.*

Louisiana *House Journal.*

Louisiana *Senate Journal.*

Maryland *Laws.*

Mississippi *Laws.*

Newsome, A. R., ed. and comp. *North Carolina Manual, 1929.* Raleigh, 1929.

North Carolina *House Journal.*

North Carolina *Laws.*

North Carolina *Senate Journal.*

Raines, C. W. *Year Book for Texas, 1901.* Austin, 1902.

———. *Year Book for Texas, 1902.* Austin, 1903.

Regulations for the Army of the Confederate States. Richmond, 1863.

Rowland, Dunbar, ed. and comp. *The Official and Statistical Register of the State of Mississippi.* Nashville, 1904.

South Carolina *Acts.*

South Carolina *House Journal.*

South Carolina *Reports and Resolutions.*

South Carolina *Senate Journal.*

South Carolina *Statutes at Large.*

Tennessee *Acts.*

Tennessee Board of Administration. *Biennial Reports.* 1918–1924.

Tennessee Board of Charities. *Reports.* 1896, 1898, 1903, 1911, 1915.

Tennessee Committee on Charitable Institutions. *Report.* 1913.

Tennessee Department of Institutions. *Biennial Reports.* 1924–1934.

Tennessee *House and Senate Journal Appendix.*

Tennessee *House Journal.*

Tennessee *House Journal Appendix.*

Tennessee *Senate Journal.*

Texas Board of Control. *Reports.* 1920–1944.

Texas *House Journal.*

Texas *Laws.*

Texas *Senate Journal.*

U.S. Bureau of the Census. "Soldiers and Widows." *Compendium of the Eleventh Census: 1890.* Pt. 3, *Population.* Washington, D.C., 1897.

U.S. Congress. House. Committee on Invalid Pensions. *Claims of Confederate Soldiers Hearing.* 64th Cong., 1st sess., Washington, D.C., 1916.

U.S. Congress. Senate. Committee on Military Affairs. *Homes for Confederate Veterans Hearing.* 64th Cong., 1st sess. Washington, D.C., 1916.

Virginia *Acts.*

Virginia *Senate Journal.*

Secondary Materials

BOOKS

Arnett, Alex Mathews. *The Populist Movement in Georgia.* 1922; reprint, New York, 1967.

Ash, Stephen V. *Middle Tennessee Society Transformed, 1860–1870: War and Peace in the Upper South.* Baton Rouge, 1988.

Bailey, Fred A. *Class and Tennessee's Confederate Generation.* Chapel Hill, 1987.

Barr, Alwyn. *Reconstruction to Reform: Texas Politics, 1876–1906.* Austin, 1971.

Bartley, Numan V. *The Creation of Modern Georgia.* Athens, Ga., 1983.

Benner, Judith A. *Sul Ross: Soldier, Statesman, Educator.* College Station, Tex., 1983.

Bradley, Chester D. *100 Years of Veteran Care, 1870–1970.* Hampton, Va., 1970.

Buck, Paul. *The Road to Reunion, 1865–1900.* Boston, 1937.

Campbell, Randolph B., and Richard G. Lowe. *Wealth and Power in Antebellum Texas.* College Station, Tex., 1977.

Casey, Powell A. *Encyclopedia of Forts, Posts, Named Camps, and Other Military Installations in Louisiana, 1700–1981*. Baton Rouge, 1983.

Chambers, Robert, Richard Longhurst, and Arnold Pacey, eds. *Seasonal Dimensions to Rural Poverty*. London, 1981.

Chesson, Michael B. *Richmond after the War, 1865–1890*. Richmond, 1981.

Coulter, E. Merton. *The South during Reconstruction, 1865–1877*. Baton Rouge, 1947.

Cunningham, Horace H. *Doctors in Gray: The Confederate Medical Service*. Baton Rouge, 1958.

Davies, Wallace E. *Patriotism on Parade: The Story of Veterans and Hereditary Organizations in America, 1783–1900*. Cambridge, Mass., 1955.

Davis, Harold E. *Henry Grady's New South: Atlanta, a Brave and Beautiful City*. Tuscaloosa, 1990.

Dearing, Mary R. *Veterans in Politics: The Story of the Grand Army of the Republic*. Baton Rouge, 1952.

Duffy, John, ed. *The Rudolph Matas History of Medicine in Louisiana*. 2 vols. Baton Rouge, 1962.

Eckert, Ralph L. *John Brown Gordon: Soldier, Southerner, American*. Baton Rouge, 1989.

Edwards, Anne. *Road to Tara: The Life of Margaret Mitchell*. New Haven, 1983.

Escott, Paul. *Many Excellent People: Power and Privilege in North Carolina, 1850–1900*. Chapel Hill, 1985.

Faber, Joseph F., ed. *Life Tables for the United States: 1900–2050*. Actuarial Study No. 87. Washington, D.C., 1982.

Fischer, David H. *Growing Old in America*. Oxford, 1978.

Foster, Gaines M. *Ghosts of the Confederacy: Defeat, the Lost Cause, and the Emergence of the New South, 1865–1913*. New York, 1987.

Foucault, Michael. *Discipline and Punish: The Birth of the Prison*. New York, 1979.

Gaston, Paul. *The New South Creed: A Study in Southern Mythmaking*. New York, 1970.

Goffman, Erving. *Asylums: Essays in the Social Situation of Mental Patients and Other Inmates*. Garden City, N.J., 1961.

Goode, Paul R. *The United States Soldiers' Home: A History of Its First Hundred Years*. Richmond, 1957.

Hahn, Steven. *The Roots of Southern Populism: Yeoman Farmers and the Transformation of the Georgia Upcountry, 1850–1890*. New York, 1984.

Hair, William I. *Bourbonism and Agrarian Protest: Louisiana Politics, 1877–1900*. Baton Rouge, 1969.

Hall, Peter D. *The Organization of American Culture, 1700–1900: Private Institutions, Elites, and the Origin of American Nationality*. New York, 1982.

Hart, Roger L. *Redeemers, Bourbons and Populists in Tennessee, 1870–1896*. Knoxville, 1975.

Hays, Samuel P. *The Response to Industrialism, 1885–1914*. Chicago, 1957.

Henry, Louis. *Population: Analysis and Models*. New York, 1976.

Hesseltine, William B. *Confederate Leaders in the New South.* 1950; reprint, Westport, Conn., 1970.

Hoar, Jay S. *The South's Last Boys in Gray.* Bowling Green, Ohio, 1986.

Horn, Stanley F. *The Hermitage: Home of Old Hickory.* 1938; reprint, Nashville,
1960.

Jackson, Joy J. *New Orleans in the Gilded Age: Politics and Urban Progress, 1880–
1896.* Baton Rouge, 1969.

Kane, Harnett T. *Dear Dorothy Dix: The Story of a Compassionate Woman.* New
York, 1952.

Katz, Michael B. *In the Shadow of the Poorhouse: A Social History of Welfare in
America.* New York, 1986.

Lancaster, Cathryn G. *Early Years of the Florida Division, United Daughters of the
Confederacy, 1896–1921.* Jacksonville, 1983.

Landry, Stuart O. *The Battle of Liberty Place: The Overthrow of Carpet-Bag Rule in
New Orleans.* New Orleans, 1955.

Linderman, Gerald F. *Embattled Courage: The Experience of Combat in the American Civil War.* New York, 1987.

Linenthal, Edward T. *Changing Images of the Warrior Hero: A History of Popular
Symbolism.* New York, 1982.

McClure, Ethel. *More Than a Roof: The Development of Minnesota Poor Farms and
Homes for the Aged.* New York, 1968.

McConnell, Stuart C. *Glorious Contentment: The Grand Army of the Republic,
1865–1900.* Chapel Hill, 1992.

McMath, Robert C., Jr. *Populist Vanguard: A History of the Southern Farmers' Alliance.* Chapel Hill, 1975.

Magdol, Edward, and Jon L. Wakelyn, eds. *The Southern Common People: Studies in
Nineteenth-Century Social History.* Westport, Conn., 1980.

Nixon, Raymond B. *Henry W. Grady, Spokesman of the New South.* New York,
1943.

Osterweis, Rollin G. *The Myth of the Lost Cause, 1865–1900.* Hamden, Conn., 1973.

Ownby, Ted. *Subduing Satan: Religion, Recreation, and Manhood in the Rural
South, 1865–1920.* Chapel Hill, 1990.

Powers, Mary G., ed. *Measures of Socioeconomic Status: Current Issues.* Boulder,
Colo., 1982.

Richardson, Rupert N., Ernest Wallace, and Adrian N. Anderson, *Texas: The Lone
Star State.* 3rd ed. Englewood Cliffs, N.J., 1970.

Riley, Matilda W., ed. *Aging from Birth to Death: Interdisciplinary Perspectives.*
Washington, D.C., 1979.

Roberts, Bobby, and Carl Moneyhon. *Portraits of Conflict: A Photographic History of
Arkansas in the Civil War.* Fayetteville, Ark., 1987.

Rothman, David J. *Conscience and Convenience: The Asylum and Its Alternative in
Progressive America.* Boston, 1980.

——. *Discovery of the Asylum: Social Order and Disorder in the New Republic.*
Boston, 1971.

Sakamoto-Momiyama, M. *Seasonality in Human Mortality: A Medico-Geographical Study*. Tokyo, 1977.

Shaw, Barton. *The Wool-Hat Boys: Georgia's Populist Party*. Baton Rouge, 1984.

Shifflett, Crandall A. *Patronage and Poverty in the Tobacco South: Louisa County, Virginia, 1860–1900*. Knoxville, 1982.

Soltow, Lee. *Men and Wealth in the United States, 1850–1870*. New Haven, 1975.

Sutherland, Daniel E. *The Confederate Carpetbaggers*. Baton Rouge, 1988.

Taylor, Joe Gray. *Louisiana Reconstructed, 1863–1877*. Baton Rouge, 1974.

Thompson, Warren S., and P. K. Whelpton. *Population Trends in the United States*. 1933; reprint, New York, 1969.

Trattner, Walter I., ed. *Social Welfare or Social Control?: Some Historical Reflections on Regulating the Poor*. Knoxville, 1983.

Waller, William, ed. *Nashville in the 1890s*. Nashville, 1970.

Webb, Mena. *Jule Carr: General without an Army*. Chapel Hill, 1987.

Wecter, Dixon. *When Johnny Comes Marching Home*. Cambridge, Mass., 1944.

Wiebe, Robert H. *The Search for Order, 1877–1913*. New York, 1967.

White, William W. *The Confederate Veteran*. Tuscaloosa, 1962.

Wiley, Bell I. *The Life of Johnny Reb: The Common Soldier of the Confederacy*. 1943; reprint, Baton Rouge, 1984.

Wilson, Charles R. *Baptized in Blood: The Religion of the Lost Cause, 1865–1920*. Athens, Ga., 1980.

Wisner, Elizabeth. *Social Welfare in the South: From Colonies to World War I*. Baton Rouge, 1970.

Woodward, C. Vann. *Origins of the New South, 1877–1913*. Baton Rouge, 1951.

———. *Tom Watson: Agrarian Rebel*. 1938; reprint, New York, 1969.

Wright, Gavin. *The Political Economy of the Cotton South: Households, Markets and Wealth in the Nineteenth Century*. New York, 1978.

Wyatt-Brown, Bertram. *Southern Honor: Ethics and Behavior in the Old South*. New York, 1982.

Wyllie, Irvin G. *The Self-Made Man in America*. New York, 1954.

Wynne, Lewis N. *The Continuity of Cotton: Planter Politics in Georgia, 1865–1892*. Macon, Ga., 1986.

ARTICLES

Anderson, Nancy N. "Effects of Institutionalization on Self-Esteem." *Journal of Gerontology* 22 (1967): 313–17.

Anderson, Richard J. "Medical Diagnoses in One Thousand Domiciled Veterans." *Journal of the American Geriatrics Society* 12 (1964): 553–61.

Butler, R. "The Life Review: An Interpretation of Reminiscences of the Aged." In *New Thoughts on Old Age*, edited by R. Kastenbaum. New York, 1964.

Chen, L. C. "Control and Diarrhoeal Disease, Morbidity and Mortality: Some Strategic Issues." *American Journal of Clinical Nutrition* 31 (1982): 2284–90.

Courtwright, David T. "Opiate Addiction as a Consequence of the Civil War." *Civil War History* 24 (1978): 101–11.

Davis, Harold E. "Henry Grady, the Atlanta *Constitution* and the Politics of Farming in the 1880s." *Georgia Historical Quarterly* 71 (1987): 571–600.

———. "Henry W. Grady, Master of the Atlanta Ring, 1880–1886." *Georgia Historical Quarterly* 69 (1985): 1–38.

Dean, Eric T., Jr. "'We Will All Be Lost and Destroyed': Post-Traumatic Stress Disorder and the Civil War," *Civil War History* 37 (1991): 138–53.

Dovenmuele, Robert H., E. W. Busse, and E. G. Newman. "Physical Problems of Older People." *Journal of the American Geriatrics Society* 9 (1961): 208–17.

Feldman, Peter, Cecelia Mulcahey, and Joseph Brudno. "A Different Approach to the Treatment of the Older Male Veteran Patient." *Journal of the American Geriatrics Society* 9 (1961): 119–24.

Franklin, John H. "Public Welfare in the South, 1865–1880." *Southern Service Review* 44 (1970): 379–92.

Friedman, Edward P. "Age, Length of Institutionalization and Social Status in the Home for the Aged." *Journal of Gerontology* 22 (1967): 474–77.

———. "Spatial Proximity and Social Interaction in a Home for the Aged." *Journal of Gerontology* 21 (1966): 566–70.

Goodman, Joseph I. "The Problems of Malnutrition in the Elderly." *Journal of the American Geriatrics Society* 5 (1957): 504–11.

Hammond, William. "Common Disorders of the Aged." *Journal of the American Geriatrics Society* 4 (1956): 215–23.

Harrington, L. Garth, and A. Cooper Rice. "Alcoholism in a Geriatric Setting: Disciplinary Problems, Marital Status and Income Level." *Journal of the American Geriatrics Society* 10 (1962): 197–200.

Hattaway, Herman. "Clio's Southern Soldiers: The United Confederate Veterans and History." *Louisiana History* 12 (1971): 213–42.

———. "The United Confederate Veterans in Louisiana." *Louisiana History* 16 (1975): 5–37.

Havighurst, Robert J., and Richard Glasser. "An Exploratory Study of Reminiscence." *Journal of Gerontology* 27 (1972): 245–53.

Holmes, William F. "The Georgia Alliance Legislature." *Georgia Historical Quarterly* 68 (1984): 479–515.

———. "The Southern Farmers' Alliance: The Georgia Experience." *Georgia Historical Quarterly* 72 (1988): 627–52.

Kapnick, Philip L., Jay S. Goodman, and Elmer E. Cornwell. "Political Behavior in the Aged: Some New Data." *Journal of Gerontology* 23 (1968): 305–10.

Klebaner, Benjamin J. "Poverty and Its Relief in American Thought, 1815–61." *Journal of Social History* 38 (1964): 382–99.

Lashley, Tommy G. "Oklahoma's Confederate Veterans Home." *Chronicles of Oklahoma* 55 (1977): 34–45.

Lawton, M. Powell, and Silvia Yaffe. "Mortality, Morbidity and Voluntary Change of Residence by Older People." *Journal of the American Geriatrics Society* 18 (1970): 823–31.

Lewis, Charles N. "Reminiscing and Self-Concept in Old Age." *Journal of Gerontology* 26 (1971): 240–43.

Lieberman, M. A. "Relationships of Mortality Rates to Entrance to a Home for the Aged." *Geriatrics* 16 (1961): 515–19.

Markus, Elliot, Margaret Blenker, Martin Bloom, and Thomas Downs. "The Impact of Relocation upon Mortality Rates of Institutionalized Aged Persons." *Journal of Gerontology* 26 (1971): 537–41.

Miller, Thomas L. "Texas Land Grants to Confederate Veterans and Widows." *Southwestern Historical Quarterly* 69 (1965): 59–65.

O'Connor, Flannery. "A Late Encounter with the Enemy." In *A Good Man Is Hard to Find*. New York, 1953.

Poole, Herbert. "Final Encampment: The North Carolina Soldiers' Home." *Confederate Veteran* (July–August 1987): 10–17.

Range, Willard. "Hannibal I. Kimball." *Georgia Historical Quarterly* 29 (1945): 47–70.

Rao, Dodda B. "Problems of Nutrition in the Aged." *Journal of the American Geriatrics Society* 21 (1973): 362–67.

Reid, Joseph D., Jr. "White Land, Black Labor, and Agricultural Stagnation: The Causes and Effects of Sharecropping in the Postbellum South." In *Market Institutions and Economic Progress in the New South, 1865–1900*, edited by Gary M. Walton, pp. 33–55. New York, 1981.

Richter, Robert L. "Attaining Ego Integrity through Life Review." *Journal of Religion and Aging* 2 (1986): 1–11.

Rutland, Robert. "Captain William B. Walton, Mexican War Veteran." *Tennessee Historical Quarterly* 11 (1952): 171–79.

Sutherland, Daniel E. "Exiles, Emigrants and Sojourners: The Post-Civil War Confederate Exodus in Perspective." *Civil War History* 51 (1985): 237–56.

———. "Southern Fraternal Organizations in the North." *Journal of Southern History* 53 (1987): 587–612.

Tobin, Sheldon S. "Preservation of the Self in Old Age." *Social Casework* 69 (1988): 550–55.

Turner, Barbara F. "Personality Traits as Predictors of Institutional Adaption among the Aged." *Journal of Gerontology* 27 (1972): 61–68.

Van de Wetering, Maxine. "The Popular Concept of 'Home' in Nineteenth-Century America." *Journal of American Studies* 18 (1984): 5–28.

Vandiver, Frank. "The Confederate Myth." *Southwest Review* 46 (1961): 199–204.

Ward, Russell A. "The Never-Married in Later Life." *Journal of Gerontology* 34 (1979): 861–69.

Williams, Emily J. " 'A Home . . . for the Old Boys': The Robert E. Lee Camp Confederate Soldiers' Home." *Virginia Cavalcade* 28 (1979): 40–47.

Young, James R. "Confederate Pensions in Georgia, 1886–1929." *Georgia Historical Quarterly* 66 (1982): 47–52.

THESES AND DISSERTATIONS

Bassett, Martha B. "The History of Beauvoir—Jefferson Davis Shrine." M.A. thesis, University of Southern Mississippi, 1970.

Bellows, Barbara L. "Tempering the Wind: The Southern Response to Urban Poverty, 1850–1865." Ph.D. dissertation, University of South Carolina, 1983.

Cetina, Judith G. "A History of Veterans' Homes in the United States, 1811–1930." Ph.D. dissertation, Case Western Reserve University, 1977.

Climer, Patricia F. "Protectors of the Past: The United Daughters of the Confederacy, Tennessee Division, and the Lost Cause." M.A. thesis, Vanderbilt University, 1973.

Davis, G. Stephen. "Johnny Reb in Perspective: The Confederate Soldiers' Image in Southern Arts." Ph.D. dissertation, Emory University, 1979.

Huffman, Frank J., Jr. "Old South, New South: Continuity and Change in a Georgia County, 1850–1880." Ph.D. dissertation, Yale University, 1974.

Lashley, Tommy G. "A History of Confederate Veterans in Oklahoma." M.A. thesis, Oklahoma State University, 1975.

Ruoff, John C. "Southern Womanhood, 1865–1920: An Intellectual and Cultural Study." Ph.D. dissertation, University of Illinois at Urbana-Champaign, 1976.

Simpson, John A. "S. A. Cunningham and the Confederate Heritage." Ph.D. dissertation, University of Oregon, 1987.

Weiler, N. Sue. "The Aged, the Family, and the Problems of a Maturing Industrial Society: New York, 1900–1930." Ph.D. dissertation, University of Illinois at Chicago, 1983.

INDEX